READY TO REBUILD

The Imminent Plan to Rebuild the Last Days Temple

Thomas Ice & Randall Price

HARVEST HOUSE PUBLISHERS
Eugene, Oregon 97402

READY TO REBUILD

Copyright © 1992 by Harvest House Publishers
Eugene, Oregon 97402

Library of Congress Cataloging-in-Publication Data
Ice, Thomas.
      Ready to rebuild / Thomas Ice, Randall Price.
      Includes bibliographical references.
      ISBN 0-89081-956-4
      1. Temple of Jerusalem (Jerusalem).   2. Temple Mount (Jerusalem)—
International status.   3. Jewish-Arab relations.   4. Bible—Prophecies—
Temple of Jerusalem.   I. Price, Randall.   II. Title.
DS109.3.I34   1992   91-37693
956.9405′4—dc20   CIP

Printed in the United States of America.

About
the Authors

Thomas Ice is pastor of Oak Hill Bible Church in Austin, Texas. He holds a master's degree in Historical Theology from Dallas Theological Seminary and is the founder and director of Bible Awareness Ministries, which follows theological trends within Christianity. He has coauthored *Dominion Theology: Blessing or Curse?* and *A Holy Rebellion: Strategy for Spiritual Warfare*.

Randall Price is a pastor at Grace Bible Church in San Marcos, Texas. He holds a master's degree in Hebrew from Dallas Theological Seminary and has done graduate studies at Hebrew University in Jerusalem. He is the founder and director of World of the Bible Tours and currently professor of Bible at Central Texas Bible College. Now completing his doctorate in Hebrew Studies, Randall is an expert on Israel's history, thought (ancient and modern), and culture.

Contents

Foreword—John F. Walvoord

A Personal Word from the Authors

Part I:
A Growing Tension

Part II:
Perspective from the Past

Part III:
Preparations in the Present

Part IV:
The Prophetic Plan

Acknowledgments

A book of this nature would not have been possible without the support and assistance of many friends both in the United States and Israel. We are grateful to those who shared their personal research and granted interviews, knowing the delicate circumstances surrounding the issues, both politically and religiously. It is our prayer that their contributions preserved in this book will inform both Christians and Jews concerning the coming days of God's prophetic program, and help prepare a generation to meet the Messiah.

We especially wish to thank *Dr. John F. Walvoord* for his many valuable suggestions and for the writing of the foreword.

Randall thanks his parents, *Mr. and Mrs. E.C. Price* for their assistance in research in Israel and continued support throughout the project.

In addition, Randall thanks the partners of the *Hebrew Study Fund* for their faithful prayers and financial support.

The authors thank *Mr. James DeYoung* for his assistance in this project while in Israel. Mr. DeYoung produced a video based on our initial research and shared in both our interviews and in additional interviews he made available to us. In addition, his help with the special photography required for this book is greatly appreciated.

Randall expresses special gratitude for the hospitality of *Aizic (Yitzhak)* and *Ita Oked* during many stays in Israel. Aizic, for more than 20 years an international journalist with the *Jerusalem Post* shared from his own extensive research on the Temple rebuilding movement.

Randall also wishes to thank *Meno* and *Anat Kalisher* for their repeated Israeli hospitality, their spiritual encouragement, and Meno's assistance as an interpreter with Rabbi Yehuda Getz.

Other thanks are due to *Mr. Steve Prentice* who provided office space for the early writing stage of this manuscript, *Mrs. Susan Magana* for her devotion in transcribing numerous recorded interviews, the congregations of *Oak Hill Bible Church* and *Grace Bible Church* for their prayers and for allowing their pastors time to complete this work, and to *Pastor Charles Bullock* and *Mr. Dan Rosema* for their assistance in the video interview of Dr. Gershon Salomon.

For their willingness to cooperate in audio and video interviews, for granting permission for photography, and their assistance in providing valuable documents, we especially thank the following individuals and institutions in Israel: *Rabbi Israel Ariel* and *Mr. Chaim Richman* of the Temple Institute, archaeologists *Dr. Dan Bahat* and *Dr. Meir Ben-Dov*, scientist *Dr. Asher Kaufman*, Western Wall Heritage Foundation Public Relations Director *Arieh Banner*, TMF Director *Dr. Gershon Salomon*, TMF associate *Ze'ev Bar-Tov*, researcher *Gary Collit*, former Director of the Israeli Government Press Office, *Mr. Mordachai Dolinsky*, Jerusalem rabbis *Rabbi Yehuda Getz* and *Rabbi Shlomo Goren*, and *Rabbi Nahman Kahane*; and for photographs of special exhibits: The History of Jerusalem Museum, The Israel National Museum, Atara L'yoshna, and Ateret Cohanim.

Finally, special thanks is given to *Bob Hawkins, Jr.*, president of Harvest House Publishers; and *Eileen Mason*, vice president of editorial, for their warm personal encouragements and their professional assistance in preparing the manuscript, and to the production team at Harvest House for their exceptional attention in the preparation of the charts, photographs, and seeing the final work through production. May the Lord acknowledge your work for Him and make the reward!

Questions or comments about the material in this book as well as requests for the *Ready to Rebuild* video should be addressed to:

Biblical Awareness Ministries
P.O. Box 90014
Austin, Texas 78709

Biblical Awareness Ministries publishes the *Biblical Perspective* and *Temple Times* (updates of the rebuilding of the Temple) newsletters six times a year. The cost of a yearly subscription is $15. A sample copy will be sent to all who enclose a self-addressed, stamped, legal-size envelope. In addition, *Biblical Awareness Ministries* has information on "Temple Tours" and various other Christian issues in the form of printed materials and audio tapes. A list of resources is available upon request.

Foreword

For many years there has been speculation concerning the question as to whether the second Temple, destroyed in A.D. 70, will ever be rebuilt. Students of Bible prophecy find clear evidence that it will be rebuilt in the end time because Scriptures predict that not only will the Temple be rebuilt but that the sacrifices prescribed by the Mosaic law will be reinstituted by Orthodox Jews. These sacrifices, in turn, will be stopped and the Temple desecrated three-and-a-half years before the second coming of Christ, according to Daniel 9:27 and many other passages.

There has been much confusion, however, among prophecy students as to the evidence for and against this future fulfillment of prophecy, and more, in particular, where the Temple will be rebuilt because the Bible itself does not give clear indication of this.

The present work is a masterpiece presenting all the various views with substantiating evidence for the findings of the authors. Randall Price is well qualified for this work because of his years of study in Jerusalem and for his work at the University of Texas in Austin where he is finishing a doctoral degree in Hebrew studies. Because he speaks Hebrew himself, he was able to converse with Jews and get many points of interest and facts that would not be readily available to others who would have the barrier of language.

Thomas Ice adds his important contribution to the work as an accomplished writer. Ice holds a Master of Theology degree from Dallas Theological Seminary and serves as pastor of the Oak Hill Bible Church of Austin, Texas.

This book is a mine of information for those concerned about prophecy, and particularly the issue of when and where the Temple will be rebuilt. Because there has been so much false information disseminated and so much misunderstanding, this book will provide a solid basis for faith and what actually can be expected in regard to the rebuilding of the Temple. It presents startling evidence that the move is already underway to provide this facility. The book is highly recommended.

—John F. Walvoord, Chancellor
Dallas Theological Seminary

A Personal Word
from the Authors

Over a century ago, Frederick the Great, king of Prussia, was having a religious discussion with his chaplain. After a time, the king demanded that the chaplain provide him irrefutable evidence that the Bible was literally true. Without hesitation the chaplain replied, "Sire, I can give you the answer you seek in a single word." Surprised at the chaplain's confidence, the king retorted, "What is this magic word that carries with it such weight of proof?" And the chaplain answered, "Israel."

Throughout history those who have sought to explain the continued existence of the Jews through exile, violent attack, and holocaust have been unable to explain it apart from God. Some divine purpose evidently sustains the Jewish people. Historians, politicians, and journalists have been forced to occupy themselves with Israel, for it has come itself to occupy a prominent position in world events. If Israel was an irrefutable proof of the veracity of Scripture in the days of Frederick the Great, when the Jewish people were scattered throughout the earth, their land under Turkish domination, and no hope of return in sight, how much more now that they are once again an independent nation after 2,000 years!

This book has been written with an eye on Israel. It has been written with the belief that what God is doing in this world, and what He will yet do, concerns the Jewish people. Further, it has been written in the conviction that we are living in the last days of human history, and that as God's purpose comes to its conclusion, Israel is again being thrust upon center stage in the divine drama.

Ready to Rebuild brings current events surrounding the plans of Israeli Jews to rebuild their Temple into sharper focus. It has not been written to be sensational, but to provide accurate information on a controversial and often sensationalized subject of genuine importance.

To this end, the authors of this book have devoted several years of research in Israel, interviewing the major leaders and spokesmen of the Temple movement, rabbinical authorities, and archaeological professionals who have direct and expert knowledge of Jewish escha-tology and the Temple Mount. We have allowed these people to voice their own, often contradictory, opinions in order to present, as much as possible, a balanced and correct interpretation of views.

We believe that the current level of interest in the rebuilding of the Temple, the first of its kind in the last 1,400 years, is of significant merit. At a time when Temple activism has provoked international conflict and has the potential to ignite a third world war, we believe that an analysis of this movement is crucial.

While we do not suggest that the Temple is being built today, nor that it can be built today, we are convinced that there is a ground swell of expectation in Israel, not simply of the radical fringe, that a Temple will be rebuilt tomorrow. Major obstacles remain for the Temple to be rebuilt; however, given the rapidly changing nature of world events in recent days, it is possible that all of these obstacles could be quickly surmounted. Control of the Temple Mount, today the single most volatile issue in the Middle East conflict, will con-tinue to escalate in prominence and demand the attention of the world.

As Christians who seek to interpret such events within the frame-work of prophetic Scripture, we offer our own conclusions concern-ing the eventual resolution of the Temple issue. We believe that these events are prophetically significant, and that the time has come for a greater study of the Word of God and preparation for the Lord's coming. As that day draws near, we know that now more than ever, the church must give itself to the task of faithfully serving our Lord through proclamation of the gospel and the edification of the saints. Our prayer is that *Ready to Rebuild* will serve as an encouragement to that end.

Thomas Ice
Randall Price
January 1992

READY TO REBUILD

The Imminent Plan to Rebuild the Last Days Temple

Chapter 1

Tomorrow the Temple?

Preparation for the Messiah began with the Balfour Declaration in 1917, followed by the "unification" of Israel in 1967; it will be completed in 1992 with the rebuilding of the Temple.[1]

—*Rabbi Leon Ashkenazi*

*S*omething momentous is happening in the Middle East today that will soon affect the destiny of our entire planet. It has not been extensively reported in our major newspapers, and few of our political analysts have connected it with the events in the former Soviet Union and Europe that are rapidly changing the course of future history. Nevertheless, this event will soon become the focal point of world controversy and usher in dramatic days of war and peace foretold long ago by the ancient Hebrew prophets.

This event is the rebuilding of the Jewish Temple in Jerusalem. Quietly, almost without notice by secular world-watchers, preparations for a new Temple have been progressing for years in the strife-worn city of Jerusalem. Except for occasional eruptions—the consequence of these preparations—which have garnered the attention of the media, little has been reported about these amazing developments that may well signal the end of our age.

15

Growing Tension

For the first time in recent history organized efforts to prepare for the rebuilding of the Temple are developing openly in Israel, and serious demonstrations by Temple activists have gained worldwide attention. On October 8, 1990, reports of a riot at the Temple Mount in Jerusalem made international headlines. Palestinian Arabs had launched an attack against Jewish worshipers at the Western Wall during the height of Israel's High Holy Days. The resulting melee left 17 Palestinian Arabs dead and many more wounded. The United Nations Security Council swiftly moved to condemn Israel for the incident. Within days after the event, a panel assembled by the Muslim Temple Mount Authority concluded that Israel had staged the attack.

To understand what really happened behind the scenes that day on the Temple Mount we must remember that Saddam Hussein had invaded Kuwait only two months before, and that the Middle East was poised for an unprecedented Gulf conflict. Intelligence reports have now substantiated the suspicion that the Temple Mount provocation was instigated by Hussein in order to shift world attention from Iraq's occupation of Kuwait to Israel's occupation of "Palestine."[2]

Almost immediately the world media carried Saddam Hussein's announcement that he would not consider withdrawal from Kuwait before Israel withdrew from "occupied" Palestinian territories. Seeking to deflect world opinion against him, he proclaimed Israel as the real invader in the Middle East. Then came the Iraqi Scud missile attacks on Israel's civilian population, an attempt by Hussein to draw Israel into the conflict and shift allied Arab allegiance to Iraq.[3] Saddam Hussein hoped to emerge as the new champion of the Palestinian people and as the leader of *Jihad* (holy war) against Israel, the old enemy of all Arab nations.

Some in the media were quick to justify Hussein's claim of Israeli aggression. One *Time* magazine writer stated:

> The one-sidedness of the carnage on the Temple Mount . . . bespeaks a state of affairs that brutalizes all concerned. For now the Palestinians are the principal victims. But in the long run, the casualties will include . . . perhaps even the viability and credibility of Israel's democracy, and certainly its support from the rest of the world.[4]

According to this writer, while Saddam Hussein's tactics were unconscionable, Israel's "imperialism," its claim to land occupied by another people, is the most serious threat to world order.

What is seldom discussed about the October 8 riot, and the intentions of Saddam Hussein in ordering it, is its linkage with the rebuilding of the Temple. On the same day, a group of Orthodox Temple activists called the Temple Mount Faithful announced that they would attempt to lay a cornerstone for the third Jewish Temple. This was the "Israeli provocation" Muslims claimed as justification for their attack, even though Israeli police had assured the Muslim authorities that the planned cornerstone ceremony on the Temple Mount had been banned and that none of the group would be allowed to enter the area.

Early that morning loudspeakers that normally sound the Muslim call to prayer exhorted tens of thousands of Muslims to "come to the Mount and sacrifice soul and blood to save the land" and to "prevent the occupation of Islam's holy places."[5] Israeli witnesses claim that there were also explicit calls to "kill the Jews."

The Temple Mount issue is at the center of the Arab-Israeli conflict, particularly in Jerusalem. Although Israel was granted statehood in 1948, and captured East Jerusalem in the Six-Day War of 1967, the government at that time allowed Arabs to retain control of Temple Mount. This was done in an attempt to pacify the Arabs, an attempt which has dramatically failed. From an Arab perspective any move by Israelis now to return to the Temple Mount would be regarded as a declaration of war against Islam. Islam is a religion of the sword, and cannot, by definition, tolerate dominance by another religious system upon land it has at any time occupied. The Arabs recognize that a rebuilding of the Jewish Temple would be the final act assuring complete Israeli sovereignty over the land and its people, a sovereignty they have never acknowledged.

One piece of graffiti used by Palestinian Arabs as a symbol of their rebellion against Israeli "occupation" depicts the Dome of the Rock as the base of an upraised clenched fist. Analyzing this symbol, Anne Marie Oliver and Paul Steinberg, experts in Palestinian symbolism, write: "[This graffiti] functions as a proclamation of Moslem possession of the most contentious site in the Arab-Israel conflict, and by extension, of Jerusalem and the land as a whole."[6] A similar interpretation could be made for the appearance of Arab handprints stained with blood on walls on the Temple Mount following the October 8 riot.

At the historic Middle East Peace Conference held in the fall of 1991 in Madrid, Spain, special mention was made of Temple Mount in Jerusalem. Israel was accused of continual acts of aggression and of attempting to blow up the Al Aqsa Mosque.

Many people believe that it is time for the Middle East to become part of the new world order. Their consensus is that "the Israeli position is the only one that puts the world in jeopardy and on the brink of danger." They claim that the most significant barrier to true and lasting peace in the region is "the resolution of *Al Quds*" (the Arab name for Jerusalem meaning "the Holy"). The speeches at Madrid made it clear that the October 8 incident at the Temple Mount was but a portent of things to come.

Today Temple Mount has been thrust to center stage as the ultimate issue for resolution in any concrete negotiations between Israel and the Arab League. As Arab and Israeli positions become more polarized in the wake of a failed peace process, desperate measures will again be used by the Arabs to wrest control of East Jerusalem from Israel.

Hotbed of Religious Passions

Since 1967, when Israel first acquired sovereignty over the Temple Mount, there has been unrelenting pressure on the Israeli government to create a Jewish presence there. Until recent years these efforts have been marginal, but with the beginning of the *Intafada* [the Palestinian uprising against Israeli occupation] and the fear that increased political pressure on the government would cause concessions and remove the possibility of Jews reclaiming the Mount, activism has dramatically increased.

Recent conversations with the leaders of some of these groups make it clear that they feel that the time for action is now. Many of these leaders believe that if the West Bank, East Jerusalem, and the Temple Mount were given away, Israel would be lost as a people. They fear that another Diaspora (dispersion of the Jews) or another Holocaust would make it virtually impossible for the Jewish people to ever emerge as a distinct nation again.

Statistics of Jewish assimilation in the United States seem to support these fears. For example, a major study by the Council of Jewish Federations has revealed that 52 percent of Jewish men and women who have married since 1985 have taken Gentile spouses, and that three out of every four children of intermarriages are being raised outside of the Jewish faith or with no religion at all. This is a significant increase over 1964 figures which show that only 9 percent of all marriages were interfaith marriages. This trend, combined with a below-replacement birthrate, a rising tide of divorce, and a virtual end to immigration is shrinking the Jewish community.

The meaning of these statistics for Jews has been interpreted by Orthodox rabbi Ephraim Buchwald of Lincoln Square Synagogue in New York as nothing less than a "death knell." He says, "There has never been a community of Jews that has abandoned ritual and survived."[7] Therefore, Orthodox Jews around the world, and especially in Israel, see the rebuilding of the Temple as the only means to bring Jews back to Judaism and preserve the durable identity of the Jewish people.

While the Palestinian uprising has escalated Jewish attempts to rebuild the Temple, the growing tension is also a direct result of the Jewish return to Israel and Jerusalem. Irving Greenberg, former chairman of the Department of Jewish Studies at City College of New York's City University and founder and director of the National Jewish Resource Center, explains:

> Now in our lifetime, the period of exile and powerlessness of Jewry is coming to an end. The Holocaust and the rebirth of the State of Israel have ended the period of exilic Judaism. *Tisha B'Av* [the day of mourning for the destruction of the Temple and of prayer for its rebuilding] cannot be unaffected by the miracle of Israel and the reunification of Jerusalem. The prophet Zechariah told Israel in God's name that after the return, Tisha B'Av and the three other fasts will become days of celebration and joy (Zechariah 8:19). While it is too early to claim that the Messianic fulfillment is here, the process of redemption now underway is discernable.[8]

For many who support the Temple rebuilding movement, the discernment of redemption has become an imminent hope. Many Orthodox Jewish leaders, both in the United States and in Israel, have been privately and publicly announcing that 1992 is the year for the accomplishment of part or all of this hope. Whether or not 1992 develops as these people expect, the fact that Jewish leaders have specific and concrete hopes is a significant recent development.

Signs of the Times

Never before in recent history has there been such an overpowering sense of destiny captivating Jewish leaders, as they prepare to welcome the coming Messiah. Never before have world events been interpreted with such prophetic conviction by Jewish rabbis and average Israelis alike in anticipation of the messianic era.

Many of these Jewish leaders are making unprecedented claims that we are about to see the fulfillment of the Bible's prophetic promises. Having been regathered from the nations, having regained Jerusalem, and having revived their ancient tongue (Hebrew), Israeli Jews are now ready for the next step: rebuilding the Temple.

For Christians, these declarations of the imminent appearance of the Messiah and of the rebuilding of the Temple produce both excitement and confusion. Many Christians expect the imminent return of the Lord Jesus and see evidence of the nearness of that coming in the current events that surround the State of Israel. They regard the rebuilding of the Temple as a scriptural condition for the fulfillment of the advent of Messiah. Others, however, look at the establishment of a Jewish Temple as a threat to their claim that God has chosen the church to replace Israel as the "people of God." They expect a conversion of Jewry to Christianity as a fulfillment of the promise made by the prophets, and view a return to the Temple ritual as an impediment to such fulfillment.

In the chapters ahead we will address each of these groups in Christianity and analyze the historical and biblical interpretations that have led to these views. Regardless of the perspective, however, the events that have engaged modern Israel since it declared its independence in 1948 are of international significance, and no one can deny the desire of the Jewish people to rebuild their Temple as a monument of their historic heritage. It is a legitimate enterprise for the fulfillment of the Jewish religious hope and an important steppingstone to the realization of the Christian destiny.

The Stage is Set

Prior to 1948, virtually the whole world opposed Jewish attempts to return to their homeland. Many Jews also opposed these efforts and thought that they would never succeed. Entire books written before 1948 (and now out of print and buried in library archives) declared that the Jewish people would never return to their homeland. Yet they did. Despite the odds against organized Zionism, the Jewish people are in their land today. Historian Heinrich Graetz reminds us, "A nation which has witnessed the rise and decay of the most ancient empires, and which still continues to hold its place in the present day, deserves the closest attention."

The remarkable parallel between Israel's successful struggle to regain its ancient land and the present effort to regain control of its Temple Mount in order to rebuild the Temple cannot be overlooked. Many people, Jews and non-Jews alike, believe that the leaders of the movement to build the Temple are pursuing an unrealistic hope. Yet these leaders, like those who dreamed of Israel's return to its land, believe that God will one day bring it to pass because the Bible declares it will be so. Even though the Temple leaders are at a loss to explain how this miracle will be accomplished in light of the current world situation, they maintain a firm conviction that one day soon there will be a Temple on the Temple Mount. They continue to hold out great hope that tomorrow may be their day, just like May 14, 1948 was the day Zionist efforts succeeded in reclaiming the land of Israel.

While sensationalism should be avoided, we can no longer deny that sensational things are occurring in the land of the Bible. Because the subject of the rebuilding of the Temple may soon occupy the attention of the world, believers need to be informed of the vital issues surrounding the Temple Mount and the progress being made to return that site to its former glory.

With each passing year more props and players are positioned for the final act of the current age of history. God has moved the main actor, Israel, onto the stage. And when that nation is moving collectively to expect its Messiah and begin again to realize its prophetic destiny, we who are Christians and share in that fulfillment ought of all people to pay attention. We have come to a turning point on the prophetic path from which we will not likely turn back.

A Nation with a Destiny

The determination among Israeli Jews, and Jews worldwide, to see the coming of the Messiah and the rebuilding of the Temple is resolute. The French general Napoleon Bonaparte once passed a synagogue and heard the Jews weeping. "What's this weeping?" he asked. When told that the Jews weep about the destruction of their Temple, Napoleon said, "A people that longs so much for its city and its Temple are bound to restore them one day!"

As weeping for the Temple has today turned to working for the Temple, is that day of restoration near? In the days before Israel's independence, when Menachem Begin was still commander of the Irgun, he announced that one of the foremost Jewish objectives in Palestine was the rebuilding of the Temple. He declared, "The Third Temple, as outlined by Ezekiel, will assuredly be rebuilt in our generation."[9] Are the Jews at last ready to rebuild? The signs that point to that conclusion are clear. They deserve our attention!

Chapter 2

Christian Controversy

But when this Antichrist shall have devastated all things in this world, he will reign for three years and six months, and sit in the Temple at Jerusalem; and then the Lord will come from heaven in the clouds, in the glory of the Father, sending this man and those who follow him into the lake of fire; but bringing in for the righteous the times of the kingdom.[1]

—Irenaeus (A.D. 185)

The Bible does not prophesy any future literal Temple or sacrificial system to be set up in Jerusalem. The Biblical prophecies of the Temple refer to Christ and His Church, definitively, progressively, and finally.[2]

—David Chilton (A.D. 1985)

*T*oday many Christians are excited about the very real potential for the rebuilding of Israel's Temple in Jerusalem. Christian publications periodically contain reports of current events relating to Jewish rebuilding efforts, and a growing number of Christians see a biblical significance in these events. However, it has not always been this way.

As we saw in the last chapter, down through history differing opinions have developed among Christians about the need for an end-times' Temple for Israel. Simply put, one group says there will be a third Temple, which will be defiled by Antichrist. The other group of believers contend that no such Temple will or should ever exist. Both views are strongly championed.

The people who contend that there will be a third Temple take Bible passages about the tribulation period literally. They believe that verses such as 2 Thessalonians 2:4, "so that he (Antichrist) takes his seat in the Temple of God, displaying himself as being God," speak of an unfulfilled, future event, which implies a Temple in Jerusalem.

Irenaeus, writing in about A.D. 185, expresses this view in the quotation that opens this chapter.

People who believe that there will be no future Temple rest their thinking on two main points. First, the destruction of the second Temple in A.D. 70 is a sign that Christianity is blessed by God while Judaism is rejected. In this view, Jerusalem and the Temple were destroyed as God's judgment upon the Jews for rejecting Jesus as Messiah. Second, the church is the new Temple of God, which He now indwells spiritually; therefore, there will never be a need for a future Jewish Temple. God's spiritual Temple, the church, forever replaces the literal, physical Temple.

Some who hold this latter view concede that a temple-like religious structure might be built, just as the Great Synagogue in downtown Jerusalem has been built, but they deny that it would have any more prophetic meaning than the erection of a new tourist hotel in the city. They believe that since Israel is no longer a "people of God," what the Jews do has no greater significance than what people in Serbo Croatia or Mozambique might do.

This viewpoint has been the one most widely held throughout the church's history, as the David Chilton quote at the beginning of this chapter exemplifies. Since we believe the Bible teaches that there *will* be a third Temple rebuilt sometime in the future, it is important to understand how the "no Temple" view developed.

A New Religion?

In the first century the Roman Empire ruled much of the world. Christianity sprang up within the empire. Rome had a policy of religious toleration toward those religions which they recognized as legal, but of religious oppression toward those that were deemed illegal. Judaism was recognized by Rome as a legal religion. In the earliest days of Christianity, Christians were viewed by the Romans as a sect within Judaism often known as "the Nazarenes," and therefore a legal sect. As time went on, there was a growing rift between Christian Jews and non-Christian Jews. The rift was complete by the time of Bar Kokhba's revolt in A.D. 132.

As Christianity developed a clear identity of its own, it was viewed increasingly as an illegal religion. Tacitus, the Roman historian, handed Christianity the ultimate insult for a religion hoping to gain tolerance from Rome when he called it a "new" religion. One of the main reasons Judaism had been accepted as a legal religion was that its advocates, like the Jewish historian Josephus in his *Antiquities of the Jews*, argued that Israel's religion was ancient. The Romans respected ancient beliefs and this helped to make Judaism a tolerated religion within an empire whose official religion was paganism. However, if Christianity was new, then on what grounds could it appeal for toleration from Rome? We will see that in the second century, Christians began to argue that the Jews were apostate, and that Christians were the "new Israel," and therefore not really new but as old as Abraham and Moses.

Since Christianity had grown out of the womb of Judaism, its first conflicts and persecutions were with its Jewish rivals. Early church apologists like Justin Martyr in his "Dialogue with Trypho," a supposed Jewish opponent, argued that Jews were no longer God's people since their Temple had been destroyed because of their rejection of Jesus as Messiah. God had a new people, the "new Israel" which was the church, the spiritual Temple in which God was now dwelling. Belief that no future, physical Temple would ever be built because God now indwelt a spiritual Temple—the church—became one of the major proofs of Christianity.

Even though some of the early church fathers, such as Irenaeus, did believe in a future Temple in Jerusalem, the "future Temple" view began to wane and the "no Temple" view began to dominate by the end of the third century. "It appeared then, as it did to later generations, that the beginning of Christianity coincided with the demise of Judaism. As long as Christianity had been in existence, it seemed, the Jews possessed neither the Temple nor the city."[3] About this time also, biblical prophecy was becoming increasingly "spiritualized" and viewed less literally, even among the orthodox.

Early church writers such as Origen, Eusebius, and Chrysostom went so far as to link the veracity of Christianity to the condition that Israel's Temple would never again be rebuilt in Jerusalem. "By the middle of the century the historical coincidence of the rise of Christianity and the decline of Judaism seemed even more certain in the Christian mind. Another several generations had passed, the Temple still was in ruins and the forty years from Jesus' death to the loss of the city merged together to form one event."[4]

By the time of Constantine (A.D. 313) the early church's desire to justify itself in the eyes of Jews and to gain acceptance from the Roman Empire combined with the shift in the literal interpretation of prophecy to produce the viewpoint that the destruction of the second Temple was permanent.[5] As if to corroborate this conviction, under the direction of Constantine's mother, Queen Helena, "Christians were beginning to transform the city of Jerusalem into a Christian city. Christian churches were being constructed in Jerusalem, notably the Church of the Resurrection (Anastasis), and for the first time in Christian history Jerusalem began to attract Christian pilgrims in significant numbers."[6]

Julian the Apostate Rises to Power

In A.D. 313 Emperor Constantine not only gave Christianity legal status, but in a moment of time pronounced this once-illegal religion as the official religion of the Roman Empire, replacing paganism. Christian morale could never have been higher. Unexpectedly, Constantine had not only converted to Christianity but also converted a whole empire into one that built churches, propagated and defended the faith, and laid the cornerstone for the development of Christian Europe—the new kingdom of God. With the establishment of Christianity as the most-favored religion, all pagan temples and statues were destroyed and replaced by Christian places of worship. Christianity was being vindicated before the eyes of her two antagonists—paganism and Judaism.

Constantine's long reign ended with his death in A.D. 361. A nephew, Flavius Claudius Julianus, replaced Constantine for 19 months, during which he attempted to return the empire to paganism in an effort to restore emperor worship. Julian, named "the Apostate" by Christians, also wrote a massive rebuttal against Christianity called *Contra Galilaeos* ("Against the Galileans," his term for Christians), and attempted to do as much as he could to obstruct Christianity.

Julianus had been educated in his youth as a Christian by the renowned bishop of Cesarea, Eusebius, but he reacted against what he saw as "Christian" persecutions of other beliefs. In response he issued an edict of universal religious toleration. Julian favored Judaism over Christianity not only because of his passion against Christians, but also because he viewed Christianity as a defection from Judaism, and because he saw Judaism fitting better with his concept of religious pluralism. By returning the ancient city Jerusalem to the Jews, Julian hoped to turn back the tide of Christianity that had swept the empire under Constantine.

The Earth Trembles

Prior to his Persian campaign, Julian wrote a letter to the community of the Jews in which he promised to abolish anti-Jewish laws and to rebuild the Temple where he would join them in worship.[7] Shortly afterward he wrote in A.D. 363 that "even now the temple is being raised again."[8] Jewish sources hint at some of the discussions that surrounded these building activities. Rabbi Acha argued that the Temple could be built even though certain sacred objects from the second Temple were missing,[9] and that the third Temple could be built before the coming of the Messiah.[10]

Christians saw this rebuilding effort as a fulfillment of Daniel 11:34 and the "abomination of desolation," which explains why they branded the emperor as Julian the Apostate. Romans saw the project as a memorial to Julian's rule. But it is probably more accurate to see this as Julian's attempt to strengthen paganism against Christianity (since both Judaism and paganism had sacrificial rites) and as a refutation of Jesus' supposed prophecy against the rebuilding of the Temple.

Just as the builders were attempting to break into the foundations to begin construction on the Temple Mount, the unexpected happened. An earthquake struck. The earthquake apparently ignited reservoirs of trapped gases below ground, and the resulting explosion destroyed all of the building materials. Philip Hammond, in studying this earth-quake, which also destroyed the city of Petra, gives an account of what the scene that day must have looked like:

> The stones were piled and ready. Costly wood had been purchased. The necessary metal was at hand. The Jews of Jerusalem were rejoicing. Tomorrow—May 20, 363 A.D.—the rebuilding of the Temple would begin! . . . Suddenly, and with-out warning, at the third hour of the night . . . the streets of Jerusalem trembled and buckled, crush-ing two hundred years of hope in a pile of dust. No longer would there be any possibility of rebuild-ing the Temple.[11]

The church told the story of this incident with some embellishments, claiming that fire fell from heaven accom-panied by a vision of Christ, as a judgment on those who sought to blaspheme the verdict of God and history. While we can understand this earthquake to be an act of divine intervention, it doesn't necessarily follow that the quake was a sign that the Jews would never build their Temple—only that A.D. 363 was not the time God had planned for the Temple's and Israel's restoration.

Still Christians hailed these events as an act of God that refuted the Jews. Chrysostom mentions "the fulfillment of the prophecy in Matthew 24, 'no stone shall be left standing upon another' as proof of the Christian claim that Jesus is God" (*Christus sit Deus* 16).[12]

Reverend Warburton of London, in 1750, wrote the most complete account in the English language of this incident in a book entitled *Julian. Or a Discourse Concerning the Earth-quake and Fiery Eruption, Which Defeated that Emperor's Attempt to Rebuild the Temple in Jerusalem*. Warburton says that God used three miracles to hinder Julian's building of the Temple:

> The first of these miracles was an EARTH-
> QUAKE, which happened at the time they were
> clearing the old foundations, in order to lay new:
> and this earthquake overthrew their magazines
> of materials. . . . The second miracle was a FIRE,
> which burnt from the foundations they were pre-
> paring; and destroyed one part of the workmen,
> and put the rest to flight. . . . Their obstinacy gave
> occasion to a third miracle. For, in the morning,
> they perceived a great number of SHINING
> STARS scattered over their habits; which they
> tried to efface, but, in vain.[13]

One early church historian, who claims that his account
of this incident was derived from eyewitnesses, adds that the
"stars" people perceived appeared in the shape of crosses
and as a result "many were hence led to confess that Christ
is God and that the rebuilding of the Temple was not pleas-
ing to Him."[14]

For the Jews, the rebuilding of the Temple had generated
such a wave of excitement and expectation that even after
their disappointment over Julian's failed attempt they continued to nurture hope of a restored Temple and their final
vindication. Nevertheless, further efforts to rebuild the
Temple were abandoned when Julian's short year-and-a-half
reign ceased and a Christian emperor regained the throne.

Symbolic Architecture

When the Byzantine Christians began their massive
building campaign during the rule of Constantine, one of
their first projects was the Church of the Holy Sepulchre
opposite the site of the Temple in Jerusalem. The site they
chose was that of Jesus' crucifixion and burial/resurrection.
The Hadrianic temple of Aphrodite had been built in the
same location, so demolishing it and erecting a Christian

monument symbolized the ascendancy of Christianity over Roman paganism.

More importantly, a statement by Eusebius in his *Life of Constantine* explains the symbolism in the church's layout: "Over the true memorial of salvation was built the New Jerusalem, facing the far-famed Jerusalem of old time."[15] As Lawrence Sporty explains:

> Eusebius is referring to the spiritual Jerusalem, specifically the Temple Mount and its spiritual center, the holy house. The New Jerusalem he refers to could not be the actual city of Jerusalem of his day either, but its new spiritual center, the basilica of Constantine. Hence, he is really saying that the new basilica arose facing the old holy house ruins.[16]

Therefore the "New Jerusalem," the new spiritual center of Christianity, was seen to have replaced the Temple Mount, the former spiritual center of the Jews, and so the Church of the Holy Sepulchre was intended to replace the Temple, both symbolically and actually.

Wilkinson in his *Egeria's Travels in the Holy Land* supports this by describing how the construction of the Church of the Holy Sepulchre was deliberately arranged to parallel the layout of the second Temple. For example, the Cave of the Anastasis (site of the resurrection) was spatially placed in relation to the site of the crucifixion in the same manner that the Altar of Burnt Offering was to the Holy of Holies in the Temple. The alignment of the basilica along an east-west axis also followed that of the Temple. Even the early liturgies and rituals conducted in the church paralleled those of the Temple.

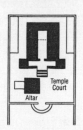
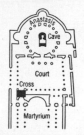

By placing the church directly opposite and facing the Temple, and in fact on higher ground overlooking the Temple, Christians dramatically emphasized the claim of Christ in John 2:19 that He would destroy the Temple. And they deliberately preserved the ruins of the Temple on the Temple Mount to reinforce this symbolism (see Figure 1).

As we can see, Byzantine Christianity viewed the church as the New Jerusalem, a viewpoint which has come to be called "replacement theology." Replacement theology supports the belief that Bible verses speaking about future references to Israel should instead be taken as cryptic references to the church. Using the destruction of the Temple as a physical proof of its claim, this approach helped the church demonstrate its ascendancy over Judaism and reinforced the "no Temple" view.

Adding Insult to Injury

While Christian architects embellished the churches of Jerusalem situated around the Temple Mount, the area of the Temple itself was deliberately left as a desolate wasteland. Pilgrim accounts describe wild animals and scavengers prowling about the ruins of the Temple. At some time during the Byzantine period (possibly at the time of Emperor Heraclius in the seventh century), the Temple Mount began to be used as a dung heap. The modern name of the gate leading to the Temple Mount entrance today, the Dung Gate, is derived from this period in history. Apparently the desolation of the site was not enough—the Christians wanted to literally heap insult upon the Jews by defiling the holy place.

When Muslim conquerors entered Jerusalem they found the Temple Mount almost inaccessible due to the large amounts of refuse that filled the entrances. On the Mount, the site assumed to be the Holy of Holies was hidden completely beneath a heap of dung. A fourteenth-century Muslim

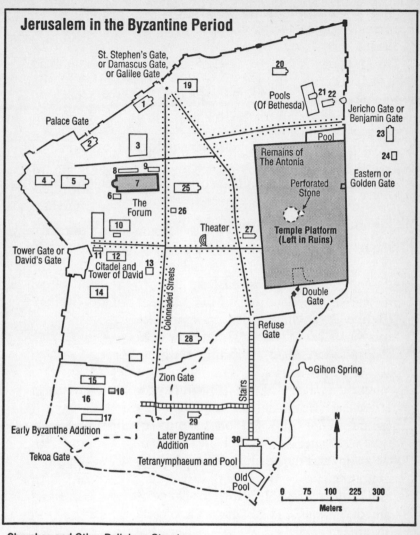

Jerusalem in the Byzantine Period

St. Stephen's Gate, or Damascus Gate, or Galilee Gate

Palace Gate

Pools (Of Bethesda)

Jericho Gate or Benjamin Gate

Pool

Remains of The Antonia

Eastern or Golden Gate

Perforated Stone

The Forum

Theater

Temple Platform (Left in Ruins)

Tower Gate or David's Gate

Citadel and Tower of David

Colonnaded Streets

Double Gate

Refuse Gate

Gihon Spring

Zion Gate

Stairs

Early Byzantine Addition

Later Byzantine Addition

Tekoa Gate

Tetranymphaeum and Pool

Old Pool

N

0 75 100 225 300
Meters

Churches and Other Religious Structures

1. Serapion Church
2. St. Georges Church
3. Patriarch's Hospice or the Smith's Market
4. Theodorus Monastery
5. Spondaean Monastery
6. Baptistry
7. Church of the Holy Sepulchre

8. Priest's House
9. Patriarch's Palace
10. Greek Monastery Church John the Baptist
11. Monastery of St. Sabas
12. Iberian Monastery
13. Syrian Monastery
14. Church of St. James
15. House of Caiaphas

16. Basilica of Mt. Zion
17. St. Stephen's Church
18. Priest's House
19. Eudocia's Palace
20. Church of Mary Magdalene
21. Church of the Paralytic
22. Church of the Nativity of St. Mary
23. Tomb of the Virgin

24. Gethsemane
25. Church of SS Cosmos and Damianus
26. Home of the Aged
27. St. Sophia's Church
28. Nea (New) Church
29. Monastery of St. Peter
30. Eudocia's Church

Figure 1: General Plan of Byzantine Jerusalem

work entitled *Muthir al-Ghiram* preserves a succinct description of the Temple Mount by first-generation Muslims in Jerusalem:

> Now at that time [of Emperor Heraclius] there was over the Rock in the Holy City a great dung-heap which completely masked the prayer niche of David and which the Christians had put there in order to offend the Jews; and further, even the Christian women were wont to throw their [menstrual] cloths and clouts in the place so that there was a pile of them there.[17]

This uncivil attitude toward the Mount wasn't limited to the Byzantines either. In 1883 British military hero Charles George Gordon arrived in Jerusalem. Gordon was a Christian whose religious enthusiasm went to the point of hallucination. He identified a hill (today known as "Gordon's Calvary") in which a garden tomb cave was located at the hill of Golgotha where Christ was crucified. Incredibly, the basis of his identification of the site was a fantastic imagery of the topography of Jerusalem. He visualized an imaginary skeleton superimposed on the city in which his site, "Golgotha" ("skull" in Aramaic) was the head. He fixed the legs of the skeleton on the City of David, and finally aligned its pelvis with the Dome of the Rock. Thus, in his sketch of this visualization, published after his death in 1885, Gordon continued the perception of the Jewish Temple as a place of dung!

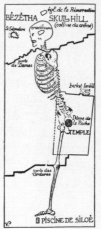

In interpreting the destruction of Jerusalem and the Temple as a permanent sign of God's disfavor toward the Jewish people and viewing any attempt to rebuild the Temple as a challenge to Christ and the church, many people, like Gordon, have gone to extremes. Christians today who have accepted the teaching that the church is Israel, and Christians are the true spiritual Jews should take note that such theology has often been used to justify anti-Semitism.

Irenaeus' View is Revived

The view that Israel's Temple would never be rebuilt dominated the church's thinking without serious competition until the early 1800's, and the permanent destruction of the Temple was used as a proof for Christianity as late as the turn of the nineteenth century.[18] Slowly, however, Irenaeus' view, stated 1600 years earlier, that there would be another Temple began to reappear.

For many Christians in Europe, events such as the French Revolution and the rise of Napoleon opened the door to a revival of biblical prophecy. By the early 1800's, increased interest in the study of biblical prophecy led to a resurgence of a more literal understanding of key prophetic passages. The more literally some of the prophecies were taken, the more other prophecies relating to the Jews also had to be taken at face value, meaning that they would be fulfilled to Jews as Jews rather than to the New Israel, the church. People began to see events like the return of Israel to their land and the rebuilding of the Temple as a part of God's future plan for Israel. However, these Christians still strongly held that the Jews must come to believe in Jesus as the Messiah in order for these things to occur.

As Bible interpreters began to think through the implications of a literal and future fulfillment of Israel's destiny, many concluded that the Bible was teaching that God has a plan for the church, which is currently being unfolded, and at the same time a separate and future plan for Israel, which is being postponed during the church age because of the Jews' rejection of Jesus as their Messiah. In the chapters to come we will show why we believe this literal approach to the interpretation of Bible prophecy is the correct one.

Although the Romans constructed pagan temples and Christians built churches, God's plan for the future calls for the reconstruction of the third Temple in Jerusalem, which the Antichrist will one day defile. As we will see, God has specific plans for both Israel and the church. But before we look to the future, let's look more personally at what the Temple meant to the Jews of the past. No other building has a richer history—or holds more significance for a people than the place they call "the house of God."

Chapter 3

One House
for One God

The Jews had a peculiar way of consecrating things to
God, which we have not. Under the law, God, who was
master of all, made choice of a temple to worship in,
where he was more especially present: just as the master
of the house, who owns all the house, makes choice of
one chamber to lie in, which is called the master's chamber. But under the gospel there was no such thing.

—*John Selden*, Table Talk (1689)

*W*hile almost every Christian has some knowledge of
the Jewish Temple, very few possess an understanding
of its significance for the Jewish people. In order to appreci-
ate the contemporary fervor over the prospect of rebuilding
the Temple, we must first gain a *Jewish* perspective of the
Temple, its purpose in the fulfillment of the Jews' unique
calling, and how the history of the Jewish people has been
affected by its absence for nearly two thousand years.

The House of God

Our English word "temple" is derived from the Latin
templum, which in turn is a translation of the Hebrew term
hekal, meaning "big house." In our English versions of the

39

Old Testament, the word "temple" is reserved primarily for the sacred Jewish building erected in Jerusalem and sometimes distinguished by a capital letter, *Temple*.

The Hebrew Old Testament, however, rarely uses this term. It prefers to describe the Temple as *bet YHWH* "house of the Lord," or *bet 'elohim* "house of God." This expression better captures the idea of the Temple as "a place where God dwells" and follows the general meaning of the Hebrew term for the Tabernacle, *mishkan*, "dwelling place."

The Ark and the Glory

The significance of the Temple, especially to the writing prophets of Israel, was its connection with the *Shekinah*, the Divine Presence. This emphasis can be seen in a brief summary of the prophets' description of the Temple: The Temple is, in their words, "the mountain of the Lord, the holy mountain" (Isaiah 11:9; 56:7; 65:11,25; Joel 2:1; 4:17; Zephaniah 3:11), wherein "the Lord dwells" (Psalm 74:2), and the Temple is "the house of the God of Jacob" and "the Lord's house" (Isaiah 2:2,3; Jeremiah 23:11; Ezekiel 8:14, 16; Joel 1:13-16; Micah 4:1,2; Haggai 1:14), the habitation of "the Divine Presence" (Ezekiel 9:3; 43:5-9; Joel 4:17,21; Habakkuk 2:20), the place where the Divine Presence reveals itself to the prophet (Isaiah 6:1; Amos 1:2; 9:1). Originally the distinction of the Temple as the dwelling place of God was associated with the presence of the Ark of the Covenant, for it represented the footstool of the Divine Presence.[1] Yet long after the Ark had disappeared, the Temple was still regarded as the place where God dwelt.

Josephus, the first-century Jewish historian, records the words of Elezar, the last of the Zealots, at Massada shortly after the destruction of the second Temple: "Where is this city that was believed to have God Himself inhabiting therein?"[2] The Roman historian Dio Cassius wrote that the Roman soldiers who burned down the second Temple were afraid to enter the Temple "for superstitious reasons" and only did so after being compelled against their will.[3]

A Transcendent God

Like the superstitious Romans, many other people misunderstood the concept of God having a dwelling place. Did God Himself live in the Temple? This was the common pagan concept. Throughout the ancient Near East, temples were built as royal residences for the gods of the people. Man's duty was to provide for the physical needs of the gods: food, water, clothing, and innumerable delicacies, and in exchange for these services, the gods were expected to provide human necessities.[4]

Israelite worship stood in opposition to this pagan concept of god and temple. The Israelite God was not a local god, nor could He be localized. He was the transcendent One, whose Being could not be limited to any physical structure and who needed no place of shelter or sanctuary.

Furthermore, the Israelite God had no need for human provision. He was the One who provided for human need from an endless store of divine supply. This understanding of God's Being may be seen in Psalm 50:9-13, where the psalmist corrects the notion that God required the Temple sacrifices for food: "If I [God] were hungry, I would not tell you; for the world is Mine and all it contains. Shall I eat the flesh of bulls, or drink the blood of male goats?" (verses 12,13). Therefore, it was alien to the Israelite concept of God to view Him as being contained in a temple in order to have His needs met by man.

When the Temple was finally built, this was explained to the Israelites who were present at its dedication: "But will God indeed dwell on the earth? Behold, heaven and the highest heaven cannot contain Thee, how much less this Temple which I have built!" (1 Kings 8:27). This statement makes it clear that God's Presence did not dwell in the

Israelite Temple in the same way a god was present in all the other pagan temples of the world. For this reason the God of Israel was not to be represented in form by an idol (Exodus 20:4; Deuteronomy 4:15-19) and placed in a shrine (Ezekiel 8:5-12) after the practice of the Canaanite religion.

The Israelite Temple, rather than being a place where *God's needs* were met, was a place where God met the *needs of His people*. The knowledge that God's Presence dwelt among them assured the Israelites of access to their God and of His provision and care for them.

A Chosen Place

The idea of God dwelling in the midst of His people is first introduced in the "Song of Moses," recorded in Exodus 15:17: "Thou wilt bring them and plant them in the mountain of Thine inheritance, the place, O Lord, which Thou hast made for Thy dwelling, the sanctuary, O Lord, which Thy hands have established." Moses, who had just witnessed God's manifested Presence in the pillar of cloud that protected the Israelites from the Egyptian soldiers, and who had passed through the divided sea on dry ground, looked forward to the time when God would permanently dwell with His chosen people in the Promised Land.

Until that time the Divine Presence appeared in the midst of the people in a *miqdash* ("holy place," cf., Exodus 25:8) known also as the Tabernacle. At various times the Tabernacle rested at a dozen places throughout the land of Israel, at sites such as Shiloh, Bethel, Dan, Gilgal in Ephraim, Mizpah in Benjamin, and Hebron. These places were recognized as spots where God revealed Himself, yet they lacked Jerusalem's particular distinction of being divinely chosen for the permanent site of the Temple.

Having a single, centralized sanctuary, first in the Tabernacle and then in the Temple, neutralized the pagan idea that Israel's God was merely a local or tribal deity. The Israelite

God was God over *all* the Israelite tribes. There was no "splitting up" of the deity in numerous shrines throughout the land, since there was only one "house of the Lord."[5] The permanent placement of the Temple in Jerusalem enforced this unique doctrine of the one true God.

A Man After God's Heart

The Tabernacle was a temporary structure, moving from place to place until the Israelites were unified politically and spiritually. This occurred when David conquered Jerusalem and made it not only the capital of Israel, but also the City of God. For the first time in Israeli history, civil and religious authority were centralized in one geographical location. First Kings 8:16 says that from the time of the exodus until the time of David, God had not chosen a city out of the tribes of Israel in which to build the Temple. This may mean that God had not chosen a place until David, for this verse and the next adds, "But I chose David to be over My people Israel. Now it was in the heart of . . . David to build a house for the name of the Lord, the God of Israel." David's desire to build God a house began to grow when he realized the inequity of his own palatial dwelling in comparison to the meager housing of the Ark in a tent (2 Samuel 7:1,2). While in the text of Scripture we do not find God specifically *telling* David the place of His choice, we do find God choosing a man who *knew* His choice (cf., 1 Samuel 13:14).

David chose Jerusalem for his capital for several reasons: First, it was territory that had not belonged to any of the northern or southern tribes, and thus represented a neutral region that would not provoke jealousy among the tribes. Second, it was strategically located and could serve as a central location for civil administration. Third, and perhaps most important, it had a historic connection with the people of Israel from the time of Abraham and was traditionally assumed to be "the mountain of God's inheritance" spoken of in Exodus 15:17.

These factors motivated David in his choice of Jerusalem as the site for the Temple. Yet David was chosen to make this choice primarily because he was a man after God's own heart (1 Samuel 13:14). The building of the Temple in Jerusalem was seen to be inspired in the heart of David by God,[6] and thereby came to be seen as the historic choice of God Himself.[7]

It has been said that "there is nothing inherent in the location of the Temple in Jerusalem. Its location was simply where it happened to be built. . . . There is no biblical etiology [explanation for the origin] for [its] location. . . . It could, in principle, have been built anywhere else and still have been the same."[8] But such a statement is contrary to the written record that Jerusalem, and the Temple Mount, were prepared as the site for the Temple from at least the time of the patriarchs. They were prepared for this purpose by repeated revelations of God to His servants.

The most important of these revelations is found in the Davidic Covenant, found in 2 Samuel 7:8-17. This passage links the promise of the building of the Temple with the covenant promise that David's royal throne would be established forever:

> I will also appoint a place for My people Israel and will plant them, that they may live in their own place and not be disturbed again. . . . The Lord also declares to you that the Lord will make a house for you. When your days are complete . . . I will raise up your descendant after you. . . . He shall build a house for My name, and I will establish the throne of his kingdom forever (2 Samuel 7:10-13).

The implication is not that the Temple would never be violated, but that the site chosen for it by David would remain forever, like the Davidic dynasty, as testimony to the unconditional nature of the divine contract. This fact is later affirmed by Psalm 132, which joins together David's choice of a site for the Temple (verses 1-5), the Davidic Covenant (verses 10-12), and God's declaration that "this is My resting place forever" (verses 13,14). In addition, the permanency of Jerusalem and the Temple Mount as God's dwelling is required for the fulfillment of prophecies ascribed to them.[9]

While God chose David, who chose the site for the Temple, He did not choose David to *build* the Temple.[10] The reasons for this give us penetrating insight into the nature of the Temple.

A Temple of Peace

David was a man of war, but the Temple was to be a place of peace. This characteristic of the Temple finds its ultimate fulfillment in the future as recorded in Isaiah 2:

> Now it will come about in the last days... many peoples will come and say, "Come, let us go up to the mountain of the Lord, to the house of the God of Jacob; that He may teach us concerning His ways, and that we may walk in His paths." For the law will go forth from Zion, and the word of the Lord from Jerusalem...and they will hammer their swords into plowshares, and their spears into pruning hooks. Nation will not lift up sword against nation, and never again will they learn war (verses 2,4).

The peace that will come to the earth will emanate from the future Temple causing instruments of destruction to be changed to instruments of production, and the nations of the world to learn the Word of God rather than war.

In token of the peaceful purpose of the Temple, none of the stones used to fashion the Temple were prepared at the site. All of the stones were dressed at the quarry so that no sound of clanging metal tools would be heard in the area of the Temple Mount and remind people of the sounds of war (1 Kings 6:7).

The Temple was to be founded in peace, by a man of peace, and be a place of peace for all who sought the true God. The sound of the clanging of swords was common to David; he had used the sword to bring death and destruction (1 Chronicles 22:8). Therefore he could not be the architect of the Temple which represented life and peace. This honor fell to David's son, Solomon, whose very name means "peace," and whose 40-year reign was one of continued peace.

At the time of the Temple's dedication, Solomon warned the people that they would lose God's blessing if their hearts were not "at peace" with the Lord (1 Kings 8:61 Hebrew). It is ironic that Solomon fulfilled his own words and set into motion the idolatrous practices that would end the first Temple. Scripture confirms this when it says of Solomon: "His heart was not at peace with the Lord as the heart of his father David had been" (1 Kings 11:4).

A Temple of Grace

Although God would not allow David to build a house for Him, He graciously promised to build a house for David. This "house" was a line of descendants who would establish David's throne forever. David's desire for the building of the Temple was fulfilled through his son, Solomon, whose birth was itself a sign of God's gracious forgiveness of David's sin with Bathsheba. The text in 2 Samuel 7 even makes provision for future sin that would threaten the Temple's existence.

Solomon would sin and be punished by men (ultimately by the Babylonian destruction of the Temple he had built), but God's grace would be displayed in that David's dynasty would continue. God's grace was the basis not only for the building of the first Temple, but for each successive Temple in Jerusalem.

God's provision for the Temple in His promise to David was preceded some 2,000 years earlier by another event that took place in the region of the Temple Mount. This was the offering of Isaac by Abraham on Mount Moriah. This place, as well as all the land of Canaan, had been given by God to Abraham forever.[11] On this spot Abraham was witness to God's grace when God substituted a ram for sacrifice in the place of Isaac. In token of this, Genesis 22:14 records: "And Abraham called the name of the place, The Lord Will Provide; as it is said to this day, 'In the mount of the Lord it will be provided.' " From the beginning of the history of the Temple Mount, grace is the attribute that has characterized the Temple.

In 1 Kings 8:31-40 and 44-53 a list is given of the various functions of the Temple. In every instance the functions relate to man's needs for judicial resolution; military, agricultural, and social assistance; and spiritual restoration. Incredibly, the function of sacrifice so commonly associated with the Temple is nowhere mentioned in this record. The primary purpose of the Temple was not to offer something to God, but to receive from Him His offer of grace.

A Temple of Prayer

Second Samuel 24 relates the story of how David sinned by taking a census to determine his military strength rather than trusting in God.[12] As a result, a plague was sent to destroy the people of Jerusalem. David went to the place where the destroying angel stood and erected an altar and offered peace offerings to the Lord. The result was that "the Lord heeded the prayers for the land, and the plague was withdrawn from Israel" (verse 25 NKJV). The place where David had prayed was the threshing floor of Araunah

(Ornan) the Jebusite, and this was purchased for the site of the Temple. A place of prayer became the place for the Temple (2 Chronicles 3:1).

When Solomon later built the Temple, he publicly explained to the Israelite population assembled for its dedication that the Temple was designed as a place of prayer. In 1 Kings 8:29,30 we read: "You said, 'My name shall be there,' that you may hear the prayer which Your servant makes toward this place. And may you hear the supplication of Your servant and of Your people Israel" (NKJV).

Furthermore, the Temple was not a place for Israelite prayers alone, but was to be a place of universal prayer for all nations. The passage continues: "Moreover, concerning a foreigner, who is not of Your people Israel, but has come from a far country for Your name's sake (for they will hear of Your great name . . .), when he comes and prays toward this temple, hear in heaven Your dwelling place, and do according to all for which the foreigner calls to You . . ." (1 Kings 8:41-43 NKJV). This universal function will ultimately be realized when the future Temple fulfills the words of Isaiah 56:7: "Even them [the foreigners who join themselves to the Lord, verse 6] I will bring to My holy mountain, and make them joyful in My house of prayer" (NKJV).

A Visible Symbol of Invisible Presence

The Temple's significance to the Jew (both in the land of Israel and those outside in the Diaspora) was that it was the one place where God's Presence was represented among His people. Shaye Cohen makes this observation: "The temple . . . served as a binding force: it represented monism and exclusivity. Only one place was suitable for God's home on earth, and that place was the temple mount in Jerusalem."[13]

Since Israel's God was the true God, and only He could answer prayer, those who would have prayer answered had to come to the Temple (or pray toward the Temple). In Temple times, the only access for both Jew and non-Jew to God on earth was through association with the Temple. Without the regular Temple service, there was no direct link between the people and their God, and no longer any sacrifice for sins.

One of Israel's sages said: "Since the day that the Temple was destroyed, an iron wall has intervened between Israel and their Father in heaven."[14] Simeon the Just declared: "The world is based upon three things: the Torah, *Avodah* [the Temple service] and the practice of *gemilut hasadim* ["charity"]."[15] Given this perspective, the destruction of the Temple undermined one of the pillars of the Jewish universe—Temple service—and caused a complete imbalance in the life of the religious Jew.

The Temple was not only prominent as a religious institution to the Jewish people, but (especially in second Temple times) also played a considerable role in the political life of the people. Even in the Diaspora, Jews fought for the right to send their contributions to Jerusalem. In fact, all other institutions, even those unrelated to the Temple service, gained moral stature from their association with the Temple.[16]

The Temple, therefore, governed the life of the Jew. Jewish life was lived in view of the festivals, the pilgrimages, the sacrificial rites, and Torah reading and study, all of which centered on the Temple. Though later, and especially after A.D. 70, the synagogue, which probably began in the Temple Court, took precedence, it was with the Temple that this institution, and all others, were organically connected. The establishment of the synagogue enabled Judaism to absorb the blow of the second Temple's destruction without collapsing, but it was never meant to replace the function of the Temple in the life and faith of the Jewish people. The synagogue is only a gathering place for the community for liturgical purposes, but the Temple was "God's house," in which His Presence dwelt, and which His priests attended on behalf of His people.

The Temple was the channel by which the religious institutions of Israel became a part of the life of the people. Stipulated hours of prayer were set according to the times of sacrifices, and even those in the Diaspora were to turn their faces toward Jerusalem and the Temple. All legal matters were decided by the Sanhedrin (the Jewish high council), who had their full prerogatives of office only when seated in the Temple, and only when the sacrificial system was operational.[17]

While it may be difficult today for Gentiles and non-religious Jews to completely understand the effect of the Temple on the life of the ancient Jew, the history of the Temple, with its emotional drama, continues to capture the interest of the modern man. It is to this story we now turn.

Chapter 4

The Temple Destroyed— The Temple Rebuilt

Beautiful in elevation, the joy of the whole earth, is Mount Zion . . . the city of the great King. God, in her palaces, has made Himself known as a stronghold. . . . Walk about Zion, and go around her; count her towers; consider her ramparts; go through her palaces; that you may tell it to the next generation. For such is our God, our God forever and ever; He will guide us until death.

—Psalm 48:2,3,12-14

As we have seen, the site of the Temple Mount was host to divine dramas with the patriarch Abraham and King David prior to the actual building of the Temple. After the Temple's construction in 950 B.C., the drama intensified as the Temple became the focal point of Israel's history.

As we capture history of the Temple, we will often distinguish the Temples as the *first* Temple and the *second* Temple. These terms refer to those periods of time in which the Temple ritual continued without interruption. Even though we will find that Herod totally rebuilt the second Temple, also known as Zerubbabel's Temple after its original builder, it was not considered a third Temple since there was no lapse in the sacrificial system for even one day during the construction. In the course of this book we will also refer to two additional Temples that will be built in the future according to the literal interpretation of biblical prophecy. The history of these four Temples is outlined in Figure 2.

The First Temple

The first Temple, built by Solomon, was initially provided for by David during his last years through the royal treasury and a collection taken from the people of Israel (1 Chronicles 29). After David's death, Solomon completed the Temple primarily through forced labor from the native Israelites (1 Kings 5:13-16; 2 Chronicles 2:2). (The relationship of the Temple to the rest of Jerusalem during this time period may be seen in Figure 3, page 54).

The pattern for the Temple, like the Tabernacle, was similar in form to pagan temples of the time. The tripartite (three-room) temple was common to the architectural tradition of many peoples of Solomon's day, such as the Syrians and Phoenicians. In keeping with the custom of his age, Solomon relied upon the Phoenician expertise of his father's supplier of material, Hiram (Huram), king of Tyre (2 Samuel 5:11; 1 Kings 5; 2 Chronicles 2:3-18). Besides materials, Hiram sent his Phoenician architects and craftsmen to advise their Israelite counterparts on building the Temple to contemporary specifications. One of these was a half-Jewish, half-Phoenician artisan named Hiram (or Huramabi), who was given oversight of the craftsmen. Credit is given to him for the vast array of decorative, cast, and overlaid objects in the Temple (1 Kings 7:13-45; 2 Chronicles 2:13,14).

A Guided Tour of the Temple

During my (Thomas') high school years our family lived in the Washington, D.C. area. Every time we had guests

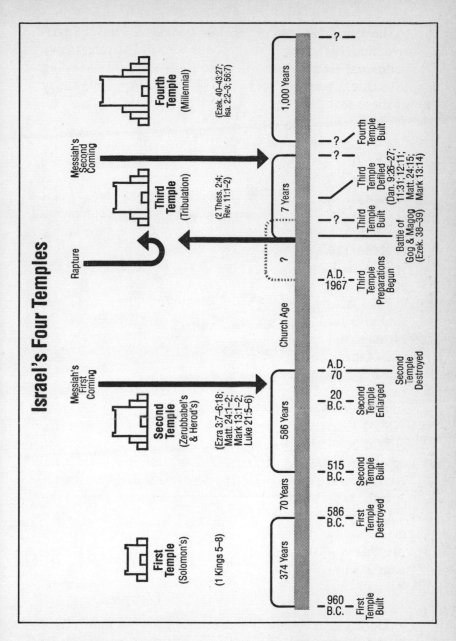

Figure 2: Israel's Four Temples

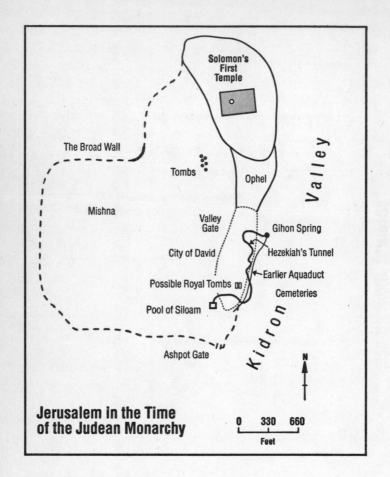

Figure 3: Jerusalem in the Time of the Judean Monarchy

who wanted to visit the sights, I was the one selected to take them around town. One place we always visited was the White House. Our guide would take us through each room and point out its importance, who last decorated it, and what historic events took place there. The guided tours added meaning to our visit, since explanations helped us understand the significance of this great American building. In the same way, one of the best ways for us to understand the significance of the Temple is to take a guided word-tour through the first Temple (see Figure 4).

Our tour begins as we approach a building of modest size, about 3,500 feet square,[1] situated on a platform approximately ten feet high. First, we ascend the ten steps leading up between the twin bronze pillars, named *Jakin* ("He [God] establishes") and *Boaz* ("in Him [God] is strength"), each about 40 feet high and 12 feet in circumference. We then come to the *Ulam*, or entrance porch, the first and smallest room of the Temple, which leads into the *Hechal*, or main room, referred to in the Bible as the Holy Place. In this, the largest room in the Temple, the interior walls are covered with elaborately carved cedar panels overlaid or inlaid with gold. The floors are covered with boards of cypress so that no stonework is seen. In addition to this, Solomon has adorned this room with beautiful precious stones.

Housed within this awe-inspiring central chamber are the magnificent seven-branched *menorah* or candelabra, the table of showbread, bearing the sacred presence bread, and the Golden Altar of Incense, where aromatic spices are burned to mask the awful stench of the outside sacrifice. Also in this room are ten tables (five on the north side and five on the south) accompanied by ten lamps on lampstands, as well as numerous implements used in the priestly service.

Going on, we are stopped from entrance into the *Devir*, the innermost room, by a double screen of a fabric veil and a wall whose only door is kept closed except on rare occasions. Access to this room, the Holy of Holies, is forbidden

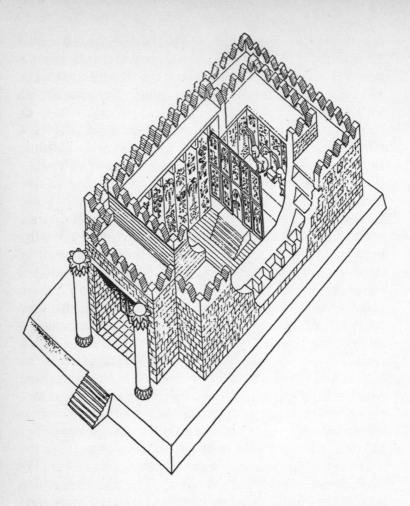

Figure 4: Solomon's Majestic Temple. The culmination of all his building projects—was intended to be the permanent home of the ark of the covenant. Though not a fragment remains today, it stood for 400 years on a hill overlooking Jerusalem. With walls 10 feet thick and crowned with a battlement, it blended fortress strength with Phoenician elegance. Two towering pillars of bronze dominated the temple facade, while the interior walls of cedar were resplendent with carvings of ivory, gold, and wood. The ark stood in the holy of holies, at the feet of two huge cherubim. These were carved from olivewood, covered with pure gold and had wingspans of 15 feet. Priests performed cleansing rituals at an enormous bronze bowl mounted on 12 bronze oxen in the courtyard. Animals were sacrificed on the spacious altar on the right side of the temple.

to all except the high priest, and to him only once a year at *Yom Kippur*, the high holy Day of Atonement. In this room, a perfect cube about 35 feet each way, covered with 23 tons of gold, stands the great Ark of the Covenant, likewise covered in gold.

The Ark rests on a bedrock platform called the *Even Shetiyyah* ("Foundation Stone").[2] The high priest rests the firepan on this rock when he enters the Holy of Holies. (Later Jewish sources posit that this large rock mass was the foundation for the entire Temple, and that it merely broke through the ground at the point of the Holy of Holies.)[3]

Passing back through the Temple and exiting down the ten steps, we end our circuit facing an open courtyard. In front of us is the great brazen altar, the Altar of Holocaust (or Burnt Offering), upon which the priestly sacrifices are made. Built upon a rock mass, it has a cave beneath where ashes and sacrificial refuse are collected.[4] Not far away lies an immense basin called the Brazen Sea. This basin, which contains an estimated 15,000 gallons of water and rests on the backs of a dozen bronze bulls, is used for the ritual purification and cleansing of the priests engaged in sacrifice. Ten rolling basins, or lavers, which look like ornamented bronze teacarts, transport the water to various places at the Temple and are stationed nearby on both the north and south sides of the courtyard.

A devout Israelite completing such a tour, his senses filled with the physical and spiritual beauty of such a splendid structure, would scarcely dream that this edifice would not last forever.

Plundered!

Though elaborately adorned and magnificently constructed, the first Temple had its rival in Solomon's palace complex. The palatial buildings, made of highgrade stones and timbers from the forests of Lebanon, were considerably larger and perhaps more resplendent than the Temple itself. While the Temple took seven years to construct, these palaces and other royal buildings took another 13 years to complete. Perhaps Solomon felt that the size of the Tabernacle should be used as an index for size of the Temple, and for this reason built the Temple in a humbler fashion than his personal and administrative dwellings. However, the difference in size may also indicate a hidden divided loyalty that grew with the years as Solomon allowed idolatrous worship centers spawned by the obligations of his political marriages to multiply.

As the practice of idolatry divided the hearts of people in Jerusalem spiritually, God announced that the kingdom would be divided politically (1 Kings 11:9-11). Indeed, the sin of Solomon's foolish son Rehoboam caused a split of the kingdom into two: Judah (Judea) in the south and Israel in the north.

The spiritual decline continued unabated in the north as its kings, beginning with Jeroboam, built alternate worship sites to keep the people from returning to the Temple in the south. They feared that if the people returned to worship at the Temple, they would be drawn back under the political influence of Judah. The idolatry of the Northern Kingdom brought it to judgment under the Assyrians in 721 B.C.

The presence of the Temple in Judah and of kings that made occasional reforms from idolatry delayed God's judgment on the Southern Kingdom for 135 years. During this period, Judah was made aware that its sin would have severe repercussions on the Temple. Evidence of this came shortly after Rehoboam recklessly divided the kingdom. Pharaoh Shishak of Egypt assaulted Jerusalem, specifically targeting the Temple and Solomon's palace, which housed 300 shields of beaten gold. He transported these and other treasures from the Temple back to Egypt (1 Kings 14:25,26; 2 Chronicles 12:2,9). The Temple and Jerusalem were spared further plunder only because the royal court humbled itself after the Lord spoke to Rehoboam and the leaders through the prophet Shemaiah (2 Chronicles 12:5-8).

After this, the Southern Kingdom proceeded on an up-and-down course of reforms and unfaithful political alliances and idolatry. The states with which Judah made alliances demanded tribute, and one source for payment was the wealth of the Temple.

The attempt to satisfy these economic obligations set about the destruction of the Temple piece by piece. King Ahaz, for example, stripped the Temple of a portion of its silver and gold, broke up the Temple furniture and utensils, and removed the bronze oxen from the Brazen Sea in order to satisfy his obligations to the Assyrian king, Tiglath-Pileser III (1 Kings 16:7-9,17,18; 2 Chronicles 28:21,24). When Ahaz went to pay his tribute in Damascus, he sacrificed to the Assyrian gods, and desiring to honor them in place of the God of Israel, had a replica of the Damascus altar made for the Temple courtyard in Jerusalem. This being done, he closed the Temple doors and constructed idolatrous altars throughout Jerusalem.

Even though Ahaz' son, Hezekiah, brought spiritual and military reform to Judah, he set in motion the final act that led to the Temple's destruction. Second Kings 20:12-18 gives an account of a tour of the remaining Temple treasures given by Hezekiah to the Babylonians. The Temple was like bait before the hungry eyes of the Babylonians, and it was only a matter of time before the bait was seized. God announced at this time through his prophets: "I will remove Judah from My sight, as I have removed Israel, and I will cast off Jerusalem . . . and the temple" (2 Kings 23:27).

Further idolatry in the face of King Josiah's reforms to the Temple and its worship signaled that the time for God's judgment was near. It came under King Jehoiakim in 605 B.C. when Nebuchadnezzar, the king of Babylon, carried Jehoiakim and thousands of the nobility and the skilled labor force (including Daniel and his friends) off as slaves to

Babylon. Because the new king in Israel was reluctant to pay tribute to King Nebuchadnezzar, and the people continued their rebellion against God, a second invasion and deportation followed in 597 B.C. This time all the remaining treasures of the Temple were removed to Babylon (2 Kings 24:13). The prophet Ezekiel was taken captive in this deportation, and he predicted the soon collapse of the city and the slaughter of its inhabitants (Ezekiel 9:1-8).

In this same prophetic context, Ezekiel saw a vision of the Shekinah glory (the Presence of God) departing the Temple and vanishing over the Mount of Olives to the east (Ezekiel 10:18,19). When the glory departed, the Temple was set apart as a common thing, ready for destruction. The final Babylonian invasion came in 586 B.C. and with it the total destruction predicted by Ezekiel. The Temple was burned, along with the palace complex, and all the houses of the city (2 Kings 25:8,9; 2 Chronicles 36:18,19).

The sorrowful attitude of Judah toward the ruined Temple was expressed by the prophet Jeremiah: "The adversary has stretched out his hand over all her precious things, for she has seen the nations enter her sanctuary. . . . The Lord has rejected His altar, He has abandoned His sanctuary; He has delivered into the hand of the enemy the walls of her palaces" (Lamentations 1:10; 2:7).

A Second Temple—
A Second Chance

The first Temple had stood almost 400 years, but the apostasy of the people brought it to an end. One of the ordinances that had been forsaken was the sabbatical rest for the land. Every seventh year the land was to have lain fallow. Because the people had violated this command for 490 years, the land of Israel would be desolate for an equivalent period (70 years for the 70 unobserved sabbath rests). Jeremiah had prophesied this, and Daniel studied his writings while in captivity, praying for his people's promised return and the restoration of the Temple (Jeremiah 25:10-12; Daniel 6:10; 9:2-19).

God encouraged the Jews in the Babylonian captivity by demonstrating to them that the Temple was still sacred to Him. When Belshazzar brought the captured Temple vessels to a party to boast of his victory over Jerusalem, the hand of God appeared and literally spelled out Babylon's doom (Daniel 5). That very night the city fell to the Persians, an empire that would be the divine instrument for the return of the Jews and the rebuilding of the Temple (2 Chronicles 36:20,21).

An Unsuspecting Player

Isaiah had prophesied that the Persian king Cyrus would be the instrument for the Temple's rebuilding: "It is I [the Lord] who says of Cyrus, he is My shepherd! And he will perform all My desire. And he declares of Jerusalem, 'She will be built,' and of the temple, 'Your foundation will be laid' " (Isaiah 44:28). Just as Daniel had understood the time of the return from *Jeremiah's* prophecy, so Cyrus learned of his part in the divine drama from *Isaiah's* prophecy (Ezra 1:1,2). Flavius Josephus, a first-century Jewish historian who wrote an account of Jewish history for the Romans records this tradition:

> By reading the book which Isaiah left behind of his prophecies; for this prophet had spoken thus to him in a secret vision—"My will is, that Cyrus . . . send back My people to their own Land, and build My Temple." Accordingly, when Cyrus read this, and admired the divine power, an earnest desire and ambition seized upon him to fulfill what was so written.[5]

With Cyrus' permission about 50,000 Jews returned to Jerusalem in 538 B.C. under the leadership of Zerubbabel.

With the help of Phoenician workmen they began laying the foundation for the second Temple after the fashion of the first Temple (Ezra 3:7-10). The Temple vessels and utensils that had been taken by the Babylonians were returned, an altar was constructed, sacrifices begun, and the observance of the biblical festivals restored (Ezra 3:1-5).

The further construction of the Temple, however, met opposition from Samaritan residents of the Northern Kingdom, and was not resumed for another 15 years. The work was finally completed in 515 B.C. after a decree from the Persian king Darius not only permitted the rebuilding, but prescribed local taxes (including those of the Samaritans!) to finance the construction (Ezra 6:1-15).

Another reason construction may have been delayed was the people's attitude when they saw the foundation for the second Temple. After it had been laid, many of the priests and Levites who were old enough to have seen the first Temple wept because they knew this edifice would only be a shadow of the former Temple (Ezra 3:12,13). No doubt this impression persisted and grew as the years passed.

But when God stirred the people to rebuild through the exhortations of the prophet Haggai, He included a word of prophetic encouragement: "The latter glory of this house will be greater than the former, says the Lord of hosts, and in this place I shall give peace" (Haggai 2:9). The first part of this prediction was fulfilled when the modest second Temple was greatly enlarged by Herod the Great, and became renown as one of the most beautiful buildings in the world. The second half of the prophecy was fulfilled in part when Jesus, the glorious Prince of Peace, entered this second Temple at His first coming (Matthew 23:37,38). The ultimate fulfillment of this peace will be brought by Jesus at His second coming, when He enters the millennial Temple to dwell with Israel as the Shekinah glory of God, administering peace to the whole world (Isaiah 2:1-4).

Pollution and Purification

For 200 years the second Temple stood as the official center of worship for Jews in the land of Israel and those in the Diaspora. During this time at least three other temples were known to have existed (two in parts of Egypt and one on Mount Gerazim). However, Jews respected the supreme sanctity of the Jerusalem Temple, and the others were quickly forgotten. Josephus accurately represents the viewpoint of Jewry at this time when he writes: "One Temple for the One God."[6]

Despite its exclusiveness, the second Temple had not yet received the "peace" predicted for it. Noncanonical documents (documents not considered Scripture) of this time tell us that under Persian rule the high priests had become the governing authority in Judea. The transformation of the priestly office into a political office had degraded the spiritual and moral character of the priesthood. Stories of political rivalries, intrigue, and murder color the narratives concerning the struggles for the office of high priest. An instance of this may be seen in the case of Johanan, the son of Joiada (Nehemiah 12:22), who assassinated his own brother in the Temple itself.

During this period, Judea was controlled by the Greeks (Alexander the Great), Egyptian Greeks (Ptolemies), and by Syrian Greeks (Seleucids). The first two rulers treated the Jews favorably and allowed continued governorship by the high priests, but during the reign of the third, under Antiochus IV (Epiphanes), strife broke out.

Two Jewish factions, Hellenist (those influenced by Greek culture) and Orthodox, contended for the high priesthood. Antiochus IV sided with the Hellenist party and appointed a high priest who encouraged pagan worship. Events surrounding this man's successor brought an invasion of Jerusalem in 170 B.C. Many Jews were killed and the Temple with its restored treasures was plundered. Antiochus further desecrated the Temple by sacrificing a pig, an unclean animal, on the Temple altar and by erecting a pagan statue in the Holy of Holies. The actions of Antiochus Epiphanes were predicted by the prophet Daniel and serve as a type of the evil directed toward Israel and the Temple that will culminate in the coming Antichrist (Daniel 8:23-25; cf., 7:24-26). Christ referred to this event as the "abomination of desolation" (Matthew 24:15).

After multiple atrocities against the Jews, including the burning of copies of the Torah, forced consumption of pork contrary to Jewish law, and compulsory sacrifice to pagan idols, an Orthodox priest named Mattathias started a revolt which his son Judas (Maccabee) successfully completed.

In 164 B.C., Judas liberated Jerusalem and purified the Temple, reinstituting the daily offerings. That day has been celebrated ever since as *Hanukkah* or the Feast of Dedication (John 10:22).

"It Is Empty!"

Judea's independence lasted nearly a hundred years, but ended in the year 63 B.C. with the triumphal entrance of the Roman general Pompey into Jerusalem. When it became apparent that Pompey meant to enter the Temple, thousands of Jews threw themselves to the ground before the general and begged him not to desecrate the Holy Place. Such a display convinced Pompey that the Temple must contain great riches or some hidden secret, and so not only did he enter the Holy Place, but he tore away the veil of separation and marched into the Holy of Holies itself. What happened next is recorded for posterity by the Roman historian Tacitus:

> By right of conquest he [Pompey] entered their Temple. It is a fact well known, that he found no image, no statue, no symbolical representation of the Deity: the whole presented a naked dome; the sanctuary was unadorned and simple.[7]

Similar to the Russian cosmonaut of our own day who said he did not see God on his trip into space, it is said that when Pompey emerged from the Temple he looked around at the Jews in wonder and exclaimed, "It is empty, there is nothing there but darkness!" It is true that the Shekinah glory was not present in the second Temple; eyes of faith rather than eyes of flesh were required to see the true God. It has been said, "To those who are [spiritually] blind He does not exist, to those who are deaf He does not speak, to those who will not seek He will not be found."[8] Pompey illustrated the confusion experienced by unbelieving rulers toward the Temple and its service. Yet when he ordered the walls of the city to be torn down, he left the Temple intact.

A Restored Jewel

Rome was now in possession of the land of Israel, and in 37 B.C. it placed Judea under the rulership of a cruel despot of Edomite ancestry by the name of Herod, whose Herodian dynasty would continue to rule for 100 years. In 23 B.C., Herod proposed the massive project of completely rebuilding the second Temple, which by this time had fallen into a state of complete disrepair. Because Herod's plans involved the demolition of the Temple, the people feared a trick— some thought he might tear it down and not rebuild it. Herod therefore had to prepare and transport all the building materials and stones to Temple Mount before touching the Temple itself.

Herod began rebuilding the Temple in 19 B.C., and the work was dedicated ten years later, although detail work continued on it for the next 75 years. His project of expansion included enlarging the Temple esplanade and constructing a huge retaining wall (of which the present Western or "Wailing" Wall is a remnant) to support this great platform (see Figure 5).

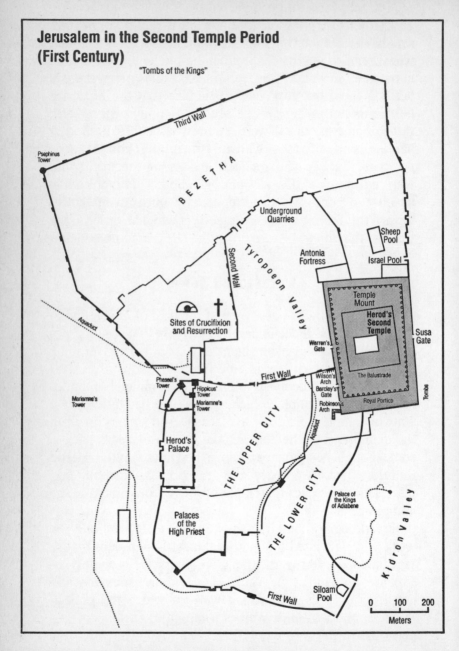

Figure 5: Map of "Jerusalem in Second Temple Period"

The rebuilt Temple was double the height of the original second Temple, and significantly wider. New compartments were added to the original design, as well as a second story above the innermost chambers. A monumental royal basilica was constructed as a place for Jews returning at the appointed feasts to buy animals for offerings. Herod also transformed the Hasmonean fortress on the northwest corner into the Antonia fortress (named in honor of Mark Anthony). This structure housed the Roman garrison, which was positioned to quell disturbances on the Temple Mount, and included quarters for the Roman procurator when he was in residence (for example, Pontius Pilate in A.D. 26–36).

The Temple of Herod, as the rebuilt second Temple was now called, revealed a conflict of interests in its architecture. On the one hand, Herod wanted to demonstrate his support of Judaism to the Jews, while at the same time proving his loyalty to Rome. This conflict was embodied in the display of the Roman eagle above the doorway of the Temple. As a bird of prey, it symbolized the character of Rome but corrupted the character of the Temple as a place of peace. Its presence was also considered a violation of the Mosaic injunction against the making of graven images.

Shortly after this image was placed on the Temple in 4 B.C., a riot occurred and the Roman eagle was torn down and hacked to pieces, much as we have recently seen the destruction of Communist statues in our own day. Herod severely punished those involved, but months later died himself of a painful disease. This was interpreted as a divine verdict on Herod, who never lived to see the completion of the work his arrogance had begun.

At the time, Jerusalem was considered, even by non-Jews, as the most famous among the great cities of the East. The rebuilt second Temple was regarded as one of the marvels of the ancient world. Josephus tells us that the Temple was made of marble overlaid with gold, and appeared from a distance as a mountain of snow glistening in the sun. One of the sages of that time wrote, "He who has not seen Herod's building has not seen a beautiful building in his life."[9] The New Testament records that the disciples of Jesus were so impressed with the Temple's construction that they sought to point out to Him its special buildings and adornments (Matthew 24:1; Luke 21:5). The pride they felt for their national treasure could not have been more intense.

The Prediction and Ruin of the Temple

The response of Jesus to the disciples' enthusiasm must have been unsettling. Instead of the expected echo of admiration, Christ announced destruction: "As for these things which you are looking at, the days will come in which there will not be left one stone upon another which will not be torn down" (Luke 21:6).

While this statement was objectionable to those Jews who believed that the Temple would never again be destroyed, and seemed incredible to the disciples, who had watched the Temple's construction all their lives, it was shared by some of the more ascetic Jews, such as those at Qumran, who felt that Herod's Temple was polluted and another Temple (of their design) needed to replace it.

Jesus' statement was based on the earlier prediction made by Daniel the prophet. Daniel had written: "Then after the sixty-two weeks *the Messiah* will be *cut off* and have nothing, and *the people of the prince who is to come will destroy the city and the sanctuary*" (Daniel 9:26). Jesus, seeing Himself as *the Messiah*, therefore saw the Romans as *the people . . . who will destroy the city and the sanctuary*. Knowing that He would soon be *cut off* (crucified), He likewise knew that the Temple's destruction would soon occur.

After the death and resurrection of Jesus, events surrounding the Temple signaled its impending doom. Tradition tells of a scarlet string hung in the second Temple's sanctuary which miraculously turned white each year on the Day of Atonement to show God's acceptance of the nation of Israel. Both Jewish and Christian historians tell us that for the final 40 years of the Temple's existence the scarlet string did not change color—a sign of divine disfavor. Christian apologists cite this as further confirmation that the nation's rejection of Jesus as Messiah meant its rejection by God and resulted in the city's and Temple's destruction. But Jewish sages contend that the problem was the result of the social and religious conditions of the time. Professors Michael Avi-Yonah and Menahem Stern write of this period:

> In the last years before the destruction, the social tension grew to such an extent that it affected the order and security of the city. In addition to the general enmity toward Roman rule, there were conflicts among the Jews themselves. On the one hand, there was friction among the different groups in the priestly oligarchy and on the other, the activities of the extremist fighters for freedom from the Romans (the Sicarii), who used violence and were not averse to killing their opponents.[10]

Because of such internal contention, the sages of Israel felt that God was displeased and had allowed their own facetiousness to bring their calamity.

Another warning of the coming destruction came with the attempted desecration of the Temple under the notorious Roman emperor Gaius Caligula around A.D. 40–41. Josephus records that Caligula ordered his own image to be placed in the Holy of Holies. He commanded that the Jews be slaughtered or taken captive if they refused to allow this. So great was the resistance by both the Pharisees and the more radical Zealots that the edict was never carried out and

Caligula was assassinated soon after. Nevertheless it was evident that a confrontation with Rome over the city and Temple was inevitable.

The straw that broke the camel's back occurred in A.D. 66, when Jewish zealots instigated riots against Rome over the misrule of the procurators. A sensational act of defiance took place in the Temple when Eleazar, son of the captain of the Temple, ordered an end to the imperial sacrifice (which had been offered to the emperor alongside the traditional Jewish service during the period of Roman rule). Rome's formidable Tenth Legion attempted to retake the Temple Mount, but failed, losing much equipment to the Jewish defenders.

The defiance, which became a full-scale revolt, soon secured all Judea in Jewish hands. Enraged by the success of this revolt, Emperor Nero sent Rome's best commander, Vespasian, with Rome's finest legions to crush the rebellion at all costs. By A.D. 69, after years of bitter fighting, the Romans had retaken all areas but Jerusalem, and Vespasian, who had recently succeeded Nero as emperor, put his son, Titus, in charge of the Jerusalem campaign.

Following a siege of Jerusalem, Titus took counsel with the officers of his army concerning the fate of the Temple. There are conflicting reports as to the orders given. The Roman historian Tacitus records that the majority of the officers were in agreement that nothing less than the total destruction of the Temple would secure a lasting peace. Therefore, on the ninth day of the Jewish month of Av in A.D. 70, the city and the Temple were burned as Daniel had prophesied.

Josephus says that Titus had given specific orders that the Temple be left intact, and that a soldier acting on impulse threw a torch through an archway of the Temple, setting the tapestries inside on fire. When the building burned, it is said that the gold on the walls melted and ran into the seams between the stones. Afterward, in an attempt to recover the gold, Roman soldiers tore apart the stone walls, fulfilling precisely the prediction of Jesus that not one stone of the Temple would be left on another.

The next year Titus made a triumphal procession into Rome before his father, Vespasian. Seven hundred Jewish captives, as well as some of the treasures from the Temple including the great menorah, the table of showbread, and a Torah scroll were paraded in front of Vespasian. Rome had conquered, the Temple was in ruins, and the Jewish people were scattered in exile.

Though the Temple was destroyed, Jewish faith continued. In the following centuries, the *Mishnah* (the earliest written collection of oral Jewish law and tradition) would record all that had been lost, stimulating hope for later restoration. Such a hope was not passive, but active, as revivals for rebuilding the Temple on Temple Mount continued in the ensuing centuries—centuries of Jewish transition.

Chapter 5

The Temple in Transition

Many different men other than Jews have sat [in Jerusalem] in the seat of power—Jebusites, Egyptians, Babylonians and Persians; Hellenist Greeks and Romans; Byzantines, Arabs, Crusaders, Mamelukes, Turks and British. But throughout the flux of these thousands of years there runs one constant thread—the unique attachment of the Jewish people to Jerusalem and the site of their holy Temple. History has no parallel to this mystic bond, and without it there would have been no state of Israel today.

—*Joan Comay*, The Temple of Jerusalem

*W*ith the destruction of the second Temple, the Jewish *world lost its center. Since the Temple and its ritual* had become an essential part of Jewish identity, only two options now existed: Jews must change their worldview, or attempt to change their world.

The Change in Worldview

As a result of most Jews being dispersed to other lands after the destruction of A.D. 70, Jews had to rethink the religious obligations that had defined their very being while in the land of Israel (the Land). It is true that communities of

Jews had been existing outside the Land for several centuries, but there had been no change in their worldview because the Temple stood in Jerusalem and their attention was constantly turned toward it. Now, throughout Judaism, a new direction had to be sought.

The new direction that post-Temple Judaism took involved a slow turning from the literal fulfillment of the Temple ritual to its inherently spiritual dimension. Although later Judaism accommodated itself to life without a Temple by transforming Jerusalem and the Temple itself into symbolic ideals, the Mishnah enshrined the literal concepts of the Temple and its ritual, preserving the permanent in the midst of change:

> The city and its Temple were permanently and untouchably enshrined in the Mishna . . . the Temple's buildings and rituals were as lovingly and as carefully detailed as if there were still Jews passing daily in and out of those precincts . . . the holiness of Jerusalem and the Temple are mapped and guaranteed.[1]

With the Mishnah as the guiding document in post-Temple Judaism, a longing for the literal restoration of the Temple was continued.

Changing the World

The Mishnah's focus upon the Temple and its ritual was never intended to replace the prophetic hope for a return to Israel's past glory with a spiritualized sense of satisfaction in *Judea Capta* (subjugated Israel) or the Diaspora (life outside the Land). Jacob Neusner, one of the world's foremost authorities on the Mishnah, notes:

> The rabbis of the Mishnah . . . do everything they can to preserve concrete facts—not merely a

generalized memory—about the [cult] which has been destroyed. That must mean they wanted the Temple rebuilt and the cult restored.[2]

This may be seen in the nature of the Mishnah itself. It is the most profoundly priestly document in Jewish literature, as four of its six tractates (divisions) center on the role of the priesthood. It affirms and reaffirms that God is served through the sacrifice in the Temple by the priesthood, that the Jewish festivals are marked in this same way, and that the daily duty of the Israelite home is to imitate the purity of the Temple priesthood. Spiritualizing the Mishnah would not explain the rabbis' intent, for spiritualization cannot accommodate the vast amount of endless details involving measurements of the Temple and directions for sacrificial procedure.

Therefore, the Mishnah is a document that, while preserving the essence of Judaism in the present, is ideally suited for the future day in which its directives can be realized and applied. Jews of the first six centuries after the destruction of the Temple looked forward to the liberation of Jerusalem and the rebuilding of the Temple. They saw their Judaism as incomplete without it. History bears the marks produced by the Jewish hope of changing the Roman and Christian world to restore the world of the Temple.

The Temple Treasured

After the destruction of the Temple, Jerusalem, a city that had depended politically and commercially upon religious life centered on the Temple, suffered stagnation and decline. The Jews who remained lost their wealth and status, and were regarded as a people who had been made a cruel object lesson by God. Only a bare platform remained to mark the site of the Temple, a reminder that the treasure of Jewish devotion, like Jewish lives, had been plundered and left desolate. Nevertheless, the Jews treasured the Temple site, for in its emptiness, it stood ready to again be filled. If at the present it could not be filled with an actual building, it could be adorned with blessings.

The hope for national return and revival that dominated these early pilgrim prayers is reflected in the *Shemoneh Esreh* ("Eighteen Benedictions"), which every observant Jew is required to pray three times daily (Berekoth 4:1). Benediction 14, in particular, is a prayer for the restoration of Jerusalem and the rebuilding of the Temple:

> Be merciful, O Lord our God, in Thy great mercy, towards Israel Thy people, and towards Jerusalem Thy city, and towards Zion the abiding place of Thy glory, and towards the Temple and Thy habitation, and towards the kingdom of the house of David, Thy righteous anointed one. Blessed art Thou, O Lord God of David, the builder of Jerusalem.

Through prayers such as this, the Temple remained in the forefront of Jewish thought in post-Temple Judaism. This Temple consciousness also expressed itself in tangible ways: Whenever circumstances favored the rebuilding of the Temple, activist movements would arise among ardent Jews. A look at some of these past Jewish struggles will give insight into the present-day movements and establish a sense of continuity between the early activists and their modern counterparts.

The Temple of Bar Kokhba

Although Jerusalem had been in ruins since the destruction of the Temple 60 years earlier, there was no ban on Jewish settlement in the area. As a result, at least 75 Jewish communities had been established in Judea. Whether or not worship resumed on the rubble of the Temple Mount is uncertain, but during this time seven synagogues were built at the foot of Mount Zion. It appears that these became the new centers for worship, although there remained a fervent hope for restoration, both of the city and the Temple.

These hopes were excited when the Roman emperor Publius Aelius Hadrian began his reign in A.D. 117. According to all indications, Hadrian did not initially entertain any hostility toward the Jews, and they in turn had expectations that their situation would be improved. The *Sibylline Oracles*, Jewish pseudepigraphal writings of this time, stated that the man whose name is like that of the sea (Hadrian— "Adriatic") would act favorably toward the Jews.[3]

Official contacts were apparently made between Judean Jews and the Roman government under Hadrian, and permission was granted to begin rebuilding the Temple.[4] Early Christian sources record that some attempt was made to raise funds for the effort, but these attempts must have met with poor success since it seems no practical work was undertaken.

Jewish hopes for a revival ended in A.D. 129 when Hadrian came to Jerusalem to begin the erection of a Roman colony on the ruins of the city. In A.D. 132 a revolt erupted under the Jewish leader Shimon bar Kosiba. The primary cause of the revolt was apparently Hadrian's unkept promise to rebuild the Temple.[5] Bar Kosiba was renamed *Bar Kokhba*, "Son of the Star," by the Talmudic sage Rabbi Akiva, who heralded him as the Messiah.

The revolt repulsed the Roman garrisons, and the Jewish rebels held Jerusalem for almost three years. During this time an independent government was established, and Bar Kokhba proclaimed himself the Messiah. So convinced was he that his conquest of Jerusalem had begun the messianic era that he began a new calendar system, counting the years from the date of his victory. Of greater significance is the probability that he began rebuilding the Temple and resumed the Temple ritual, perhaps including the reinstitution of sacrifice.[6] Rabbi Gamaliel, who lived during the Bar Kokhba revolt, is said to have offered his Passover sacrifice in the new Bar Kokhba Temple.[7]

The principal evidence for a Bar Kokhba Temple stems from coins minted by Bar Kokhba that bear a picture of the facade of the Temple and the name of Eleazer, a high priest appointed by Bar Kokhba. Based on this evidence, Rabbi Leibel Reznick believes that Bar Kokhba actually completed the Temple. He argues that without a functioning Temple, Bar Kokhba would not have appointed a high priest or issued coins bearing the image of the structure. In addition, Reznick notes that any person claiming to be Messiah would attempt to rebuild the Temple (Ezekiel 40–47).[8] Bar Kokhba's reign ended when Hadrian recaptured Jerusalem in A.D. 135. The emperor issued restrictive edicts against Jewish study of the Torah and made any observance or religious practice a capital offense. In order to demonstrate that the Jews had not succeeded in saving their people or their Temple, Hadrian destroyed the Bar Kokhba Temple[9] and erected a temple to the Roman trio of Juno, Jupiter, and Minerva, along with an equestrian statue of himself (see Figure 6).[10] This was an official statement of the continuing triumph of the Roman empire.

Today you can see a Roman gate inscription of the time (located near the present American consulate) which states that a Roman "holy place" stood on the Temple Mount. Most scholars assume that this holy place was Hadrian's pagan temple, and that it was built on the site of the Jewish Temple since Hadrian built similar shrines on Christian holy sites. Jerome, one of the church fathers, was of the opinion that the equestrian statue was over the site of the Holy of Holies.[11] Modern scholars such as John Wilkinson disagree: "It is clear that a political and religious statement was being made . . . in the statue, undoubtedly of Hadrian, *overlooking* the ruins on the Temple Mount."[12] Wilkinson further argues

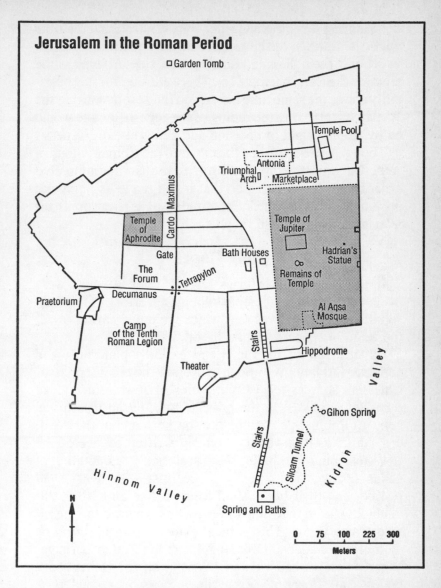

Jerusalem in the Roman Period

- Garden Tomb
- Temple Pool
- Antonia
- Triumphal Arch
- Marketplace
- Cardo Maximus
- Temple of Aphrodite
- Temple of Jupiter
- Hadrian's Statue
- Gate
- Bath Houses
- Remains of Temple
- The Forum
- Tetrapylon
- Praetorium
- Decumanus
- Al Aqsa Mosque
- Camp of the Tenth Roman Legion
- Stairs
- Hippodrome
- Valley
- Theater
- Gihon Spring
- Stairs
- Siloam Tunnel
- Kidron
- Hinnom Valley
- N
- Spring and Baths

| 0 | 75 | 100 | 225 | 300 |
Meters

Figure 6: General Plan of Jerusalem in the Roman Period

that Hadrian was an astute ruler, who realized that the time might come when the empire would wish to allow the Jews to rebuild their Temple. Leaving the site in ruins while erecting the Roman temple elsewhere allowed for this possibility and at the same time attested to the absoluteness of the Roman victory. Any rebuilding of the Jewish Temple would be by Roman right of decision and generous forgiveness.

Though Hadrian turned the city into the Roman colony of Aelia Capitolina, Rome did little more than maintain civil order there. It was satisfied that it had made its point and prevented Jerusalem from continuing as a focal point for Jewish nationalism and revolt.

Holy Hopes

In the following centuries several other attempts were made to organize a Temple rebuilding effort. The most significant of these was that which we noted earlier under the reign of Emperor Julian in A.D. 363.

Julian arranged for funds and building materials, and appointed Alypius of Antioch to oversee the reconstruction. Christian sources tell of multitudes of Jews returning to Jerusalem to assist in the project. In 1969 an inscription beneath Robinson's Arch on the southern end of the Western Wall was discovered. Probably written by one of the Jews returning to rebuild, the inscription is a quotation of Isaiah 66:14: "And when you see this, your heart shall rejoice, and their bones shall flourish like an herb." Undoubtedly those returning to Jerusalem expected the messianic era to begin. This is most evident from the writer's deliberate change in wording from the Isaiah passage. Whereas Isaiah had written "When you see this . . . *your* bones shall flourish" (KJV), the inscription reads "*their* bones." Meir Ben-Dov notes: " 'And when ye see this' refers to the people who will behold the inscription, whereas 'their bones' are those of the dead about to be resurrected."[13]

With the rebuilding of the Temple underway, the End of Days was near, and with it, the national resurrection of the Jewish people predicted by the prophets. All Jews believed the Day of Redemption was at hand!

After Julian's failed attempt, further efforts to rebuild the Temple were sporadic in nature.

The yearning for the revival of the Jewish kingdom was again aroused when the Empress Eudocia, the pagan daughter of an Athenian professor of rhetoric, who converted to Christianity in order to marry Emperor Theodosius II, settled in the city in A.D. 443. She changed the physical face of the city with her many building projects, but for the Jews her greatest fame came when she granted them permission to return to the Holy City and to resume prayer on the Temple Mount.

The Jews interpreted the empress' intentions as a sign that a restoration of Jerusalem and the Temple was imminent. These holy hopes were spread throughout the Jewish communities in Rome and Persia by a letter dated A.D. 438 from the heads of the Galilean Jews to the Jewish community in Egypt. This encyclical letter reveals that a renewed messianic expectation was in the Land:

> To the great and mighty Jewish people; from the priests and elders in Galilee—many greetings! Know that the end of the exile of our people is near and all our tribes shall be gathered together. Lo, the Rulers of Rome have decreed that our city, Jerusalem, shall be returned to us. Come quickly to Jerusalem for the Feast of Tabernacles, for the kingdom is at hand in Jerusalem.[14]

To the Jews' disappointment, the day of deliverance was not to come. As the Jews convened at the Temple Mount a number of their party were killed in a stoning. The Christian account says that a miracle happened, and that stones came from heaven to prevent the Jews from rebuilding their Temple. The Jews who were struck by the stones saw the matter differently. Those who survived had 18 of the followers of an anti-Semitic monk named Barsauma arrested and charged with murder. However, the powerful bishop of Jerusalem at this time, Juvenal, had positioned Barsauma so that he could not be harmed, and the matter eventually turned against the Jews and their hope for restoration.

In A.D. 614, the Persians shattered the Byzantine defenses and entered Jerusalem. The Jews of Jerusalem helped the Persians defeat the Christian emperor Heraclius, and as a result, the Persian king Chosroes II appointed a Jew named Nehemiah as governor of the city. This was seen as an act of divine providence, for in the fifth century B.C. the Persian king Artaxerxes had also made a Jew named Nehemiah governor of Jerusalem. The earlier Nehemiah had been the first rebuilder of Jerusalem and had repaired the walls of the city to protect the newly restored Temple.

To add to this coincidence, Chosroes II granted the Jews permission to rebuild their Temple. It appears that the Jews enjoyed a brief period of influence, from A.D. 614–617, in which they resumed liturgical rituals. The Jewish pseudepigraphal *Book of Zerubbabel*, gives an account of this reclamation of the Temple Mount and remarks that the Jewish leader "made sacrifices." The only suitable place for such ritual would be atop the Temple Mount.

It is unclear how far work progressed on the rebuilding of the Temple, if it was begun at all, during these years. Whatever work was begun was soon halted as the Persian shah changed his mind and revoked his permission, perhaps due to political pressure from the substantial Christian influence in the Persian court in Iraq.

Going even further, the Persians installed their own governor and expelled the Jews from the city. Only 15 years later, the Byzantine emperor Heraclius recaptured the city and built an octagonal church on the Temple Mount, thus "defiling" it and dashing Jewish hopes of rebuilding the Temple.

The hope of rebuilding the Jewish Temple in Jerusalem since these early efforts has revived only in the past few decades. God has put a stirring in the hearts of His people to return to their ancient land. Combined with many other significant world events, it appears that the time of Israel's redemption and the rebuilding of the Temple is close at hand. But one major obstacle remains in the path to rebuilding—the presence of a third party on the Temple mount.

Chapter 6

The Temple and Islam

The mosques on the Temple Mount were built by the order of God. . . . Our sovereignty is not subject to compromise.

—*Adnan Husseini*,
senior Wakf (Muslim) official

Now I have heard Muslims say that not in a million years can they make peace with Israel. From their point of view they cannot make peace. But from an Islamic point of view they are mistaken. And if they persist in their refusal to accept Israel it is due to sheer enmity and hatred; it has nothing to do with true religion.

—*Asher Eder*,
scholar of comparative religion

*I*N A.D. *638, Islam invaded the Holy Land. Since that time, Jerusalem and its Temple Mount have come under the* influence of a religion that until recently has precluded any thought of rebuilding the Temple. Both Islam and Judaism claim that the Temple Mount is sacred. In addition, Muslims know that if Israel rebuilds the Temple, it will be impossible for Islam to regain control of all Israel, one of its cherished goals.

The violence that erupted on October 8, 1990 on the Temple Mount was evidence of the Muslim belief that Jerusalem is *Al-Quds* ("the Holy One"), that it is exclusively sacred to their religion, and that Jews have no right to it. Indeed, the instruction in Muslim schools for generations has been to this effect. Yassar Arafat has boldly stated: "Give [show] me one Arab who would betray Jerusalem, one Palestinian who would betray the . . . Muslim holy places."[1]

Gaalyah Cornfield reveals this prevailing attitude when he writes:

> For the Moslems the history of the Mount began with Muhammad's vision of his night's journey from Mecca to Jerusalem and thence, with a spring, that left a mark, much revered, on the surface of the . . . Temple Mount, up to heaven. Over that spot, the present "Dome of the Rock" was built, everything lying beneath it being, to the Moslem, irrelevant, even the insights of archaeology in the last hundred years, even the results of contemporary excavations being conducted now. Even these, to the descendants of the Moslems who walled up the historical underground passages and kept "infidels" and curious away, are unimportant.[2]

Aside from Mohammed's vision, why is it that Islam, which originated in the Arabian peninsula so far removed from Palestine, came to invest Jerusalem with an aura of sanctity? And does Islam have a historical religious right to Jerusalem and the Temple Mount?

Mohammed's Jewish-Christian Connection

When Islam invaded the Holy Land it had to subjugate a Christian and Jewish population. As the Muslim rulers entered Jerusalem and later began erecting structures on their sacred sites, these newly conquered subjects of Islam might well have wondered what connection their Holy City had with the Muslim faith. No doubt the sacredness of Jerusalem to Islam is derived from Judaism and Christianity, since both Jews and non-orthodox Christians were among the teachers of Mohammed. This sanctity grew through time. In A.D. 632, Islamic armies stormed out of the Arabian peninsula, capturing Jerusalem in A.D. 638 during the reign of 'Umar, the second caliph after Mohammed. This Arab conquest of Jerusalem and the attention paid to Arab building on the Temple Mount was the result of a number of factors. First was Jerusalem's close location to the early capital of the Islamic empire—Damascus. Even though Arabia was the cradle of Islam, Syria was more involved in world issues of that day. Religious factors were also important and what city had greater religious significance than Jerusalem? Miriam Ayalon, professor of Islamic art and archaeology at the Hebrew University explains:

> Indeed, the fact that Jerusalem was already important to the two monotheistic faiths from earlier times, and the fact that Islam considered itself as the last of the revelations . . . made it legitimate for Islam to absorb and identify with former beliefs obtaining there. Jerusalem could not be ignored. The Temple area . . . offered an ideal space to establish the monuments of the new rulers. Moreover, the very fact that some of the preexisting Byzantine buildings remained in Jerusalem and could provoke admiration, or eventually jealousy, required a Muslim response.[3]

Therefore, after almost 60 years of occupation, the Umayyad caliph 'Abd al-Malik built in A.D. 691–92 what is known today as the Dome of the Rock.

Many conjectures surround the purpose of the Dome's erection. Some people believe the Dome was built as a commemoration of an Islamic event or place of prayer for a caliph (such as 'Umar, after whom it has been popularly called the Mosque of Omar). Others assert that it was built in competition with a rival caliph in Mecca, or as an attempt to replace the Ka'ba (holy stone in Mecca) and divert the Hajj (Muslim pilgrimage to Mecca) to Jerusalem.[4] However, the Dome of the Rock, called *Qubbat as-Sakhra* in Arabic, was originally designed only as a monument to what had previously existed on the Temple Mount. It was "a precious container for the Holy Rock."[5]

'Abd al-Malik's act thus preserved the site and unintentionally honored the sacred tradition of the Temple site in Jewish history. This fact may not have escaped mystically inclined Jews who saw the cleansing of the Temple Mount from the debris heaped on the Mount by earlier Byzantine Christians and its Islamic adornment as a divine sign. Though the history of this period is sketchy, we know that the Umayyad caliphs were tolerant of the Jewish faith and that Jews were allowed to take up residence southwest of the Temple area. Some of these Jewish families were given the responsibility of making lamps for the buildings and lighting and cleaning the Temple Mount. On festival days, Jews would march around the walls of the Temple Mount and pray at the gates. Such allowances, coupled with the sight of renewed splendor on the Temple Mount, caused a Jewish messianic movement to develop that anticipated the rebuilding of the Temple. An example of this Jewish hope may be seen in *Nistarot de Rabbi Shimon bar Yohay* (an apocalyptic book written soon after the Arab conquest):

> And the second king who will emerge from Ishmael shall conquer all the kingdoms and shall come to Jerusalem and prostrate himself [before the God of Israel] . . . He shall be a friend of Israel

and help them build up the Temple. He shall make even Mount Moriah and call Israel to build up [there] the Temple. In his day Israel shall be saved and the offspring of David [the Messiah] shall come forth.[6]

The height of this messianic fervor was an armed revolt under a self-proclaimed messiah, Abu 'Isa of Isfahan, which 'Abd al-Malik suppressed, ending Jewish expectations under Arab rule for a restoration of the Temple.

Countering Christian Influence

Another purpose for the Dome's erection was as an act of propaganda and rivalry—to the Jews, but more especially to the Christians whose presence was manifested in their massive religious architecture, especially in Constantine's great basilica. The historian Muqaddasi, a native of Jerusalem, offers just such an explanation:

> So he ['Abd al-Malik's son al-Walid] sought to build for the Muslims [in Damascus] a mosque that should prevent their admiring these [Christian churches] and should be unique and a wonder to the world. And in like manner, is it not evident how Caliph 'Abd al-Malik, noting the greatness of the Dome of the Holy Sepulchre and its magnificence, was moved lest it should dazzle the minds of Muslims and so erected, above the Rock, the Dome which is now seen there.[7]

What we know of the history of the time supports Muqaddasi's statement. We know that the original primitive wooden structure built to house the Rock was satisfactory to the first generation of Muslims, who were accustomed to the simplicity of Mohammed's mosque in Mecca. However, the splendor of the Christian churches that filled Jerusalem, and were built in close proximity to the Temple Mount, called for a response from second generation Muslims who had grown up as conquerors. Indeed many Quranic (Koranic) inscriptions, written explicitly to counter Christian doctrines and warn Muslims against Christian errors, decorate the walls of the mosque. This is important because Jesus is seen as a prophet in Islam, and because the influence of the Christian city at that time was great.

In the beginning the Rock itself had no religious meaning to Islam. It was only after some time, and most likely in order to attract visitors to Jerusalem, that the stories of Jerusalem being the place of final resurrection and of Mohammed's night journey were invented. In fact, the name of Jerusalem is not mentioned even once in all of the *Qur'an* (also *Koran*, the holy scripture of Islam).

Some Muslim authorities have argued the "Night Journey of Muhammad" refers to Jerusalem when it says that he went to Al Aqsa, the name of the mosque which today is built south of the Dome of the Rock. However, the word *Al Aqsa* simply means "far corner," and it is supposed that it was originally located in the east corner of Mecca, not in Jerusalem. If it was 'Abd al-Malik who built the Al Aqsa Mosque (some say it was Caliph Walid in A.D. 705–715), he probably used this story to justify his propagandistic campaign, and because he needed a mosque to match the beauty of the Dome of the Rock. Shelomo Dov Goitein notes that "most of the traditions about Jerusalem and its sanctuary had no foundation in old Muhammedian stock."[8]

Muslim prayer, even today, is in the direction of Mecca, not Jerusalem. According to an early account, when Ka'b al-Ahbar proposed to the Caliph 'Umar that the place of prayer in Jerusalem should be fixed north of the Dome, so that Muslims would turn during their prayers toward the Rock at the same time they turned toward Mecca (which lies to the south of Jerusalem), the caliph rejected his advice because he considered it a Jewish scheme to coerce Muslims to prostrate themselves toward an object of Jewish worship, the Holy of Holies in the Temple. He is said to have retorted to Ka'b: "By Allah, Oh Ka'b, in your heart you are still a Jew, for I have seen how you took off your shoes [before entering the Temple Mount], but we Muslims were not ordered to sanctify this Rock, we were only ordered to turn [in our prayers] towards the Ka'ba [in Mecca]."[9] There are records of early caliphs who deliberately avoided the site of the Rock, or who prayed with their backs to it to show their religious indifference.

Another reason the Muslims may have built the Dome was to counter Jewish and Christian traditions. It is quite possible that both the Dome of the Rock and the Al Aqsa mosque were built over the ruins of either synagogues or Byzantine churches. It is fairly certain that Emperor Justinian had built a Christian basilica in the sixth century on the site and with the same dimensions as the later Al Aqsa mosque. The octagonal shape of the Dome of the Rock, unique in Islamic architecture, may imply the use of a former Byzantine foundation or may simply be the result of Christian architects employed by 'Abd al Malik.

In this same vein, a Muslim cemetery was placed in front of the Golden Gate, considered the original eastern entrance to the Temple. This was intended to keep the Jewish (and Christian) Messiah from entering through it, since passage through an unwalled cemetery incurs defilement. If the Jews could not enter the gate, they could not rebuild the Temple on the Temple Mount as prophesied.

Hidden Acknowledgments

The point we want to make by showing how Jerusalem became sacred to Islam and why Muslims felt it necessary to build on the Temple Mount is that there is no historically justifiable claim for Jerusalem or the Temple Mount as a holy place in Islam. It was not until A.D. 1187, when the Crusaders were finally dislodged by the Muslim leader Salan-ad-Din (Saladin), that Jerusalem was confirmed as the third holiest place in Islam (after Mecca and Medina). As we have noted, nothing in the Qur'an supports this reverence. In fact, the Qur'an actually supports the historic claim of the Israelis to the land. In Sura V, v. 21, citing the words of Moses in the story of the spies, it is written: "Oh, my people, enter the Holy Land that has been promised to you."

By contrast, the Temple Mount is the one and only holy place in Judaism, and is backed by at least 3,000 years of recorded history. Despite the fact that Islam has dominated the Temple Mount for 1,300 years, Jews have continued to direct their daily prayers toward it, and to look forward to the day when the Temple could be rebuilt. An example of this can be seen in the thirteenth-century statement of the Jewish sage Nahmanides in a letter to his son:

> What shall I say of this land . . . the more holy the place the greater the desolation. Jerusalem is the most desolate of all. . . . There are about two thousand inhabitants . . . but there are no Jews. . . . People regularly come to Jerusalem . . . to see the Temple and weep over it. And may He who deemed us worthy to see Jerusalem in her ruins, grant us to see her rebuilt and restored.

Many Muslims realize the prior claim Jews have to the Temple Mount. Even though their modern historians rewrite history to teach that nothing occupied the site before Islam, those who live in Jerusalem daily pass by the excavated remains of the great entrance stairs to the Temple and the Huldah Gates at the Southern Wall. To this we must add another statement from the Qur'an which speaks not only of the Temple, but also of a Jewish return. In Night Journey 8 it is written:

> We sent against you [Israel] our servants to
> discountenance you, and to enter the Temple, as
> they entered it the first time, and to destroy
> utterly which they ascended to. Perchance your
> Lord will have mercy upon you; but if you return,
> we shall return.

Some people have said that it was because the Arabs
knew these passages and believed that the Jews would one
day return to the Temple Mount to rebuild that they were
able to abandon the Temple Mount without major conflict
during the Six-Day War in 1967. It may also be for this
reason that through unusual political-religious diplomacy,
some significant internal upset, or military assertion, it
might be possible to see Islam one day leave the site without
controversy.

By whatever means Islam is forced to abandon the Temple
Mount, its presence through the centuries has providen-
tially preserved the site for the Jewish return to the Land.
And having now returned, many Jews are awaiting the day
when they will finally ascend their Holy Mount and rebuild
their fallen sanctuary.

Chapter 7

Why Rebuild?

Build Your house as at the first, set Your Temple on its foundations, allow us to see it built and make us joyous in its establishment, return Priests to their service and Levites to their songs and music, and return Israel to their pleasant places, and there we will ascend and be seen and bow down before You.

—*Ancient Jewish Holiday Prayer*

*F*or 2,000 years Jews the world over have successfully maintained their faith without the Temple. Why should they want to rebuild it now? The answer is that not all Jews do want to rebuild the Temple. Conservative and Reformed Jews, for example, claim that the rebuilding of a literal Temple is unnecessary. Viewing Judaism as an evolving religion, they see no reason to return to the past. Hebrew University professor and rabbi Pesach Schindler explains: "We have respect for the past, but it has no operational significance. With the establishment of the State of Israel, we have all our spiritual centers within us. That is where the temples should be built."[1]

Others who study the past contend that there has always been a vital historical link between the physical return to the Land and a literal rebuilding of the Temple. Historian David

Salomon affirms, "It [the desire for a rebuilt Temple] was the essence of our Jewish being, the unifying force of our people."[2] This perspective is advanced by modern Temple activists to justify their efforts:

> The hope for the rebuilding of the Temple was born on the very day of its destruction almost 2,000 years ago. Rabbi Akiva comforted his weeping colleagues by proclaiming that if the prophecies of destruction have come to pass, the fulfillment of the prophecy of redemption and rebuilding is certainly to follow. In the course of 2,000 years, the Jewish people have never forgotten the Temple. . . . The dream of rebuilding the Temple spans 50 generations of Jews, five continents and innumerable seas and oceans. The prayer for rebuilding is recited in as many languages as are known to humanity. These prayers . . . now gain a new dimension with the return of the people to the Land of Israel. . . . This new dimension is: a possibility [of rebuilding the Temple].[3]

The *Amidah*, a prayer whose edited form goes back to shortly after the Temple's destruction, is recited three times daily by religiously observant Jews, and includes both a petition for the return of Jews to Israel and for the rebuilding of Jerusalem and the reinstitution of the Temple service. On sabbaths and festivals an additional petition is made for the speedy rebuilding of the Temple and the revival of sacrifices in a restored Temple. Therefore, every prayer of the Jewish people for the redemption of Israel ties together the Land and the Temple as an inseparable hope.

In the "613 Commandments" (a rabbinic collection of the biblical precepts and prohibitions), approximately one-third relate to or are dependent upon the presence of a

Temple in Jerusalem. Commandment number 20 of the mandatory commandments (the first 248) specifically calls for the rebuilding of a Temple. Because the observance of these commandments is obligatory for all Jews, some people believe that since 1967, when control of Jerusalem was regained by Israel and the possibility finally existed, it has been a sin that the Temple has not been rebuilt. Others interpret the "sin" not as a failure to actively work toward rebuilding, but as a lack of desire for the Temple. Maimonides, the medieval philosopher and codifier of Jewish law, contended that every generation of Jews was obligated to build the Temple if its site was ever taken. With the establishment of Israeli sovereignty over the Temple Mount, it is clear that a historical mandate now exists for the Temple's rebuilding.

Other spokesmen for the rebuilding of the Temple consider nationalistic and religious reasons for beginning preparations at the present time. As for nationalistic motives, the need to unify the Jewish people is foremost. In Temple times, the Temple served as a symbol of national unity. It is said that during the time of the second Temple the Romans would strengthen their garrisons when the Jewish pilgrims came to the Temple, because those were the times when Jewish nationalistic feelings ran high.[4] In those days, too, the Temple was the political center for the nation, since the religious and political elements had been combined in the office of the high priest. Today, no greater rallying point can be found to foster Jewish unity than rebuilding the Jewish Temple. It is attractive even to many secular Jews because of their ethnic heritage and in view of the security it would afford the nation.

On religious grounds, Jerusalem and the Temple are essential to Judaism. Pinchas Peli, professor at the Ben Gurion University of the Negev, states:

> It is somehow strange to speak about Jerusalem
> in the Jewish faith, since Jerusalem is not only a

city holy and central within the faith of Judaism, but it is the faith itself. . . . We cannot picture a Jewish faith without Jerusalem. . . . A Jew cannot say Grace after the meal without referring to Jerusalem: "Please, O Lord, have mercy upon us, upon Israel Thy People, and upon Jerusalem Thy City. Build Jerusalem the Holy City speedily in our days." . . . At the time of the destruction of the First Temple, they [the Jews] took a sacred oath (Psalm 137): "If I forget Thee, O Jerusalem, let my hand forget its cunning, let my tongue cleave to the roof of my mouth, if I remember Thee not, if I set not Jerusalem above my chiefest joy." This oath has never been forfeited.[5]

The need for a new Temple is also appealed to on the basis of the biblical prophets and their promise of Israeli ascendancy and the establishment of world peace, events which, as we will see, cannot occur apart from the rebuilding of the Temple. Temple activist Gershon Salomon argues from this perspective when he declares that the Temple must be rebuilt as a prelude to Israel's redemption:

I cannot imagine an Israeli state or Israeli life in this country without the Temple Mount in the center of this life, without Jerusalem in the center of this country, as a capital of national, spiritual, and moral life. The Temple Mount is for us the place of life. . . . The Israeli people must renew their life as God chose for them to be, a people who have a biblical mission to fulfill the principles of God . . . and the Temple Mount is the primary condition for the fulfillment of this historical mission. . . . More than this, the Temple Mount . . . must be . . . for all the world, a center of belief in God, of prayer to God. . . . So the

> redemption of all the world is connected to . . . the
> redemption of the Temple Mount . . . and the re-
> building of the third Temple.[6]

Whether the Temple is viewed only as a national symbol, a rallying point for Jews in Israel and the Diaspora, or seen as a prophetic hope essential to the fulfillment of the mission of Judaism, since the liberation of Jerusalem and the Temple Mount, the *possibility* of rebuilding has existed. While some attempts were made after 1967 to organize rebuilding discussions, it was not until Arab aggression increased in 1987 with the Palestinian uprising that Temple rebuilding movements began to visibly organize. Fearing a loss of what they had fought for in 1967, either through greater Arab imperialism or peace resolutions, groups with the goal of seeing the Temple Mount restored as a place of Jewish worship began to multiply. The urgency that is embraced by all of these groups is expressed by Nahman Kahane, rabbi of the Young Israel Synagogue and head of the Institute for Talmudic Commentaries:

> All Jewish history as far as we're concerned is
> one big parenthesis until the Temple is returned.
> Life without the Temple is not really living.[7]

Chapter 8

Gathering Momentum

I believe [that the time for the erection of the third Temple] could be close. In Isaiah [60:22] it says, "In its own time I will hasten it." With regard to my own research I felt at many times that it was being very much hastened.

—*Dr. Asher Kaufman*

*W*hen we talk about Temple activism and preparations for rebuilding the Temple, we must emphasize the word *preparations*, since direct access to the Temple Mount is impossible both politically and religiously.

Many of these preparations are educational in nature. They are being carried out by Jewish groups that, despite theological differences, have in common the belief that a third Temple will one day be established in Jerusalem. Some of the groups see it as their responsibility to Judaism to fulfill the command to rebuild the Temple in this generation. Other groups feel that only the Messiah can locate the true site of the Temple and initiate its rebuilding, and so they work in areas of scholarly research to raise the spiritual consciousness of Jewry toward the hope of a third Temple. All groups working toward the day when the Temple can be rebuilt stress with equal conviction that while they have no idea how the Temple will rise, it will rise soon. Rabbi Nahman Kahane says:

> There are two views about the next Temple. One is that the Temple will come down from heaven in a miraculous way, without human intervention. The majority think that it will be a building which is built with human intervention. . . . You have to have the political background, you have to have the capability, *but this could happen tomorrow.*[1]

For the past decade, research concerning the Temple—its ritual and its requirements—has been amassing through both individual and institutional efforts. Let's look at some of these efforts and organizations, and their current contributions toward preparing a Jewish people ready to rebuild.

Let the Temple Be Built!

One of the major problems faced by Jewish groups making any type of preparations for the Temple is the problem of perspective. For many Jews the Temple is a relic of the past that they feel they can get along without. Jews involved in preparations for rebuilding, however, feel that the Jewish people, and all humanity, are living below the spiritual level God intended, and that the reason for this is the absence of the Shekinah (Divine Presence) from the world. One speaker stated the concern succinctly: "The Shekinah is brought about only through the Temple. . . . In terms of our mission as a people, we cannot in any way reach our spiritual status without the Temple."[2] Realigning Jewish thought so that the Temple is once again central is the goal adopted by the Society for the Preparation of the Temple.

To help realize this goal, the group publishes a bi-monthly journal *Yivneh Ha-miqdash* ("Let the Temple Be Built!").

This journal is a forum for scholarly dialogue and Temple-related subjects researched and published throughout Israel and the world (see Figure 7). This organization also sponsors a prayer service on the Temple Mount, which will be discussed later.

What to Wear

With the return of the Jewish people to the land of the Bible, there has come a renewed call for a return to a biblical lifestyle. Outside of Israel it was not possible to observe the festival calendar or to continue many of the prescribed rituals that depended upon the presence of a Temple and functional priesthood. As many Jews have sought to fulfill these biblical commandments in the Land, they have had to do extensive research to discover lost knowledge about specific biblical injunctions.

One example of this is the commandment in Numbers 15:37-40, which requires a blue-colored thread to be included among the cords of the fringed garments. While this commandment applies to all religiously observant males, it especially applies to the Temple garments of those who conduct the ritual service. One of those who has researched the matter of the exact colors produced by certain dyes mentioned in Talmudic sources is former Chief Rabbi Isaac Herzog.[3] He has concluded that the biblical blue (*techelet*) used for dyeing religious items in ancient times was made from the *segulit* snail. Because of the rarity of these snails, it was reserved for royalty and the wealthy. In A.D. 300, one source records that one pound of blue-dyed silk sold for the equivalent of $96,000. Therefore, the use of this color on the single thread of the fringed garment of the common man gave him a touch of royalty.

According to the Talmud (Menahot 44a), the shores of ancient Israel were once said to have been inundated with these snails (only once every 70 years, however). Many

יבנה המקדש

בטאון
התנועה
לכינון
המקדש
02-71904

בס"ד,   גליון 10028   - מיוחד -   כתובת המערכת-ת.ד. 4נב"ע

דבר העורך

שלום רב! לפני עשרים ושלוש שנים, לראשונה מאז מרד בר-כוכבא, נכנסו חיילים יהודים להיכל... אך שלא כבראשונה את המקדש הם לא טיהרו. הם שחררו רבים ממרחבי ארצנו ובראש ובראשונה את עיר קדשנו. לאחר רוממות הרוח בא מפח הנפש.

שר הבטחון דאז משה דיין נטל את מפתחות העזרה - אותם המפתחות שלפני אלפיים שנה זרקו הכהנים השמימה בעת שריפת בית המקדש, אותם המפתחות שהוחזרו זה עתה ע"י אבינו שבשמים - הוא נטל את המפתחות ומסרם ברגע של חולשה ורפיון לידי צוררי ישראל. משך אלפיים שנה חיכה עם ישראל לרגע הנשגב הזה של שחרור מקום המקדש והנה בשבריר שניה אנו הורסים את הכל -

במו-פינו אנו ועקים לרבונו של עולם: אנא, אל תיקח אותנו ברצינות! זה נחמד להתפלל וללבכות וגם לצום ארבע פעמים בשנה, אבל לעשות משהו בפועל זה יותר מדי, עוד לא הגיע הזמן וגם עדיין איננו מוכנים!

לא פלא שהחמשך לחטאים הנוראים הללו לא איחר לבוא, שהרי עבירה גוררת עבירה - את חברון ואת שכם לא אינכלאסנו; את אופירה ואת חבל ימית הרסנו במו-ידינו (דבר ללא תקדים בהסטוריה); על יהודה ושומרון הכרזנו כשטח כבוש; את סיני מסרנו למצרים; והנורא מכל - גם בתוככי ירושלים עיר קדשנו ישנם מקומות (ובעיקר אלו הסמוכים למקום המקדש) שהינם "מחוץ לתחום" לישוב יהודי. ומי יודע אם חלילה לא הסכימו גם בבית דין של מעלה לפסק זה, כי הרי - "פלסטין של מלך לא כיבשת ואתה כובש לך ארצות" (ספרי עקב)?! -   ומה לנו כי נלין על כי מוקד האינתיפאדה נמצא בהר בית קדשינו.

לאור כל אלה קמנו, קבוצת יהודים החרדים לדבר ה' והחפצים באמת ובתמים לעשות את דברי תורתינו הקדושה, והקמנו תנועה אשר באמצעותה אנו פעולים להחזרת כבוד השכינה למקומה, על ידי הפצת דעת תורה ברבים.

הגליון הנמצא בידך הינו דוגמא בלבד. עד כה הוצאנו לאור שלשים ושנים גליונות. בכל גליון יש כארבעים עמודים. כל גליון מכיל חומר רב ומגוון. הצטרף עוד היום אלינו והיה שותף למלאכת קודש זו.

בברכת "אקם"
המערכת

thought this to be exaggeration until in late October 1990, segulit snails in huge quantities were found all along beaches on the Mediterranean coast of Israel. This unusual appearance of the snails, coming at the conclusion of Israel's first generation as an Independent State, has been hailed by some Orthodox Israelis as a sign of the imminent coming of the messianic age since it heralds the possibility of the revival of the Temple priesthood.

Restoring the Temple Vessels

Utilizing the research of Herzog and others to produce actual priestly garments, as well as authentic implements for the Temple service is the task of the Temple Institute. No organization in Israel has received more attention in its efforts toward rebuilding the Temple. In its October 1989 issue, *Time* magazine presented a two-page article on the rebuilding of the Temple that focused on the Temple Institute. In the same year ABC's "20/20" program aired a segment about the Temple Institute on its nationwide program. In addition, almost every wire service has posted some story about the Institute's activities, and several Christian television programs have done extensive reports on the vessels in preparation. The Temple Institute tourist center itself has drawn thousands of Jewish and Christian tour groups, as well as countless Israelis.

The Temple Institute's founder is 52-year-old Israel Ariel (see photo section). Rabbi Ariel was one of the first paratroopers in 1967 to reach the Western Wall buttressing Temple Mount. His first army assignment after the war, ironically, was to guard the Dome of the Rock, the very object that prevents the rebuilding of the Temple! A biblical and Talmudic scholar, Ariel is a researcher whose published writings include an *Atlas of the Land of Israel: Its Boundaries According to the Sources*, the first of a projected four-volume work which argues that the original boundaries of the land promised to Abraham extend west to east from a point near the present Suez Canal to the Persian Gulf, and north to south from northern Syria along the Euphrates River to a boundary line running from Eliat on the Red Sea to the border with Persia. Within these boundaries today fall the countries of Egypt, Jordan, Lebanon, Syria, and portions of Iraq and Saudi Arabia. According to Ariel, when the Temple is rebuilt and all those outside the land of Israel return, these lands will provide the necessary room for the increased population.

Rabbi Ariel recognized that the main spiritual center of Judaism was restored to the Jewish people in 1967, but its treasures were not. According to tradition these objects from antiquity were either destroyed, hidden under the Temple Mount, or taken by Roman conquerors to Rome. Rumor also persists that many of these objects (e.g., the menorah, table of showbread, and Temple utensils) lie in a repository in the Vatican, and that the Vatican's anti-Semitic stance prevents their return to Israel. Whatever the case, Ariel believes that the restoration of objects used in the Temple service will awaken Jews throughout the world to their biblical heritage and ultimately prepare them for the rebuilding of the Temple. This ambition culminated in the opening of the Temple Institute in 1988.

Outside the visitor's center of the Temple Institute, a sign advertises "Exhibition of Temple Vessels" in Hebrew, and "Treasures of the Temple" in English. Once inside, the visitor is told that the vessels manufactured by the Temple Institute are not replicas, but usable vessels, destined for future service in the third Temple. At present, 53 of the 103 vessels the Bible says were used in the ancient Temple have been or are in the process of being constructed (see photo section).

Among these are the golden crown of the high priest, the priestly garments, a copper washbasin (laver) for the purification of the priests for Temple service, implements for sacrificial service, the high priest's lottery box, a set of incense utensils and incense spices, and silver trumpets for calling worshipers to the Temple. The 12 gemstones to be set in the breastplate of the high priest are currently being researched and prepared by a local craftsman.

In addition, a six-foot high wax replica of the gold menorah stands in the group's bookstore not far away (see photo section). The menorah project is the culmination of three years of research begun by Israel Ariel. Soon, a bronze original will be made from the same mold by Haem Odem, a craftsman who emigrated from Soviet Georgia to Israel. The cost of constructing a gold-electroplated menorah with its 94.6 pounds of gold is estimated at $10 million.[4]

These reconstructed vessels serve only an educational purpose at present, but the Temple Institute is working in other ways to see that their utilization in a rebuilt Temple can become a reality. Zev Golan, the Institute's director, has said:

> Our task is to advance the cause of the Temple and to prepare for its establishment, not just talk about it.[5] . . . We believe that all of our hopes and all of our attempts . . . will cause some activity in the heavens, and with God's help, the day will come soon when we will build the Temple.[6]

Toward this end, the first bi-annual Conference on Temple Research, jointly sponsored by the Temple Institute and the Ministry of Religious Affairs, was held October 18, 1989. This conference brought together rabbis, scientists, archaeologists, and the public to clarify Temple-related issues.

The Temple Institute also maintains a research room for Institute architects and engineers who feed their research data into computers to prepare blueprints for the future Temple. Some of these plans, which have involved years of debate over *halakah* (prescribed ritual), present innovative

קבלת הדם

הכהן המקבל את הדם עומד כנגד השוחט
באלכסון, פניו לקרן דרומית מזרחית ואחוריו
למערבית צפונית. מחזיק בידו הימנית מזרק ומקבל
את הדם היוצא מיד אחר השחיטה.

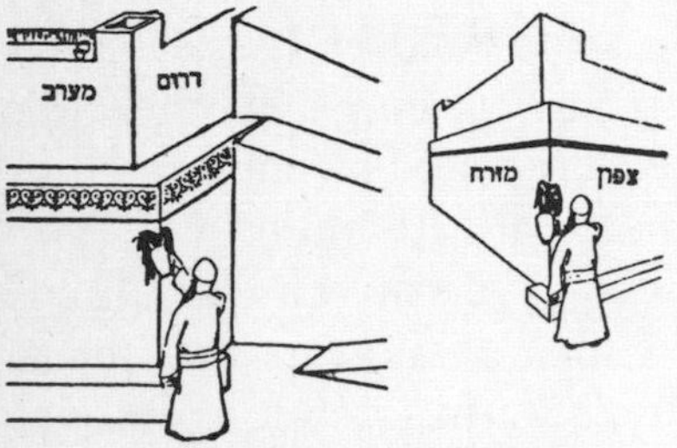

הולכת הדם וזריקתו

אחר שקיבל את הדם במזרק מוליכו לקרן מזרחית
צפונית של המזבח, כשהוא נעמד על רצפת
העזרה, וזורק הדם בחלק התחתון של המזבח
למטה מחוט הסיקרא באופן שהדם יתפשט לשתי
רוחות המזבח — צפון ומזרח. אח"כ מוליך את
הדם לקרן מערבית דרומית של המזבח, וזורק על
הקרן כנ"ל.

חטאות פנימיות

סדר ההזאה בחטאות הפנימיות: הכהן מוליך את
הדם להיכל, ועומד בין המזבח למנורה כשפניו
למערב ואחוריו למזרח, אך אינו נכנס בין המזבח
למנורה, אלא עומד מחוץ למזבח כשהמזבח לפניו,
ומזה שבע פעמים כנגד אמצעיתה של הפרוכת.
אח"כ נותן ד' מתנות על ד' קרנות מזבח הזהב,
ומתחיל בקרן מזרחית צפונית, וממשיך — צפונית
מערבית, מערבית דרומית, דרומית מזרחית. שיירי
הדם היה שופך על גג היסוד המערבי של מזבח
החיצון נגד פתח ההיכל.

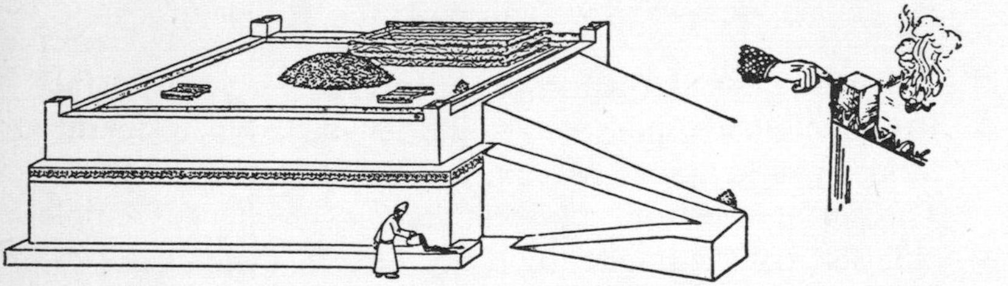

Figure 8: Temple Sacrifice Instructions. Examples of instructions given to priests on the proper procedure for offering sacrifices in the third Temple. Taken from the Hebrew text *Summations and Illustrations* by Rav Shalom Dov Steinberg, pp. 7, 22.

approaches to rebuilding the Temple in modern times. For example, an electric-current table on display offers a solution to the problem of using electricity in the Temple.

In recent years, to educate and promote its cause, the Institute has developed an aggressive media campaign. It has also begun a traveling exhibition and established a more permanent exhibition in the United States. To communicate the restoration agenda, it has produced several video presentations, and printed illustrated booklets and postcards of the new Temple objects.

Preparing a Temple Priesthood

Several related groups in Jerusalem are currently preparing men for future priestly service in a restored Temple. One of these, the *Ateret Cohanim*, has established a yeshiva (religious school) for the education and training of Temple priests (see photo section). Motti Dan [HaCohen], who claims descent from the priestly line, started the school in the 1970's to research regulations related to Temple service. At one time or another the school is said to have had as many as 200 men in active preparation for the priesthood. Several texts for a renewed sacrificial system are studied by these priests, as illustrated in Figure 8.

Another organization also pursuing research with respect to the Temple priesthood is located in the Young Israel Synagogue in the Old City. This synagogue has the distinction of being the synagogue nearest in proximity to the Western Wall, which is the place nearest to the Temple Mount. Called the Institute for Talmudic Commentaries, the organization is headed by Rabbi Nahman Kahane. The purpose of the Institute is primarily to conduct and publish research associated with priestly activities and the Temple. Rabbi Kahane, who himself belongs to one of the lines of priestly families, maintains a computerized data base on all *cohanim* (priests) in Israel. His list contains thousands of names along with the addresses and professions of those listed. "This way," says Kahane, "when the Messiah comes, I can say, 'Here, Mr. Messiah, here's your data base.'"[7]

The problem of identifying a prospective priest is more complicated than finding someone whose last name is Cohen or Levi. When Rabbi Kahane was asked how he could know if someone was legitimately from a priestly family, he explained:

> No one really knows who the original cohen are. Within the context of cohen, the cohanim, there are certain families which are "blue-bloods." However, though you might be in the blue-blood family, the possibility remains that there could have been an invalid marriage 500 years ago, e.g., to a divorcée, or a convert. So, even though we don't know for certain who is a cohen, whoever has the tradition in his family that he is a cohen is a cohen. We don't check the credentials, we don't even have the ability to check his credentials. The premise is that no one is going to lie about it [being a cohen] . . . because it makes life more difficult. You're limited in whom you can marry, in where you can go, and there are many more such limitations.[8]

Rabbi Kahane's brother, Meir, was at one time head of the anti-Arab Kach Party and a controversial member of the Knesset (he was assassinated in 1991 by Arab terrorists while speaking to followers in New York). Although Rabbi Kahane has declined an invitation to take over his brother's movement because he is not sympathetic with its philosophy, he is considering following in his brother's political footsteps. There is a reported groundswell among the

Orthodox that favors him as a replacement for mayor of Jerusalem when present mayor Teddy Kollek retires in 1996. Currently he is preparing to run for a seat in Israel's parliament, the Knesset. Kahane, an ultra-Orthodox Jew who supports the State of Israel, believes his chances of winning are reasonably good. One can only speculate how Kahane's political position might affect future efforts toward the rebuilding of the Temple.

Messianic Marketplace

The proliferation of various individuals and groups who support and advance the views of Temple rebuilding is steadily increasing. Every year Jerusalem sees new industries that promote in some way or other the messianic concept of a third Temple era. Two such industries are those of *Beged Ivri* and *Harrari Harps*.

Beged Ivri: Clothing for the Third Temple Era

Beged Ivri, which means "Hebrew Clothing," is the brainchild of Reuven Prager, a 32-year-old Orthodox immigrant from Miami, Florida who believes he is from priestly descent. Prager's shop, on the second floor of a business tower near the ultra-Orthodox community of Mea Shearim, advertises "Clothing for the Third Temple Era." This clothing, made by Prager as a levitical function, is designed according to biblical and historical sources and purports to be "authentic dress worn in biblical times." Prager believes that the current generation is unique because of the return to the land of Israel, which will be followed by the rebuilding of the Temple.[9]

In a 1989 interview, *Hadassah* magazine reported:

It is the image of the rebuilding of the Third Temple which led Prager to wonder at the appearance of Jews when they came to Jerusalem to pray during the days of the First and Second Temples. Prager believes that Jews should start dressing that way again in preparation for the Third Temple.[10]

By Prager's account, he one day looked out over the Temple Mount and visualized people coming to pray at the third Temple. This inspired him to create fashions to help advance that day. His store contains pictures and literature relating to the rebuilding of the Temple.

Prager walks the streets of Jerusalem daily dressed in his biblical garments. He has issued statements for others to join him in a return to the past—in preparation for the future. One of his statements reads:

> We don't believe in lip service. We don't believe in sitting in a foreign land saying "next year in Jerusalem" when it could be this year in Jerusalem. We don't believe in relegating the Holy Mitzvah of Tzitzith to a shmata worn under gentile apparel and ignoring the Divine Commandment of Techelet [the biblical blue used to color a thread included in the fringes of a four-cornered garment].

In addition to making "third-Temple era" apparel, Prager has proposed the revival of the ancient Jewish marriage ceremony, a ceremony from the end of the first Temple period which was lost after the destruction of the second Temple.[11]

To work toward the realization of this goal, Prager has established a nonprofit organization registered with the Ministry of the Interior, has obtained a copy of the ancient bridal crown made of pure gold, and is raising funds to build the royal wedding litter described in the Song of Solomon. This effort, along with his clothing, is intended to reviv

Temple consciousness and pave the way for the establishment of the third Temple.

Harrari Harps: Music for the Messianic Age

During the time of the first and second Temples, half of the 38,000 Levite priests played on two types of harps, singing melodies that no one else was permitted to learn. This secret knowledge was passed from father to son until the destruction of the second Temple. Since that time the special knowledge of this music has been said to be "hidden." Because of the sacredness of the music of the Temple instruments, most Orthodox Jewish communities do not use any instrumental music in their synagogues as a sign of mourning over the Temple.

But after a 2,000-year absence, the sounds of the biblical harp have returned to Jerusalem. The return began when Micah and Shoshanna Harrari were in California, building and repairing stringed instruments and studying harp-making. They were planning to immigrate to Israel when they heard that the mayor of Jerusalem had said, "Jerusalem needs a harpmaker." Answering this need, the Harraris decided to research the biblical harp. They discovered that the harp of King David was considered a symbol of Israel, and believed that its recreation would serve as a symbol of the future of Israel as foretold by the prophets of old.

A story is told that when they had first made their replica of the ten-stringed harp of David, and tuned it to the ancient Hebrew mode, a rabbi came by to see it. When he saw and heard it he exclaimed that this was a fulfillment of prophecy, for the Talmud said that this harp was a symbol of the world to come, and that when the harp was again sounded in Jerusalem the Messiah would come!

The Harraris believe that they are part of the divine plan in ushering in the days of the Messiah and world peace, for it is also written of this harp that the *Shir Hadash* or New Song, whose main theme is a world of no more war, will be sung upon it. They also believe that it is the *Asora*, the mythical harp spoken of in Jewish literature "whose song will rise on the day when the world that is to be will be recreated in one harmonious whole."[12]

The messianic hope connected with the Harraris' harp was mentioned in an article written about the instrument in Jerusalem's magazine of the arts, *Art and Judaica*: "One can almost picture a latter-day scene with the same sounds [as when David brought up the Ark] as the Messiah enters Jerusalem from the Mount of Olives."[13]

One of the Harraris' ten-stringed harps is included among the vessels on display at the Temple Institute, and the Harraris also display and distribute pictures and information about the preparations to rebuild the Temple in their shop. Located next door in the same courtyard is an outlet store of Reuven Prager's Beged Ivri.

Beged Ivri and Harrari Harps are but two examples of the work of a new generation of Israelis who view the rebuilding of the Temple as a near event, and who are seeking to change their own lifestyles and influence others to get ready for the coming of the Messiah and life in a third Temple era.

One thing is certain about the immediate future: This recent preparation will only grow stronger in coming days. As research and education continue, more pronounced demonstrations of the growing Jewish hope are also capturing the interest of the world. Each element adds to the momentum, making the Israeli people increasingly ready to rebuild.

Chapter 9

Activity on the Mount

People can think what they want, but God is doing what He wants to do; the Will of God must be fulfilled, and the Will of God is that this place, which He chose to be His home, will again be His home. It will be a place for the third Temple, and after this Temple will be rebuilt by the people of Israel, then this place will become a place of prayer for all the nations.

—*Gershon Salomon*

*I*n order for the Temple to be rebuilt, the political situation must allow for complete *Jewish sovereignty over the* Temple Mount. In order for complete Jewish sovereignty to be gained over this area, some activists believe that a return of Jewish presence in the Old City as close to the Temple Mount as possible is essential. Recently the Ateret Cohanim group tried to occupy St. John's Hospice in the Christian Quarter of Jerusalem's Old City, a site near the Church of the Holy Sepulchre and in the proximity of the Temple Mount. On Good Friday, April 13, 1990, Jewish families, all members of Ateret Cohanim, settled into four buildings owned by the Greek Orthodox Church. Immediately, a protest made the following headline in the *Jerusalem Post*: "All Churches Protest Old City Settlement."[1]

Newspapers throughout the world received the wire service announcement, and looking for good "Easter press," U.S. papers presented the story as an instance of Jewish aggression against a Christian holy site. The truth, however, was that the "holy site" was a neglected and abandoned group of buildings that the church had advertised for sale for two years. The church had rejected bids by two Christian groups in Jerusalem of $2 million each, because they wanted more money. Ateret Cohanim apparently met their lease price and legally moved onto the property. However, as soon as they occupied the buildings the Christian community in Jerusalem protested that the move violated the church's standing as a traditional Christian historical site. The Israeli courts, always careful to avoid religious conflicts, decided that the Jewish residents had to vacate the premises until the issue could be settled through litigation.

Although both Jews and Muslims had previously purchased property from the Greek Orthodox Church (in fact a large number of the shops in the Christian Quarter are Muslim owned), the Ateret Cohanim members are considered Messianic Jews, and their settlement efforts are viewed with caution by the Israeli government and with opposition by Muslims and anti-Zionist Christian denominations. Former President Chaim Herzog, in a letter to the primate of the Greek Orthodox Metropolis, pointed out the inconsistency of the affair when he wrote:

> It is extremely alarming, to say the least, to note the manner in which the neglected, abandoned, misused hospice, suddenly becomes a Holy Site. . . . I have not noted any Church protest anywhere in the world at the sale of property in the area of the Church of the Holy Sepulchre to Moslem inhabitants in Jerusalem. The voice of the protestors, it is sad to note, was raised only because of the Jewish identity of the buyers or lessees.[2]

Joining their sister organization in settlement efforts is *Atara L'yoshna*, meaning "[restoring] the crown to its original [form]," a name reflecting the group's desire to return Jewish life to its former state with a rebuilt Temple. This organization has been legally purchasing property in the Arab Moslem Quarter "in order to create a Jewish environment." Already more than five sites have been purchased and occupied.

Atara L'yoshna's connection with Temple preparations goes back to earlier days when members of the group met with Rabbi Nahman Kahane and members of what is now the Ateret Cohanim group for Temple and priest-related studies. A division occurred which separated the two groups, though Atara L'yoshna's goal of the resettlement in the Moslem Quarter is still publicly linked to the rebuilding of the Temple. The group maintains a Study and Tourist Center located near the Western Wall in the Herodian section of the new Jewish Quarter, just around the corner from the Temple Institute. The Study and Tourist Center displays replica models of the Tabernacle, the first and second Temples, various Temple furniture, including an Ark of the Covenant (see photo section), a menorah, a collection of incense spices, and other items relating to Jewish tradition. The largest model, occupying center stage, is clearly labeled "The Third Temple" (see photo section). This third Temple model is based on the dimensions of the millennial Temple given by Ezekiel (whose plan is displayed beside the model). The placement of this model is such that a visitor looking through the window behind the model can see the Temple Mount and catch a glimpse of the Dome of the Rock, the traditional site of the Temple. The implication is that the two images should be joined in the mind, not as a past, but as a future symbol.

One of the most controversial and widely publicized settlements near the Temple Mount has been that of the El Ad housing association. In early October of 1991, this group, along with four members of the Knesset, occupied five buildings in the eastern Jerusalem village of Silwan. Until that time the village, which occupies the ancient site of the biblical Shiloah, had been 100 percent Arab. Thousands of members of the *Shalom Akshav* ("Peace Now") movement staged a protest in Silwan against the action. Jerusalem Mayor Teddy Kollek opposed the move saying it threatens to cancel the upcoming twenty-fifth anniversary of Jerusalem's unification. Coming also at the same time as the Middle East peace talks, the Shamir government has tried to avoid personal responsibility in the matter by making it a decision for the Israeli courts.

The settlement of Silwan was probably a right-wing attempt to abort the peace negotiations. Any attempt at negotiations that would further compromise Israeli sovereignty over the Temple Mount is also opposed by Temple movement activists, many of whom support the settlement not only because the Silwan is in the area of the ancient Israeli capital from King David's time, but because it is located just below the Temple Mount and contains the Pool of Siloam, the source for the water-libation conducted yearly in the Temple.

As these groups continue their attempts to purchase property near the Temple Mount, one can be certain that protests will follow. As this happens, it will be important to remember the connection between the reported protests and the underlying reasons for the conflict: the preparation for the rebuilding of the Temple.

Pilgrimage to the Mount

While some groups are attempting to establish a Jewish presence *near* the Temple Mount, others believe that the establishment of a religious Jewish presence *on* the Temple Mount is necessary as "a preparatory step to the erection of the third Temple."[3] As an initial move in this direction, the

Society for the Preparation of the Temple has reinstituted the concept of pilgrimage to the Temple Mount.

Orthodox Judaism maintains that the Temple Mount is off-limits to everyone, Jew and non-Jew, because of its sanctity. But as the Society for the Preparation of the Temple points out, this restriction applies only to a Temple precinct 500 cubits by 500 cubits, and since the Temple Mount platform is about four times that size, it is possible to visit the Temple Mount without trespassing on the Holy of Holies and violating the rabbinical ban. As one spokesman for the Society put it: "We don't know exactly where the location of the Temple or the Holy of Holies were, but we do know where they were *not*." The group takes a once-a-week walk around the Mount (avoiding possible sites of the Holy of Holies) as a spiritual exercise and to demonstrate to both Jews and the Muslim authorities that the site of the former Temple is spiritually important to them.

A Synagogue on the Mount

Another proposal for a Jewish presence on the Mount is the building of a synagogue on the eastern wall of Temple Mount near the Golden Gate. This plan has been advocated by former Ashkenazi Chief Rabbi Shlomo Goren (rabbi of the German and European Jews) and Sephardi Chief Rabbi Mordechai Eliahu (rabbi of Jews from Spain and Portugal). Based on his 1967 survey of the Temple Mount, Goren, like the Society for the Preparation of the Temple, concluded that some areas were permitted for Orthodox access. He had long argued against the common belief that the second Temple was built on the site of the present Dome of the Rock, and had even debated this when he was 17 years old with then Chief Rabbi Cook. When Goren took Israeli soldiers up on the Temple Mount after the Six-Day War to help determine the Temple's location, he received much criticism. But armed with this information, Goren promoted the building of a synagogue on the Temple Mount.

Eliahu likewise proposed plans for the synagogue, which when built, would be higher than the Western Wall and both the Dome of the Rock and the Al Aqsa Mosque, and would have its wall overlooking the Temple site constructed entirely of glass.

Cooperating with this effort, Gershon Salomon, founder and leader of the Temple Mount Faithful, originally planned to gather a team of architects to undertake the design. But in August 1991, Salomon indicated that he was no longer involved with this effort because he felt that the construction of a *synagogue* would further delay the actual building of the third *Temple*. He stressed that nothing should impede the immediate establishment of the Temple on the Temple Mount.

Goren disagrees with the idea that a synagogue would slow the establishment of the Temple. He insists that the building of the Temple "is a heavenly process; we are not responsible for it; all is planned by heaven!" It is his belief that the Temple cannot first be built by human hands, but only after heaven reveals the way. This is not to say that Rabbi Goren is passive about the Temple. Every Yom Kippur since 1967 he has held services at the Mahkama police station (located on the Temple Mount) which include special elements unique to the Temple service. These services draw hundreds of worshipers and such notables as former General Chief of Staff Moshe Levy, who has attended every year since he headed the Central Command.

The Temple Mount Faithful

The most-publicized activist group in the land of Israel today is known by its full name as the Temple Mount and Eretz Yisrael Faithful Movement (TMF). As mentioned, the organization is headed by 53-year-old Gershon Salomon, a tenth-generation Jerusalemite who serves as professor of Oriental Studies at the Hebrew University in Jerusalem (see photo section).

Salomon is an observant Jew, who has become a vegetarian in keeping his view that all men and animals will return to an Edenic lifestyle in the messianic age (Isaiah 11:6-9). He was seriously wounded in 1958 during the Sinai campaign, but returned to duty in the Six-Day War in 1967. On the fourth day of this battle when Jerusalem was reunited, Salomon was present at the newly liberated Temple Mount. Of that moment, which has shaped his direction ever since, Salomon says:

> I was in the first Israeli paratroop unit who made it through to the Temple Mount on the fourth day of the War. My feeling, and every soldier's feeling, was the same upon entering this place for the first time. We went first into the Dome of the Rock, and once inside I started to cry like a little child. Then, all of the soldiers which were around the Rock started to cry. We could not stop ourselves. We stayed on the Temple Mount for long hours—we could not move. You cannot understand this moment for us! This place was the place of the Temple, the heart and soul of the Jewish people. I felt that I was very close to Abraham, Isaac, Jacob, King David, and the prophets. It was the most important day of my life, and it follows me every moment of my life. . . . I felt that we had completed a special mission that all of the generations since the destruction of the Temple in A.D. 70 asked us to fulfill.[4]

Salomon believes that his life was spared and that he was allowed to be present at the liberation of the Temple Mount because God had a divine mission for him in connection with the Temple. To fulfill his mission, which he sees as the historic mission of the Jewish people, he founded the TMF.

The stated purpose of the movement is to realize "the true destiny of the land of Israel which is both a full return of the People of Israel to the Temple Mount, historic Jerusalem, and Greater Israel, and a renewed linkage between the People of Israel and their vision, ideology, faith, and roots in the renewed Zionist struggle."[5] Salomon clarifies the focus of the group in connection with the Temple Mount when he says that their central goal is to take the Mount from the Arabs, "and then to rebuild again the third Temple in its right place, on the Rock in the center of the Temple Mount, a Temple that will be again a center of religious, national, spiritual and moral life for Israel."

His movement came into existence in reaction to the Israeli government's return of jurisdiction over the Temple Mount to the Muslim authorities. Salomon explains his motivations for founding the TMF in view of this dramatic event:

> This organization was founded after the Six-Day War when the Israeli army, by the will of God, liberated the Temple Mount. . . . We felt that a long dream of almost 2,000 years of Diaspora was fulfilled, and that the people of God had come back to their home, the Temple Mount. But, in one moment, the Defense Minister of Israel, Moshe Dayan, destroyed this dream, and gave back the keys of the Temple Mount to the enemy of yesterday and tomorrow, the Arabs. The Gates to the Temple Mount were closed to Jews, and they were not allowed to come and pray and to express their feelings and to worship God. This was a great crisis for the Jewish people, and so we decided to try and change this terrible decision.[6]

Salomon speaks candidly of the intentions of his group. In an April 1991 *Jerusalem Post* interview, when Salomon was asked what he would do if he had the freedom to accomplish his mission, he replied: "I would remove the Moslem presence from the Temple Mount, announce to the world that the Temple Mount is the center of the Jewish People, and start building the third Temple."[7]

Putting on the Pressure

In 1987 the TMF entered a court action with the Israeli High Court.[8] The general purpose of the action was to compel government officials to assert Israel's sovereignty over the Temple Mount more forcibly. The specific nature of the complaint was that the Muslim governing authorities on Temple Mount had and were deliberately destroying and concealing ancient visible remains of Solomon's Temple, the second Temple, and Crusader structures. The TMF argued that these acts were motivated by a Muslim desire to obliterate all historical Jewish connections to the site, and thereby remove any basis for an Israeli claim to the Temple Mount.

The TMF accused the government and the municipality of ignoring these acts of Arab imperialism. It further charged that effective Israeli sovereignty over the Temple Mount had been abandoned because no building permits had been required for the numerous Muslim constructions on and around the Mount.

Support for these charges was furnished by Dr. Asher Kaufman, a physicist who has developed a theory about the specific location of the first and second Temples. He contended that 35 remains—rock outcroppings, remnants of walls, and mosaics from the Temple periods had been removed or obscured. (Much of Kaufman's evidence has been published in a special editorial section of the popular *Biblical Archaeology Review* in 1983,[9] and in an updated article in 1991.[10]) Kaufman's concern was that valuable archaeological artifacts, as well as the only existing clues to the Temple's location, were being lost. Further evidence was supplied by Dan Bahat, the official district archaeologist for Jerusalem at that time.

On June 16, 1991, three High Court justices conducted an on-site study of the claims (from a distance, since they observed the boundaries prescribed by Orthodox Jews). Kaufman presented his evidence, as did representatives of the Antiquities Authority (Israel's governmental department which directs all archaeological excavations) who dispute Kaufman's findings. When the High Court ruling is handed down, it will seek to maintain a workable balance and prevent future eruptions of tension on the Mount.

While the Israeli court's view is not yet known, the view of the Arab governing authority, the *Wakf*, is patently clear. In an interview with the *Jerusalem Post* concerning the High Court investigation, Adnan Husseini, a senior Wakf official, stated: "The mosques on the Temple Mount were built by God. . . . Our sovereignty is not subject to compromise."[11] When asked about the claim that Jewish archaeological remains were being destroyed, Husseini, who is also in charge of engineering projects on the Temple Mount, denied the allegation, stating that there were no signs of an ancient Jewish presence on the Mount, therefore there could have been no efforts to obliterate them. Such a statement is in keeping with the general Muslim view that there was no historic Jewish occupation of the site before the Muslim period beginning in the seventh century A.D. The Wakf boycotted the court's final hearing, stating that it was not bound by Israeli law regarding the protection of archaeological sites. It is such claims by the Arabs that have provoked the action by the TMF.

Laying the Cornerstone

Certainly the most aggressive action to foster Temple rebuilding has been the TMF's efforts to lay a cornerstone for the third Temple. The first attempt occurred on October 16, 1989. As Salomon explains:

> On our most holy day, Sukkot, we felt that we must take the first step for rebuilding the Temple. I and my friends, as well as every Israeli and every Jew in all the world, felt that God had performed a great miracle in bringing us back to our historical country. . . . The land of Israel and the State of Israel is now rebuilding again every day more and more, [and so] we felt that we must take the second step, which was the will of God, to build His house again on the Temple Mount. We decided to bring the first cornerstone for this Temple, after 2,000 years. . . . We brought it with us to put it on the Temple Mount, [but] the police and the government decided not to allow us to do it.[12]

I (Randall) was present with the TMF when this first attempt was made. It was truly an amazing thing to behold. Not since Temple times had such a procession taken place openly in Jerusalem. Marching from the Western Wall Plaza down to the site of the ancient Pool of Siloam, the group consisted of people displaying political placards, Israeli flags, and a large banner that read "The land of Israel is Ours!" Some in the group carried reconstructed vessels prepared for use in the future Temple such as the copper washbasin, the silver *mizrak* (used to carry the blood of the sacrifice to the altar), and a silver menorah. Several played musical instruments like those once used by the Levites in Temple worship. Leading this parade, along with Salomon, was a man named Yehoshua Cohen, wearing the woven linen garments of the Temple priests (see photo section).

Moving down the same road on a flatbed truck was the

newly hewn cornerstone (see photo section). Salomon describes the preparation and purpose of this cornerstone:

> We brought this cornerstone from an area in the south of Israel, in the desert, called Mitzpe Ramon. It is a very beautiful place in the land of Israel where the character and color of the stone is very similar to those from which the first and second Temples were made. We also brought the cornerstone from this area because the Torah was given to the people of Israel in the desert, in Mount Sinai, not far from this place in the Negev. This stone is almost four tons in weight, and we believe that the third Temple, which must be a beautiful building, should be started with such stones. The Bible would not allow us to use iron [implements] to [quarry] this stone because it is disrespectful to beat the holy stones used for God's house. We [quarried] this stone with *even tzor* [flint], a special stone called Shamir (the same name as the Prime Minister of Israel), used to work other stones. We prepared this stone very carefully because it will be the first stone of the Third Temple.[13]

The group entered the area of the Pool of Siloam, passing through the Arab village of Silwan. Curious-but-cautious Arab onlookers kept their distance while the TMF began their ceremony. This ceremony consisted of Yehoshua Cohen drawing water from the spring (see photo section), and a blessing called the *shehehianu* (thanksgiving for having reached a special occasion) recited by Salomon. The conclusion of the ritual, held on the street above the pool's entrance, was the climactic consecration of the cornerstone with the water from the spring. The group then returned to the Western Wall Plaza to lay the cornerstone, but were turned back by police at the Dung Gate entrance.

What had just transpired was in accordance with the traditional *Simhat Beit Hasho'eva* or "Celebration of the Water-drawing Place" ceremony. In order to understand the significance of the TMF's performance of this water-libation ceremony, let us go back to the days of the second Temple in which it was said "whoever did not see this ceremony never saw a real celebration" (Succa 5:1).

In Temple times this ceremony lasted six days, with the seventh day as a climactic celebration. On this day the blowing of the ram's horn trumpets accompanied bands of Sukkot worshipers who paraded through the narrow streets of the Holy City toward the Temple Mount. In the Temple courtyard stood three giant candelabra that shined so brightly that the entire city was illuminated. Rabbis and their disciples danced to the accompaniment of musicians while a choir of thousands of Levites sang the 15 Songs of Ascent from the Psalms—one for each of the 15 steps—as they climbed from the Courtyard of the Women to the Courtyard of the Israelites situated in front of the Temple.

The water-libation ceremony began with a specially appointed priest being sent to the Pool of Siloam with a golden pitcher to bring back water from the pool. This pool's water comes from Gihon Spring, through which David entered to defeat the Jebusites and take Jerusalem (2 Samuel 5:8). [14] Having this connection with David (hence, with the Davidic Covenant) and being the water for the life of the city, the pool had messianic associations. Here, too, in ancient days fullers washed clothing (Isaiah 7:3), a figure drawn upon by the prophets to illustrate the Messiah's purification of the millennial Temple's servants (Malachi 3:2,3).

Returning to the Temple this water was poured over the corner of the altar, a ritual based on an oral tradition dating to the time of Moses (Taanit 3a, Sukkot 44a, 44b). The significance of the pouring of water was both *symbolic* and *prophetic*. Its *symbolic* purpose was as a prayer for rain, since the summer was about to end and the rainy season begin. This prayer for rain demonstrated Israel's dependence upon the Lord, an act of faith that will be required of all nations in connection with this ceremony in the millennial Temple (Zechariah 14:16-19).

Its *prophetic* purpose was messianic, looking forward to the outpouring of the *Ruach Ha-Kodesh* ("Holy Spirit") upon Israel and the nations in the messianic era (Ezekiel 36:27; Joel 2:28). In this regard, the seventh-day climax of the water-pouring ritual was called *Hosanna Rabba*, the Day of the "Great Hosanna." At this time the people waved their palm branches while the Levites chanted the *Hallel* (Psalms 113-118). The name of this day—Hosanna—comes from the closing words of Psalm 118 which reads: "Save now, I beseech thee, O Lord. . . . Blessed be he that cometh in the name of the Lord" (Psalm 118:25,26 KJV). This prayer for the speedy advent of messianic redemption accompanied the entire water-drawing ceremony.

This forms the background for the New Testament account of Jesus' arrival described in Matthew 21:9 and John 7:37-39. Keeping this messianic imagery as well as that of the light given off by the Temple menorahs in mind, we can better understand Jesus' messianic fulfillment as He rode into the Temple precinct through the Eastern Gate entrance. He was greeted by shouts of *hosanna* ("Save us please!"), and then proclaimed to the crowds that He was the true giver of the "water" and the "light" of the world (John 7:37,38; 8:12).

For the Temple Mount Faithful, this ceremony proclaimed the prophetic promise to rebuild the Temple and renew its ritual. However, they included a significant "addition" to this ceremony. They poured the water libation on their cornerstone (as the first and only existent part of the third Temple), with a prayer that the messianic redemption would come, the Temple would soon be built, and the water could be properly poured on the Altar.

Recent Demonstrations

Two additional attempts to bring the cornerstone to the ramp leading to the Moghrabi Gate to the Temple Mount have also met with police resistance. Salomon feels that the police and the government who denied permission for the laying of the cornerstone actually believe in the act, but cannot permit it because of the fear of Arab reprisals.

The fears of the authorities are well founded. On October 8, 1990, the second attempt resulted in a riot on the Temple Mount and the death of 17 Palestinian Arabs. As we have already discussed, the riot was planned to draw attention away from Saddam Hussein's occupation of Kuwait and to the Palestinian cause; it was used as justification for terrorism.

On July 21, 1991, the Jews celebrated Tisha B' Av, the annual day of mourning for the destruction of the first and second Temples. Salomon and the TMF appropriately chose this day to go to the Temple Mount in yet another attempt to lay the cornerstone for the third Temple. Although this effort was also blocked by police, Salomon did ascend to the Temple Mount at the site of the Mahkama police station and offer prayer as a symbolic gesture of Jewish presence. Earlier Salomon had related that he truly felt that this Tisha B' Av would be the very last one in which the Jews had to mourn, clearly implying that he expected such progress toward rebuilding the Temple that Jews would be able to rejoice over the Temple's restoration in the future, rather than express remorse over its ruin.

In August 1991, Salomon made a trip to the United States to inform and to enlist the support of Jewish and Christian groups in the TMF cause. Bringing with him video and slide presentations of the TMF's progress, and accepting invitations to speak to any interested group, Salomon was featured on numerous television programs, including Pat Robertson's "700 Club," and radio talk shows. He also spoke to many Jewish organizations and churches throughout the country. This show of support has encouraged Salomon that a spiritual revival of interest in Israel's destiny and the Temple's rebuilding exists, and that his belief that the realization of his goals for the Jewish people are not far away.

On September 24, 1991, the TMF attempted again to lay the cornerstone directly on Temple Mount. The parade began as usual at the Dung Gate and descended to the Pool of Siloam for the water-libation ceremony. On their return with the cornerstone to the Dung Gate the participants were met by a large crowd of Jews who pled with them not to attempt to lay the cornerstone in view of the upcoming Middle East peace conference. The effort was further rebuffed by police refusal to allow the ceremony to proceed within the walls. Despite another setback, Salomon has announced that he fully expects that the rebuilding of the Temple will commence in the Jewish year 5752 (1992).

These failures to lay the cornerstone have not weakened Salomon's resolve:

> In the right day—I believe it is very soon—this stone will be put on the Temple Mount, and be worked and polished . . . and will be the first stone for the third Temple. Just now this stone lays not far from the Temple Mount, very close to the walls of the Old City of Jerusalem, near Shechem [Damascus] Gate . . . and this stone watches over the Temple Mount. But the day is not far that this stone will be in the right place—it can be today . . . or tomorrow, we are very close to the right time.[15]

The groups that are committed to the varied courses of action we have described intend to continue to attempt the laying of a cornerstone, to settle, and to pray on the Temple Mount—and to increase their activity until their fervent hope is realized.

Chapter 10

A
Purified
Priesthood

These [red heifer] ashes must be found before Israel can
have a priesthood . . . and before the orthodox Jew rec-
ognizes Israel as being authentic. . . . The first book in
the Moslem Bible, the Koran, is called Parah, "the
Calf," and it pertains to the ashes of the red heifer. The
Moslems believe whoever finds this will rule the world.
So this could have political implications as well. This
could settle the jihad, "the holy war."[1]

—*Vendyl Jones*

*O*ne of the most interesting issues in the rebuilding of the
Temple is the problem of ritual defilement, which every
Jew has incurred because their land has been dominated
by Gentiles. Without ceremonial purification, no one is
thought to be able to enter the Temple precincts on the
Temple Mount to rebuild the Temple. Resolution of this
issue is also critical to the priesthood, since the priests'
ability to function in their prescribed office depends on it.
The only remedy for this state of impurity is the ceremony
of purification, which requires the ashes of sacrifice from a
particular type of red heifer.

This presents a double problem. First, there are no red
heifer ashes available today, and second, only a person who

131

is ceremonially pure can conduct this ceremony, and no such person exists. Therefore, even though priests are trained, and even if red heifer ashes are produced, no one is currently qualified to purify them for service.

Holy Ashes

According to Numbers 19:1-22, the ashes of the red heifer (Hebrew *parah adumah*, "red cow") required for the purification of the priests and people of Israel were deposited in a "clean place" outside the camp of the Israelites. Then the ashes were mixed with water as a ceremonial cleaning agent.

In Temple times the ashes were kept in the House of Stone located near the Eastern Gate.[2] Even after the Temple was destroyed and Temple sacrifice ended, a supply of ashes was available and continued to be used as late as the Amoraic period (A.D. 200-500). According to the rabbis, only nine (some say seven) red heifers were actually burned in Jewish history, and the tenth, and last, will be prepared by the Messiah.[3]

At present there are two schools of thought concerning the ashes of the red heifer. The first is that some of the ashes from the time of the second Temple still exist. The second is that a suitable red heifer can be found and new ashes made.

The Missing Urn

About a decade ago, Vendyl Jones, a onetime Baptist minister who now rejects cardinal doctrines of the Christian faith, popularized his theory that ashes from the second Temple period are still in existence after he began digging in a cave near Qumran. Acquiring credibility by association with the late professor and archaeologist, Pesach Bar-Adon, Jones has been digging in what he believes is the "Cave of the Column" mentioned in the Copper Scroll. The Copper

Scroll is an archaeological item found in 1952 in a cave along the shores of the Dead Sea, although not deciphered until many years later. It contains a text in Hebrew and Aramaic script inscribed on thin copper sheets that describes the hiding of Temple implements outside Jerusalem and makes mention of another scroll that lists 67 other places where items are hidden. Most scholars believe this is a fictitious account, but others, like Jones, take it seriously and have launched archaeological excavations based on the scroll's cryptic message. Among the items listed is a jar (called in the text a *kalal*). Jones theorizes that this jar is the ceremonial jar (also called *kalal*) mentioned in the Mishnah as containing the ashes of the last red heifer. So far the only item of interest uncovered has been an ancient flask of oil, which may have connection with the Temple service, by archaeologist Joseph Patrich of the Hebrew University while conducting a survey of Judean desert caves.

Other Seekers

Another American searching for the ashes of the red heifer is Gary Collitt. Collitt, a Christian, believes that Vendyl Jones is incorrect in his identification of the cave where the kalal is buried and is working at an alternate site. Following his own theory of location, and utilizing aerospace technology in his search, he feels certain that he is on the verge of success. Explaining his methodology and discoveries, Collitt says:

> As we looked at the necessity for Temple restoration, and the need for the ashes of the red heifer, and as we looked at the evidences, we became convinced that to the north [in the wadis of Zumdotrim, where Vendyl Jones is digging] was not the right area, but in the Wadi la-Chippah. Wadi la-Chippah means "the dome of the bridge" or

"the covering over." In Judaism, it is important that God is "over us." [This site] is very important because it identifies with Jerusalem in the scroll. The two caves [here] are orientated east and west in a [fashion] typical of the Temple. . . .

[Aerospace technology] can take pictures of a particular site on earth, and then analyze [them] to reveal what is 60 feet below the surface. A private organization that was into molecular frequency research offered this NASA-type technology to us. . . . They gave us readings . . . [for instance] of a library in a room-cave 40 feet down that they said had standing pottery and scrolls in the pottery.

Collitt believes the special geographic situation of his site additionally confirms it as the location of the red heifer ashes. He states:

[Our site] is located next to Sakakah, one of the six wilderness cities from the time of Joshua . . . and may have been the capital. . . . Other writings tell us that Jeremiah took the Ark of the Covenant to Mount Nebo, and the east-west orientation of our cave site aligns with Nebo. Jeremiah went over there with the Ark of the Covenant, and it says he turned and beheld the inheritance of God, meaning he looked back at Israel, then went further and hid the Ark in a hollow (i.e., man-made, carved) cave. We believe that cave was between these two caves at one time. After the Babylonian captivity, the Ark of the Covenant was taken back to Jerusalem where it resides [today].[4]

Collitt believes that the ashes of the red heifer would be a great evangelistic tool to turn Israelis to Jesus, since the red heifer typifies Christ. He hopes to find New Testament manuscripts among the scrolls in the cave site he is planning to excavate. He believes that such a discovery would lead to world revival.

No Biblical Command for Finding Ancient Ashes

Despite the sincerity of Jones and Collitt, and the possible treasures they may unearth, many authorities have substantial reservations about the existence and necessity of the original ashes of the red heifer.

One reservation involves the location of the ashes. Some historical sources suggest that the ashes may have been carried from Jerusalem to Yavneh with the Sanhedrin during its wanderings after the destruction of the second Temple. They may have ultimately been deposited somewhere in the Tiberias region. Another source indicates that the ashes may have been included with the treasures supposedly buried beneath the Temple Mount in Jerusalem.

A point of greater contention is the belief that the original red heifer ashes were mixed with each new red heifer sacrifice. The basis for these "ashes of continuity" is the statement in Numbers 19:10 that the red heifer ritual was to be a *huqqat 'olam* ("perpetual statute"). Jones believes that ashes of the red heifer had to be passed down from sacrifice to sacrifice in perpetuity. But he has misread the text of Scripture. The text reads: "It shall be a perpetual statute to the sons of Israel." This means that the sacrifice itself will be perpetual, not that perpetual ashes are necessary as Jones mistakenly advocates. In the construction of the sentence, "perpetual" modifies the noun "statute." For Jones' view to be correct, "perpetual" would have to modify "ashes," which it does not.

Therefore, nothing in the text or in extrabiblical tradition explicitly states that such continuity with the original ashes is required. For this reason, the recovery of the ashes of the red heifer is not considered important by some Temple activists, including members of the Temple Institute. Chaim Richman, manager of the Temple Institute, explains:

> This is not a Jewish concept. There is apparently in Christian tradition a concept that we would need those original ashes, and that [not to have them] is an impediment. Why do I think that [this is a Christian tradition]? Because so many [Christian] groups have come to me and have said, "Well, what about those original ashes?" that I really have to clarify that there is no prerequisite in Judaism that we have those original ashes. . . . If we found a jar, how could I know for sure that it was the authentic one? On the other hand, if we now have a cow that is authentic, in every way, and meets all the criteria of Maimonides, that would be fine.[5]

The Temple Institute believes that they *have* found a means of producing an authentic red heifer today. Originally, the red heifer project was aimed at the transfer of red heifer embryos from a herd in Sweden and their implantation into select heifers on a kibbutz in Israel. About a year ago, however, Clyde Lodt, a Christian rancher, sent the Temple Institute a pictorial scrapbook and video of red Angus cattle raised on his ranch in Mississippi. Israel Ariel believes that he has identified some unblemished, genuine red heifers that will meet the biblical requirements (see photo section). Funds are being raised to transport a group of these heifers and care for them after their arrival in Israel.

The Temple Institute, then, is preparing vessels and garments for the Temple service, and seeking to produce a valid red heifer in Israel for the future purification of the priests and worshipers in the Temple. The leaders of this organization firmly believe that we are in the *achari ha-yamim* ("last days") which include the coming of the Messiah. They expect the building of the Temple to begin shortly.

An Undefiled Generation

Once the ashes of the red heifer become available, it will be necessary to find someone who is ceremonially pure to perform the purification ritual for others. A very unique solution has been proposed to meet this problem. The Talmud gives advice on raising a generation of children, never exposed to ritual impurity, who can grow up and perform the ceremony of the red heifer. Chaim Richman of the Temple Institute explains this concept:

> The Torah describes how in the time of the Temple there were certain courtyards, which because of their unique geological make-up, were shielded from ritual impurities. Stone prevents the penetration of impurities, and that is why there are rock walls in the [Jewish] cemeteries, and why the ashes were kept in stone vessels. In these courtyards the wives of the cohanim [priests] went to give birth, and they left the child there until he reached a certain age. [To reproduce this today] there have to be all the services for those children in the courtyard—nursery, grocery, everything. It's a whole concept of a society within a society . . . but, it seems to me to be the only vehicle for preventing children from being exposed to impurities. This is obviously a mammoth undertaking . . . but this work may in fact be being done right now.[6]

Reports concerning this work are not reliable, but what has been rumored is that special Israeli houses have been built on double arches to raise the dwelling off the ground so that it does not come into contact with the land of Israel. This is because the Land itself is defiled, and contact would cause the inhabitants raised in the house to also incur ritual impurity. It is claimed that children born to priestly families are being kept there in a state of quarantine and trained to perform the ceremony of purification. If such places exist, these children are awaiting the day when the right type of heifer becomes available and they are able to fulfill their destiny as priests, preparing the way for the rebuilding of the Temple and the renewal of Temple service.

Chapter 11

An Ancient
Tunnel Uncovered

This gate, and the Coponius gate, a little bit further
[north] from it in the Western Wall that we discovered
ten years ago is a secret. The big vault that we saw [inside
it] is one of the entrances to the Temple. [And as for the
Ark of the Covenant], we know exactly where it is!

—*Yehuda Getz*
Chief Rabbi of the Western Wall

*T*he Western Wall, known to Jews as Ha-Kotel ("*the
Wall*"), and popularly as the "Wailing Wall" has been
the subject of hundreds of books. It is the Temple's only
remnant and monument to Israel's glorious past that has
survived the thousands of years. One book explains: "Some
people . . . relate to the Wall as the holiest place in Judaism
and a temporary substitute for the Temple."[1]

But the relatively small above-ground section of the Wall,
originally part of a retaining wall of the vast platform that
supported the Temple and palace complex built by Herod, is
not the only remnant that has survived the millennia.

Since 1867 when Charles Warren discovered an ancient
entrance gate to the Temple Mount north of Wilson's Arch,
it has been known that the entire length of the Western Wall
is in existence. Because of the presence of a long hall

running alongside the Wall, thought to have been used by Temple priests, the excavated remains have been popularly called the Rabbinic Tunnel. The recovery of the entire Western Wall, and of four entrances to the Temple, has been sponsored by Israel's Ministry of Religious Affairs and is now directed by the Western Wall Heritage Foundation. Under the oversight of archaeologist Dan Bahat, a team of workmen finished unearthing the wall in 1986, and the site was opened for tourism in July 1991. Until then, few visitors to the long-exposed 200-foot vestige of this wall, the Wailing Wall, had any idea that the full length of the wall continued another 1,000 feet underground (see photo section).

If you were a visitor, upon entering this ancient Western Wall concourse you would pass through an immense subterranean hall that dates from the time of the second Temple. Serving today as an exhibition hall, the area contains a large-scale model of Herod's Temple, designed by Bahat to conform to new evidence unearthed in the Western Wall tunnel excavation.

As you move through the entrance to the tunnel itself, a huge stone section of the Western Wall is visible. This section of wall, named by scholars the Master Course, contains one of the largest building stones ever discovered in Israel (see photo section). Of Herodian origin, it is 40 feet long, ten feet in height and depth, and weighs approximately 458 tons. By comparison, the largest stone in the Great Pyramid of Cheops in Giza weighs only 20 tons.

Moving along the extremely narrow thoroughfare of the Western Wall, you come to ancient entrances to the Temple. At the northern end lies a quarry from which the stones for building the Temple were cut, and an enormous Hasmonean canal cut in the bedrock that supplied water to the Temple Mount. The Western Wall excavations have also uncovered a great Herodian bridge that doubled as an aqueduct, bringing water from Solomon's Pools in Bethlehem for the daily cleansing of the Temple and its courts.

Truly, the Western Wall Tunnel is one of the most exciting excavations to ever be revealed to the public in the land of Israel. Yet the significance of this excavation is much more than historical. Brochures distributed to visitors reveal something of the religious fervor for the Temple awakened by the Western Wall Tunnel. They contain the following explanation of the purpose of the project:

> From the time of the Temple's destruction we have been unable to ascend the Temple Mount to stand in the presence of the Shechina [Shekinah]. Foreign domination and the constraints of Halacha which prevented access to the Temple Mount shifted the focus and longings of the Jewish people for their heritage to the Western Wall. For hundreds of years the indignity of destruction concealed the major part of the Western Wall. . . . In 1967, soon after the liberation of the Old City of Jerusalem, the Ministry of Religious Affairs undertook the task of clearing the Western Wall Plaza area. The Ministry also initiated a project to expose the full extent of the hitherto concealed Wall—a project with a goal beyond mere scientific and archaeological curiosity. . . . These finds will one day provide the setting for a learning center fostering an awareness of Jewish History and an appreciation of the ideals nurtured in Jerusalem and the Temple. Here is a realm rich in roots—it was on this mountain that Abraham was warned not to "lift your hand against the youth," Isaac. Here one can imagine the songs and music of the Levites. The stones evoke memories of King David and Solomon, of Ezra and Nehemiah, of the Maccabees and the Sages. Kings and

prophets walked along these paths. Here at the foot of the Western Wall, more than any other place on earth, the memories of Jewish past mingle with the hopes of Jewish future.[2]

These words convey the desire to increase public awareness of the significance of the Temple Mount, not only in terms of the past, but also with a view to the future. A sign once placed near the site's entrance stated this connection more clearly:

With every stone revealed we come to know better how the Western Wall links the last days of our ancient kingdom with the beginnings of our future. This Wall which survived as a remnant of the Holy Temple will be the first wall of the rebuilding of the next Temple, the "House of prayer for all peoples."[3]

The importance of this newly developed site for future Temple preparations cannot be overlooked. First, the site is important because the scientific excavations greatly increased our knowledge of the evolution of the Temple Mount. New information concerning the location of the first and second Temples will be gained from these excavations as well. This knowledge will serve those who are researching the precise dimensions and measurements for the future rebuilding of the Temple.

Second, this site, which now draws Jews and Gentiles from around the world to the closest access to the ancient Temple precincts, will help to promote a renewed interest in the Temple and its rebuilding as a part of Jewish heritage. As interest increases, a new awareness will develop toward the realization of a third Temple era. The public will be prepared for a greater access and presence on the Temple Mount itself.

The Discovery of an
Ancient Temple Entrance

A report of the Western Wall Tunnel excavations has not yet been published, and in fact significant remains have not been completely explored.[4] In addition, certain aspects of the excavation have been kept carefully guarded. One of the most fascinating is the discovery of an ancient entrance to the Temple, the nearest of all Temple entrances to the Holy of Holies.

On two separate occasions in 1981, Yehuda Getz, Chief Rabbi of the Western Wall (see photo section), and Rabbi Shlomo Goren, along with a group of students, entered a passage that serves today as a cistern to the Mount. Rabbi Getz describes the events of that day:

> Our job was to discover the original stones of the Temple [in] the Kotel [wall]. . . . When King Solomon built the Temple, he built the Western Wall as a frame. . . . Between this frame and the actual wall of the Temple there was a [stone] filling to fill the gap in between. We discovered that underneath this frame all the stones are connected with the frame of the Temple. [It] was planned [here] to build a synagogue that would face the Holy of Holies. . . . While trying to build the synagogue, a little bit of water [seeped out] along the Western wall. Our workers wanted to discover [where it came from], so they moved one of the stones and a huge amount of water went out . . . and they saw a big room. . . . It was thought that these kinds of rooms might have been built by the Turks for just collecting water, [but then] they saw an arch . . . and a beautiful hall. This big vault that we saw was one of the main entrances to the Temple, probably the second

Temple. Another gate entrance—one of the four gates mentioned by Josephus—we also discovered ten years ago, and its location is a secret.[5]

The entrance Getz had discovered is called Warren's Gate. Though accidentally discovered over a century ago by Charles Warren during the first probes ever attempted underground at the Temple Mount, its exact location had been lost or concealed ever since. Warren never revealed how he had found it or how he knew it to be one of the four ancient entrance gates to the Temple mentioned by Josephus.

It was rediscovered and identified by the British explorer and excavator Charles Wilson (who named it Warren's Gate) beneath the obscure Gate *Bab-el-Mat'hara*, which was an Arab latrine until 1967. The vaulted passageway within was used as a water reservoir or cistern. Historical sources tell us that this gate led directly onto the Temple courts and was used for bringing in wood, sacrifices, and other materials for the Temple rites. Dan Bahat, in a personal interview, explained the historical significance of this site:

> This gate is the most important of all the gates because it is the nearest gate to the Holy of Holies. The eastern extremity of this passage is even nearer to the Holy of Holies, and this is why it was preferable for Jews to pray inside this vault. For over 450 years it was the holiest place where people came to pray, or in other words, from the Arab conquest of 638 A.D. till the Crusader conquest of 1099 A.D., it was the central synagogue of Israel's Jewry. It was called the "Cave" because it has the form of a cave, a kind of an underground vault penetrating into the Temple Mount, and thus it played a very important role in Jewish life

in Jerusalem in the early Arab period simply because of its proximity to the Holy of Holies. When the Jews returned to Jerusalem after the Crusader rule, the Jews wanted to come back into [Warren's Gate], but the whole area was filled in with Islamic buildings, so they chose the second best site, the Western Wall further down [from the site of the Temple].[6]

There is little doubt that this passage is one of the most significant historical remnants of Temple times known today. But within this passage even greater remains may wait to be revealed.

A Secret Chamber— The Lost Ark?

The entrance gate to the Temple may not have been the only secret uncovered by the two rabbis and their team. Rabbis Getz and Goren relate that deep within this passageway they discovered a secret chamber, in which they believe are hidden the treasures of the Temple, including the Ark of the Covenant. Rabbi Goren describes this thrilling discovery:

> I started digging just beneath the Temple Mount from outside, just a few years ago. We were very close to the place on the Temple Mount, where the Holy of the Holies was located. We were very close, beneath the Holy of the Holies. We believe that the Holy Ark made by Moses, and the table from the Temple, and the candelabra made by Moses, along with other very important items, are hidden very deep underneath the Holy of the Holies. We started digging and we came close to the place; we were not more than 30 or 40 yards away.[7]

Rabbi Getz adds his own excitement about that day, saying:

> When we discovered these [treasures from the first Temple] I was so moved—I wanted to go in and see these things ... but it was not yet the time.[8]

Getz' conclusion that it was not yet "heaven's time" to reveal those secrets to the world was painfully confirmed when the men were attacked during their discovery. As Rabbi Goren explains:

> Unfortunately we came so close that the Arabs started rioting and attacked us, and the government became afraid. They stopped us, and built a wall [to prevent further entrance].

Reports published at the time say that when word came to the Muslim authorities (the Wakf) that they were about to uncover the Ark, the Wakf stopped the excavations by sending the mob of Muslims to attack the excavators. Chaim Richman of the Temple Institute suggests that the Wakf had definite motives for the attack:

> They were afraid that if the Jews found these objects that it would be the surest sign of all of a Jewish presence on the Temple Mount. It wasn't some sort of mystical tradition. They were afraid that if these things were uncovered that we would rebuild the Temple. [It is part of] an orchestrated effort to destroy and eradicate any semblance of Jewish presence around the Temple Mount.[9]

The border police and the army say they had to intervene to keep Getz, Goren, and their men from being killed.

Rabbi Getz still says to this day that he knows exactly where the Ark is located. He does not want to reveal the precise location for fear that the Muslims would steal or destroy the Ark and other Temple treasures. He has confirmed that the Ark's supposed hiding place is known to the Israeli government, but that it decided the issue was too politically volatile and closed the case, allowing Arab authorities to block the entrance. The announcement would eventually cause worldwide media attention to be focused on the already sensitive Temple Mount area and could provoke "premature" action by fringe groups wanting to build the Temple.

In addition, there are religious complications, since no one at present is able to touch the Ark due to ceremonial defilement. For the time being, if the Ark is beneath Temple Mount, it will remain locked in secret behind an entrance blocked with three meters of concrete and steel. Getz and Goren agree that the matter cannot be resolved by human agency, and are willing to wait for the Messiah to reveal it when He comes.

Are There Temple Treasures in Ethiopia?

The traditional view that the true Ark is hidden beneath the Temple Mount has recently met with competition. Since the May 24, 1991 airlift of 14,300 Falasha (Ethiopian Jews) to Israel (code-named Operation Solomon), a popular story has circulated that the Ark of the Covenant is in Ethiopia and will be secretly returned to Israel when the remaining Falasha make the exodus from the capital of Ethiopia, Addis Ababa.[10] The claim that the Falasha supposedly have had the Ark from the time of Solomon and that it would be returned when the last Ethiopian Jew was transported to Israel has been promoted by Grant Jeffry, a Canadian evangelical prophetic researcher.[11]

Israeli government officials who have worked with the immigration of the Falasha were unaware of this rumor. Other people who had heard it, such as Chaim Richman of the Temple Institute, had been told the story by Christian tourists (who apparently had read Jeffry's book or heard his teaching on this subject). Richman has attempted to verify this story and has concluded that it has no basis in Jewish tradition or actual fact. The consensus among Temple researchers in Israel is that the Ark is exactly where Getz and Goren claim—buried deep under the Mount in a chamber entered by the now-sealed Warren's Gate.

Other Voices

The importance of the discovery of this hidden vault beneath the Temple Mount is apparently being downplayed to the general public. When Public Relations Director Ariel Banner was asked during a tour of this area why this entrance was sealed, he replied that it was simply to show the Arabs that the Western Wall Heritage Foundation has no religious interest in this site. However, just above the gate, Rabbi Getz has a new synagogue with the gate as one of its walls! And just a few steps to the north of this gate, a place for prayer has been prepared at the point located opposite the Holy of Holies. While the official statement must be that no religious interest is being sanctioned by the government, it is clear that it is sympathetic with those who have now imbued the site with a sanctity rivaling the Wailing Wall.

Other individuals are also hesitant to reveal any knowledge of the existence of the Ark. Rabbi Kahane has said that Rabbi Goren could not possibly have any knowledge of the Ark's location. Dan Bahat has said that the Ark must have been looted or destroyed by Nebuchadnezzar in the sixth century B.C., and that "any hope of finding it today is nil." Concerning the claim that Temple treasures are buried within the Warren Gate passageway, Bahat says:

No Jew ever [in the early Arab period] would have thought of treasures of the Temple deposited in this place.... In any case, some of the treasures of the Temple were brought to Jerusalem around 540 A.D. when Emperor Justinian inaugurated a church [there]. Since he could not come personally to Jerusalem, he sent these Temple objects [from Rome], and they are probably buried somewhere in the Jewish Quarter where this church stood. No one ever mentions the possibility of bringing them back into the Temple Mount itself. So, from this point of view, it [the treasures] are lost. [12]

Whatever Israeli officials may say, the concrete patch covering Warren's Gate and verbal denunciations of religious interest will not satisfy the Muslim authorities forever, especially as thousands of tourists now walk through the more than 1,150 feet of tunnels underneath the Temple Mount and prayer services are regularly conducted at the site. Furthermore, if the Ark of the Covenant is indeed buried within reach of this passageway, this site will cause even greater excitement in the near future. Rabbi Getz concludes: "The treasures of the First Temple are under the Mount, and we know exactly where they are.... [13] The time will come when we will enter."

Chapter 12

Searching for
the Sacred Site

We have to know where the original place of the altar was. Since no one knows where the altar was, no one is going anywhere on the Temple now.... The Temple now . . . is off boundary to everybody. All of the different opinions . . . all of the discrepancies . . . surround only one question: Where is the place of the altar? That's the whole problem.

—*Rabbi Nahman Kahane*

*T*he precise location of the Temple is perhaps the most controversial subject engaging students of the Temple Mount. The subject of intense investigation and debate, several theories about the original site of the first and second Temples vie for acceptance today. All of the proposed sites respect the dimensions of the Muslim Haram es-Sharif (the platform on which the Dome of the Rock stands), which generally follows the square outer perimeters of the Temple complex as recorded by Josephus and the Mishnah (in the tractate Middot), and maintain the same east-west orientation. However, they differ significantly in their placement of the Temple within this enclosure. What are these competing theories, and what questions do they raise about the exact location of the Temple? Most importantly, can the location of the Temple be identified today for rebuilding tomorrow?

No Excavation Allowed

The problem facing all who attempt to investigate the original location of the Temple is the lack of sufficient archaeological evidence. Some of the leading archaeologists of the last half-century have given their verdict as to the impossibility of making a precise determination. Dame Kathleen Kenyon, a British archaeologist who excavated extensively in the Temple area, concluded: "Absolutely nothing survives of the Temple built by Herod."[1] In like manner, the Israeli historian and archaeologist Michael Avi-Yonah stated: "The location of the actual Temple, the central problem, cannot yet be ascertained."[2] As far back as 1887 J.L. Porter wrote: "The Temple is gone. Not a stone, not a trace, remains."[3]

Beside the lack of structural remains, several other problems compound the first.

First, as we have noted, Jewish religious law forbids any Jew from stepping foot on the *'azarah*, the sacred precinct or enclosure of the ancient Temple. Since all Jews today are ceremonially impure, to do so would violate the sanctity of the entire Temple Mount.

Second, the Moslem Wakf, governing authority of the Temple Mount since 1967, has stringently precluded any access to the Temple Mount to non-Muslims for religious purposes. Any investigation of a former Jewish holy site would certainly be interpreted in this regard. Furthermore, the Israeli "Protection of Holy Places" law supports the Muslim position and makes it a crime to in any way desecrate a holy place, which would certainly occur if the site were excavated. For these reasons, no archaeological excavations are likely to be conducted on the Temple Mount. Yet archaeological excavations are seemingly the only way to decisively resolve the question of the Temple's location.

Third, since material evidence cannot be obtained through archaeological research, the primary sources for information about the Temple's location have been historical writings. The earliest recorded description of the Temple site is that given by Josephus. His measurements of the area conflict in many respects with those given in Middot, which was composed a hundred years later. In addition, one of the most detailed sources for information concerning the Temple Mount of the fifth century A.D., *Nehemiah's Jerusalem Atlas*, has provided vital clues to archaeologists, yet its accuracy in determining surviving remains and locations of certain landmarks has been questioned.

Further complications arise when we consider a source such as the Temple Scroll, a parchment discovered with the Dead Sea Scrolls at Qumran, which dates to the time of the second Temple and gives detailed patterns for the rebuilding of the Temple. As promising as this data might appear, the Temple it proposes is quite different from any recorded in Scripture or the extrabiblical sources,[4] and therefore does not offer significant advances to the study of the Temple Mount.

For these reasons, it has generally been thought that no one will be able to locate the exact site of the Temple today. However, in recent years new light has been shed on the subject and new proposals offered. Meir Ben-Dov, one of the premiere archaeologists of the Temple area has noted that "hardly a month goes by without at least one research paper being published on one aspect or another of the Temple Mount."[5] Even while I (Randall) was writing this chapter, I received a call from Jerusalem about a lecture presented in the Old City that same evening on new research by an Israeli architect concerning the Temple's location! Let us now consider some of this research and the proposals that have been made to identify the exact site of the Temple.

Three Possibilities

While archaeological investigation cannot be conducted on the Temple Mount, extensive excavations have been made around the outer perimeters of the area. Kathleen Kenyon, who said no trace of the Temple remains, also said, "Much of Herod's work can still be traced in the great platform that supports the Dome of the Rock, so from the present structure back to Solomon there is no real break."[6] In the area of this platform, over a century ago, extensive probes and tunneling excavations were conducted by British explorers. Though restricted by Muslim sensitivities, they nevertheless discovered the important structural remains that form the basis of our knowledge of the site today.[7] In recent times, excavations conducted in other parts of Jerusalem by Yigael Shiloh have revealed the extent and location of the original palace complex of David and Solomon. Excavations at the Southern Wall, first directed by Benjamin Mazar and then by Meir Ben-Dov, and those at the Western Wall directed by Dan Bahat, have greatly improved our understanding of the Temple's location. In addition, the identification and examination of visible structural remains around the Temple Mount, many of which have been accidentally or purposely destroyed since their discovery, have led to new theories about the ancient Temple's placement. Based in part on the results of these excavations, and additional private research, two theories have been advanced alongside the traditionally accepted view of the Temple's location at the site of the Dome of the Rock (see Figure 9).

A Southern Location

A Franciscan scholar, Father Bellarmino Bagatti, published his *Recherches sur le Site du Temple de Jerusalem* in Jerusalem in 1979.[8] He concluded from his study of the ancient documents and his personal exploration and measurements that the ancient Temple must have occupied a site

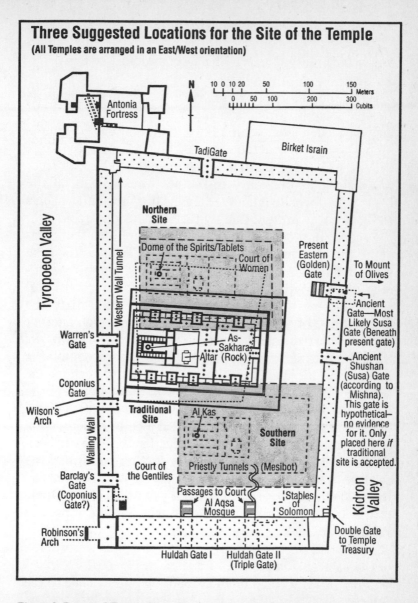

Figure 9: Proposed Temple Sites. Three proposed sites for the location of the ancient Temple. The Holy of Holies is indicated in each site by the Al Kas Foundation (Southern), As-Sakhara "the [Sacred] Rock" (Traditional), and Dome of the Spirits/Tablets (Northern). Location of the Temple Mount gates based on Mishnah (Middot 1:3), Josephus (Antiquities 15:401), and excavations.

to the south, somewhere between the Dome of the Rock and the Al Aqsa Mosque. This was not a new view, but Bagatti supported his arguments with new considerations and original data.

First, the ancient topography of the Temple Mount, as gleaned from historical sources, suggests that the Temple may have been situated at a lower elevation on the Temple Mount, rather than at the supposed highest point, the Rock under the Dome. Bagatti also contended that the rock face, now having its boundary in the northwest corner of the Temple platform, originally extended further south and was cut back to its present line by the Romans or Arabs.

Second, in order to determine the square area that composed the huge platform upon which the Temple stood, he measured the length of the southern Herodian wall, beginning at the southeastern corner. Moving northward 920 feet, he came to a point in the eastern wall where the original line of the rampart ends and from which another wall, a short distance from the former wall, begins its northerly course toward the northeastern corner of the enclosure. This junction in the wall seemed to determine the course of an east-west wall, the northern boundary of the Temple. Looking across the present enclosure in this direction, he saw that the ground revealed a definite depression along the supposed wall line. The fact that the area had been planted with trees by the Muslims further confirmed the absence of solid rock at this level. Apparently, the area had been filled in by the seventh-century builders of the Dome of the Rock. Since this wall line was south of the present Eastern, or Golden, Gate, this gate was excluded from the Temple area, a fact which agrees with Josephus' description of the eastern Temple enclosure.

Third, Bagatti read in an account of a pilgrimage to the Temple site in A.D. 438 by Barsauma and his pilgrim group that the Jews gathered together to venerate their ruined Temple. While the exact place that they prayed is not given,

Bagatti interpreted the statement "at the gates which lead to Siloam"[9] to refer to the Huldah Gate entrance at the southern wall (adjacent to the present Al Aqsa Mosque), which indeed leads downward to the Pool of Siloam. From this he concluded that the Temple was situated nearby at this southern location.

Fourth, Bagatti claimed that the Dome of the Rock had no real historical significance, neither being venerated by Israel during Temple times, nor by Jews or Christian pilgrims from the Temple's destruction to the early Islamic period. In his opinion, the Rock beneath the Dome only received its sacred character in the seventh century because of a political-religious rivalry between Jerusalem and Mecca. He reasoned that since the rock had no religious importance, it could not have been the site of the Temple.

Two other lines of evidence have been advanced to support this theory. First, the presence of numerous underground reservoirs in the proximity of the Al Aqsa Mosque agrees with descriptions of reservoirs that supplied the enormous amounts of water used in the Temple rituals. Many of these reservoirs are completely built with masonry and vaults, which suggests that their earlier use was as secret escape tunnels or hidden chambers. The historical sources speak plainly of such hidden passageways and rooms used by the Temple priests. The presence of these underground features at this site lends credence to a southern location for the Temple.

In addition, a comparison can be made of the plans of second-century Roman architecture with the historical account of Hadrian's erection of a temple and statues in or nearby the Temple. When the architectural layout of the Roman temple complex is compared with the present layout of Muslim buildings on the site, it can be seen that the location of the Roman sanctuary approximates the site of the Al Aqsa Mosque, rather than the Dome of the Rock.

Bagatti's work has broken some new ground for Temple research, but it has some weaknesses. His interpretation of the A.D. 438 account of Jewish prayer being at the southern area is no proof that the Temple was located nearby. As today, so in earlier times Jews would not venture near to the Temple to pray for fear of violating the sanctity of the site.[10] Too, since the site had been desecrated, both by destruction and later by pagan monuments, Jews could not have prayed there.

Bagatti's rejection of the Rock as having sacred associations until the seventh century goes against the longest and strongest traditions recorded of the Temple site. The earliest pilgrim accounts seem to present a description of a venerable "Perforated" Rock whose only known counterpart is the Rock beneath the Dome.

Third, while reservoirs and passageways are located in the southern region, they are also abundant around the area of the Dome of the Rock. Since these winding passageways likely connect, they may well have been entered from another location in the northwest.

A Northern Location

When I (Randall) was a student of archaeology at the Hebrew University in 1979, I was fascinated by a published interview with a Dr. Ze'ev Yeivin, (now deputy director of the Department of Antiquities), who happened upon Arab construction work on the Temple Mount almost ten years earlier and had made some drawings of an exposed ancient wall near the Dome of the Rock. Since archaeological excavations cannot be made in this area, such rare findings are of great significance.

Another man who was fascinated by the discovery was Asher Kaufman, who today has identified the section of wall seen by Dr. Yeivin as the eastern wall of the Temple's Court of the Women, whose entrance faced the Eastern Gate. Dr.

Kaufman was much intrigued by the research of Bagatti. He accepted his evidence that the Dome of the Rock could not be the site of the Temple; however, he rejected his theory of location. Developing his own theory based on Bagatti's leads, he first presented his views in the 1977 issue of the Jerusalem journal *Ariel*.[11] In his initial research he had sought to locate and analyze ancient blood samples that he believed had flowed from the sacrificial altar in the Temple into the Kidron Valley below. This eastern location had been referred to in the Mishnah tractate Middot, and led to an additional "Temple landmark" on the Mount of Olives, the spot where the priests offered the sacrifice of the red heifer and sprinkled its blood toward the Altar (directly across the valley). Kaufman concluded that the alignment of this site with the Temple would not permit a location at the present site of the Dome of the Rock.

His next investigation sought possible structural remains on the Temple site both above and below ground. While his only access to the evidence beneath the Temple Mount consisted of reports by British explorers conducted a century ago, his survey on the surface produced some relevant new discoveries. Of special merit was a particular rock mass near the northeastern steps leading up to a small Muslim cupola (a dome-shaped covering with open sides that houses a section of exposed rock) on the Temple Mount.

Based on a study of these remains, which he concluded were originally the northwest corner of the Court of the Priests, he determined that the site of the Temple was at this northeastern corner, and that the east-west line aligning the Mount of Olives with the Eastern Gate and the Temple exactly bisected this small cupola at the place of the Holy of Holies (see photo section). He noted that the bedrock inside the cupola (and extending a little outside) is the only such bedrock appearing on the Temple Mount esplanade. The rest of the area around the Dome of the Rock had been paved with stone. Was this the *Even Shetiyyah* ("Foundation Stone") that protruded in the ancient Holy of Holies? Significantly, this bedrock appears to be pitted, a detail that agrees with the description by the fourth-century Pilgrim of Bourdeaux of the Foundation Stone, called in his account the "Pierced Stone" because it had numerous imprints of the hobnails of soldiers. Of further importance was the Arabic name of the cupola: the Dome of the Spirits (or Tablets). Since Arabic titles often preserve original place names, were these dual titles reminiscent of the Divine Presence that accompanied the Ark and the tablets of the law stored within it which once rested in the Holy of Holies?

If Kaufman's theory is correct, it places the location of the first two Temples only 330 feet from the Dome of the Rock. While the Dome of the Rock has traditionally been believed to have been built on the Temple site, Kaufman now argues that the exact knowledge of that location was unknown to the Arab caliph who erected the Dome. His most recent research has led him to conclude that the ancient identifications of the Rock under the Dome as the site of the Temple have no historical validity in any source.[12] This agrees with an old story that the guide who directed the caliph to the site of the Rock was a Jew who, knowing the original location, deliberately deceived him so that a Muslim mosque would not be built over the site of the Temple.[13]

Dr. Kaufman's theory, which should be seriously studied because of his extensive research, has been published in numerous Israeli journals and in two American archaeological magazines.[14] While this theory represents a radical departure from the traditional location of the Temple accepted by all Israeli archaeologists, it has been adopted by some lay scholars outside of Israel. One of these scholars, Lawrence D. Sporty, who is the attending psychiatrist and senior lecturer in the Department of Psychiatry and Human Behavior at the University of California at Irvine, recently published two articles supporting Kaufman's theory in *Biblical Archaeologist*, the official quarterly of the American Schools of Oriental Research.

Using a comparison of landmarks and historical literary sources from the pre- and post-destruction periods to test the Kaufman hypothesis, Dr. Sporty arrived at the same conclusions. He argues that a centrally located Temple would have isolated troops stationed in the Antonio Fortress, blocking their access to disturbances around the compound. He maintains that the geographical references in Josephus, the Letter of Aristeas, and the Mishnah tractate Middot support a location of the Temple near to the Antonio Fortress at the northwestern corner of the compound (Kaufman's view). He further argues that the Dome of the Rock acquired the legends and traditions as the site of the Temple because of its proximity, and that the Church of the Holy Sepulchre was built as a symbolic rival to the Temple directly facing the Holy of Holies, a view Kaufman also put forward.

Kaufman's theory has especially attracted the attention of prophecy-minded Christians, who believe a northern location removes the major obstacle for the rebuilding of the Temple today. If, they say, the Temple could be built alongside the Dome of the Rock, then the only thing standing in the way of Temple construction is a negotiated settlement with the Arabs to share the Temple Mount. Those who argue this position find support for their view in the prophecy concerning the measuring of the third Temple in Revelation 11:2. This passage states that "the court outside the Temple" (where according to Kaufman, the Dome of the Rock stands) is to be "left out" of the Temple's measurements, "for it is given to the nations" (in this case, Islam). However, simply moving the location of the Temple and excluding the outside court area from Jewish occupation would not resolve the problem of rebuilding the Temple. The very presence of an Islamic shrine on the Temple Mount defiles the Mount and makes entrance to the Mount for construction impossible. In fact, those in the Temple movement in Israel are quite emphatic that not only must the Dome of the Rock be removed, but also the Al Aqsa Mosque, which according to traditional reckoning (with the Temple at the site of the Dome of the Rock) would be in the Court of the Women. The Arabs, incidentally, are equally emphatic about the impossibility of sharing the Temple Mount with a Jewish Temple. Given this, it is possible that the reference in Revelation 11:2 to giving "the court which is outside the Temple" to the nations is a means of preventing the Temple itself from being destroyed when the nations "tread under foot the Holy City for forty-two months" (the last half of the tribulation period).

Although Kaufman's theory of location has an impressive body of recent research in its favor, the archaeological community in Israel has rejected it. The fact that Kaufman is not trained as an archaeologist and cannot claim to have excavated in the area of the Temple does not necessarily endanger his view, since actual excavation is impossible. Yet a significant topographical objection has been raised by archaeologists to Kaufman's main theory that the Temple stood north of the Dome of the Rock. Based on his expertise as a Jerusalem geographer and recent findings at the Western Wall, archaeologist Dan Bahat articulates this objection:

> If we take Asher Kaufman's theory of the [location of the] Holy of Holies, it will force the entire Temple to be built beyond the northern valley of the Temple Mount, and this is an impossibility because of the great depth of the valley below. Moreover, Charles Warren discovered an enormous moat in this northern area, and if we accept Kaufman's theory, half the Temple would have to be built within this moat.[15]

Kaufman is aware of this objection and believes evidence exists for the immense structural support his location requires. However, at this point, the contrary argument of tradition and the evidence from topography favors a cautious approach to the acceptance of his view.

The Traditional Location

The tradition that has come down through the ages from the earliest pilgrimages to the Temple has been of a location for the Temple in or near the present site of the Dome of the Rock. Even so, scholars have been divided over the question of whether the Dome of the Rock marks the spot of the Altar of Sacrifice or of the Holy of Holies (see photo section). As Rabbi Reznick puts it: "The Dome of the Rock is a shrine built to protect the treasure within the rock. But what, exactly, is that rock?"[16]

If the Holy of Holies was on the Rock, then the Temple must be shifted to the east to accommodate room in the back of the Temple, as indicated by historical references. If the Rock is the site of the Altar of Sacrifice (the successor of David's altar),[17] then the Holy of Holies would be located to the west. Both positions have considerable arguments in their favor.

The Rock as the Site of the Altar

Many scholars identify the Rock as the base of the Altar of Sacrifice and place the Holy of Holies to the west of it. Tradition lends support to this theory. In the *Midrashim* it is written that the Rock is the *Even Akkidah*, the "Stone of Binding" and marks the place where Abraham bound his son Isaac and laid him on an altar, but that the Holy of Holies was built over the place where the ram was caught in the thicket, a short distance away. Tradition further contends that the Rock is not only the place where the offering of Isaac was attempted, but that it was also the threshing floor of Arunah the Jebusite which King David purchased and upon which he pitched the Tabernacle.

Structural features which seem to argue for the Rock being the place of the Altar of Sacrifice are the bored hole for the drainage of blood and fluids, the cave directly below this perforation which was said to collect the ash and drainage from above, and extensive reservoirs and aqueducts beneath the floor, including a canal running north, that would carry away the refuse and water used in the rituals. How else can these features be explained if this is not the site of the Altar?

Against this theory it has been argued that if the Rock supported the Altar, the Holy of Holies would occupy an area where the ground slopes away rapidly. If this is so, an artificially raised platform must have been raised to prop up the sanctuary; however, there is no substantive evidence for this conjecture.

New Evidence for the Rock as the Site of the Altar

Immediately after the liberation of the Temple Mount in 1967, Rabbi Goren assembled a team to carefully measure the distances from the outer walls (assumed to be the compound enclosure of the second Temple) to the place of the inner walls within which stood the Temple. These measurements were compared against those given in Talmudic sources (principally Middot and Shekalim) and found to agree. Based on this survey, the location of the Temple, the Altar of Sacrifice, and the Holy of Holies, could be calculated. Rabbi Goren concludes:

> The Holy of the Holies is not . . . beneath, nor is it located within the Dome of the Rock. The Moslems are mistaken. I made the measurements right after the Six-Day War, and I came to the conclusion, and it is 100 percent [certain], that

the Holy of the Holies is outside the Dome of the Rock, to the west side.[18]

Believing he knows the exact location of the Temple does not mean that Goren entertains any ideas about its immediate rebuilding. As noted, the obstacles of impurity and his belief that the next Temple will descend directly from heaven prohibits such activism. Goren awaits a prophet who must first come and confirm his survey by personally identifying the exact locations. Evidently his only use of this survey has been the precise determination of the boundaries of the sacred precinct for those Jews wishing to pray on the Temple Mount without bringing ritual defilement to the site of the Temple.

Goren's survey, however, is the basis of the Temple Mount Faithful's claim that the Temple could be built "tomorrow." Conversations with Gershon Salomon, leader of the Temple Mount Faithful, repeatedly point to Salomon's reliance on this survey. Goren's claim to have exactly pinpointed the Holy of Holies is significant, for such an identification makes possible the rebuilding of the Temple when conditions permit.

Unfortunately, Israeli archaeologists seem either unaware of Goren's survey or do not recognize its validity. For the most part, these archaeologists believe that the location of the first and second Temples was the site of the Dome of the Rock. This is also the official position of the Israeli Antiquities Authority.[19] Some Israel archaeologists go even further to state their certainty, in opposition to Goren, that the Rock itself marks the location of the Holy of Holies.

The Rock as the Site of the Holy of Holies

The alternate theory to the Rock as the site of the altar is the Rock as the site of the Holy of Holies. This speculation is favored by many scholars and by Jewish legend.[20] The

Rock is called the *Even Shetiyyah*, the "Foundation Stone" because in the Talmud it is recorded that "after the disappearance of the Holy Ark a stone was left, called the Rock of Foundation, rising three fingers high above the ground and on it the High Priest placed the censer on Yom Kippur."[21] Legend says that this is the foundation stone of the earth "because from it the world was built up."[22]

Rabbi Shaul Schaffer offers a harmonization of the two theories:

> This Rock, which in the time of King Solomon was a few feet higher at its peak than now, rose above the floor of the *Devir* [the Holy of Holies] (like the top of an iceberg) and on it he built the Temple. Even the Outer Altar stood on it at its eastern extension. In the course of centuries, when the place lay waste, erosion wore away some of the Rock, whilst violence and souvenir-taking tore off more.[23]

Despite the support of the traditional sources, this view also has a disadvantage. If this rock in the Holy of Holies stood higher than the floor of the Temple (which would have been built around the original hill), how could the walls of the Holy of Holies have been built on the hilltop? The position of the Holy of Holies at this spot would cut across the Court of the Women to the east of the altar, and this is not verified in any of the historical sources. Furthermore, we are left without any explanation for the cave and the canal under the stone.

In an interview at his Western Wall excavations in July 1991, Dan Bahat unequivocally stated his professional view of the Temple's location:

> I will say right now that the Temple is standing exactly where the Dome of the Rock is today on

the Temple Mount. I want to say explicitly and clearly that we believe that the Rock under the Dome is the precise site of the Holy of Holies. [To be more accurate], the Temple extended exactly to the place where the Dome is today. The "Foundation Stone" [the Rock within the Dome] is actually that stone which comprised the Holy of Holies.[24]

This is not only the professional view, but the traditional view as well. Chaim Richman of the Temple Institute says:

We have a tradition that has been passed down in an unbroken chain from our fathers that the Rock, the stone underneath the Dome of the Rock, is the "foundation stone."[25]

Dan Bahat agrees with this when he says:

If this site were not the site of the Temple, we would not have the sanctity that has been bestowed upon that stone for centuries. The church fathers describe how the Jews were coming every year to that place, and the Moslems chose to build their sanctuary on the very same stone because they were aware of the Jewish tradition. . . . Omar, the Moslem conqueror of Jerusalem, was brought by a Jew straight to that stone and not to another one. So the tradition is quite clear about the tradition of this place.[26]

The Rock Between the Altar and the Holy of Holies

Another arrangement of the Temple site that attempts to resolve the objections to the two theories presented above has been recently proposed by David M. Jacobson.[27] Rather than attempting to fix the position of the Temple by the enigmatic Rock, as most in the past have done, Jacobson has sought to deduce it from the remains of the enclosure that Herod constructed around the Temple. These remains, Jacobson argues, reveal that Herod's enclosure did not have the same boundaries as the present irregularly-shaped Muslim platform. He accepts that the outline of Herod's enclosure is preserved in the boundaries of the present platform on three sides, but proposes that the original Northern Wall ran parallel to the Southern Wall, commencing at the eastern edge of the Antonia Fortress and terminating at its junction with the Eastern Wall. Having fixed on these boundaries, Jacobson deduced the position of the Temple based on the geometrical order of construction governing the area of the enclosure.

This geometrical construction plan superimposed on the Temple area places the focal point of the Temple platform at the center of the great sacrificial altar. While this *could* mark the Holy of Holies, it would leave insufficient space for the Court of the Women to the east. Starting with this location, Jacobson used the measurements provided in both the Mishnah and Josephus to draw a plan of the Temple outward from the Altar based on a scale of one cubit to 18.55 inches. His plan revealed the Altar centrally located in front of the Temple, in a position that allowed visibility of the Sanctuary entrance from the summit of the Mount of Olives (as prescribed by Middot 2:4). Aligning the Holy of Holies along a common axis with the Altar placed it a little to the west of the Rock, yet allowed the Rock to be within the Sanctuary itself. This coincides with Josephus' testimony that the Temple was built on top of the mountain,[28] and agrees with the tradition that identifies the Dome of the Rock with the Temple.

Given this interpretation, the Rock itself cannot be the summit of Mount Moriah, but simply a natural feature that acquired the distinction due to its proximity and its identification by Christian pilgrims as the Pierced Stone. By the time of the Arab conquest the symmetrical layout of the Herodian enclosure was becoming lost under the buildup of the centuries, and the original relationship between the Altar of Sacrifice and the Holy of Holies had been obscured. The true summit was probably reduced in height as a result of the extensive construction efforts of Hadrian on the Temple Mount. The Rock shows signs of such past quarrying. Jacobson's alternative plan for the Temple would account for the objections to the two traditional approaches and would find general support from Rabbi Goren's survey.

Accelerating the Search

While we cannot say with absolute certainty whether the Dome of the Rock is on the precise spot of the Altar of Sacrifice or the Holy of Holies, we do believe that the Temple was on this site. Archaeological research based upon existing remains around the Temple compound is being conducted at the present time that may shed further light upon this subject.

It is possible future explorations with radar and laser equipment inside the Western Wall tunnels will contribute more precise measurements. If satellite technology can be employed using molecular frequency generation to "see" beneath the present surface of the enclosure from a safe distance above, many more clues to the exact location may be determined. Such methods only await financial support and government permission.

Some people are hopeful that the renewed excavation at Tel Hazor, where Yigael Yadin believed he had located the ancient royal archives of the city before his death, will provide literary clues to resolving the longstanding debate. Already in the summer of 1991 the dig, under the direction of Ammon Ben-Tor of the Hebrew University, had uncovered an Akkadian tablet from the late Canaanite period.

There is anticipation that future excavations may uncover these archives, which might have records of Solomon that would provide specific information about his building of the first Temple.

The search for an answer to the exact location of the Temple has accelerated in the past decade, and more research is being conducted in this subject than ever before in recent history. The fact that some of the experts believe they have located the precise site gives rise to the hope that perhaps the convincing evidence, that final resolution that will make possible the rebuilding of the Temple, will make headlines in our papers tomorrow!

Chapter 13

Why
the Delay?

Notice and Warning: Entrance to the area of the Temple
Mount is forbidden to everyone by Jewish Law owing to
the sacredness of the place.[1]

—*The Chief Rabbinate of Israel*

A *s we witness the various attempts underway to prepare*
for the building of a new Jewish Temple, we may be
seeing the beginning of the fulfillment of the biblical prophecies concerning Israel's messianic future. We may indeed
be approaching the "last days" that will usher in the glorious hope of Christ's return. Yet how can we explain the
1,922-year delay or how it will ever be possible, in view
of the present Middle East situation, to realize this objective?

Our earlier study of Jewish history in the land of Israel
revealed that several unsuccessful attempts have been made
in the past to rebuild the Temple. While these efforts were
genuine (although often tainted with political motives), and
the Scripture promised that a Temple should be rebuilt, the
timing for this event was not God's timing. Now as we look
at history and the present situation in Israel, we also find
several other reasons why the Temple has not been rebuilt.

Wanderers
in the World

For the last 2,000 years, while other nations developed rich civilizations, the Jewish people wandered throughout the world without a homeland. In the Diaspora the Jewish communities were scattered among different ethnic nationalities and cultures and spoke different languages. Though religious Jews maintained a dream of returning to the Land and seeing the Temple rebuilt, their primary task was one of survival. Added to this is the horrible history of persecution. No people have suffered as the Jews have suffered. They were simply unable to unite to organize a return under these conditions.

A small number of Jews felt obligated to remain in the Land due to religious conviction. However, their state was worse than those Jews in the Diaspora. They suffered terribly under their Christian, Muslim, and Turkish rulers. Poor, often prevented even from visiting their holy sites, they were in no position to issue a call to world Jewry to return, even if world Jewry had been in a position to respond.

Not only was anti-Semitic persecution aimed at reducing the economic and social status of the Jew, it was directed especially at attacking and destroying their religious faith and heritage. Yet aside from the attempts by other religions to convert Jews and ban their literature, the Diaspora itself caused Judaism to become more pluralistic. Different traditions arose within Judaism that separated Jews from each other. Today there are ultra-Orthodox, Orthodox, Conservative, and Reform Jews within Judaism, and each of these, especially among the more orthodox, are separated into further divisions. This complicates the matter of working together to rebuild the Temple. The ultra-Orthodox and the Orthodox, for instance, refuse to accept the liberal Reform Jews.

Loosening the
Cords of Tradition

As generations of Jews were raised within a non-Jewish culture and were less and less exposed to their traditions, many assimilated the Gentile lifestyle. These Jews adopted the beliefs and traditions of their new nationalities and consequently lost their desire to return to Israel and rebuild the Temple. In fact many such Jews in various parts of the world actively opposed Zionism when it was proposed by Theodor Herzl in 1897. Even today nonreligious Jews, while generally supportive of the State of Israel, oppose the religious Jews in Israel who seek a return to stricter observance of Jewish law. They feel that talk of building a Temple is both fanatical and destructive.

A Difference of Interpretation

Added to the weakening of tradition are conflicts in theological perspective about Temple rebuilding. Even among the ultra-Orthodox themselves there are several interpretations concerning how the Temple can be rebuilt. The Jewish sages, speaking from the distant perspective of the Diaspora, taught that the Temple must await the coming of the Messiah. The medieval rabbi Rashi declared that the Temple would descend directly from heaven after the coming of the Messiah. Maimonides also argued that only the Messiah could build the Temple. The prayer at the afternoon service on Tisha B'Av reflects this thinking: "For You, O Lord, did consume it [the Temple] with fire, and with fire You will in the future restore it." Rabbi Goren, as one representative of this position, maintains: "The Temple will not be built by mortals."[2] Rabbi Nahman Kahane likewise contends that only "the Messiah can come and tell us where the Altar [of Sacrifice] is, and where the Temple should be built."[3]

The Israeli government agrees with this position and maintains that their actions to prohibit Jews from worshiping on the Temple Mount are based on these rather than political grounds. This position was put on record during the investigation that followed the fire at the Al Aqsa Mosque in 1969. The Arab representative charged that the Israeli government deliberately set the fire in order to rebuild the Temple. The Israeli representative in the debate denied the allegation firmly:

> The Temple Mount is so holy that the devout amongst us would not even tread on it. According to the [halakah], the Temple will be rebuilt when the Messiah will have come. It is, therefore, inconceivable that we ourselves should make any plans for the rebuilding of the Temple.[4]

Other groups, however, believe the Temple may be built at the present time by whatever means possible. Proponents of this position note that the Babylonian Talmud has conflicting opinions about the matter and that the Jerusalem Talmud permits the Jews to construct an intermediate edifice before the messianic era. Some scholars cite the Sifrey (a rabbinic commentary) on Jeremiah 50:5 in regard to seeking the house of the Lord. There it is said:

> Seek—means on the instructions of a prophet. You might infer from this that you should wait until the prophet tells you so. But the Torah says "unto His habitation shall you seek and to there shall you come," meaning that you should first search for the site and then the prophet is to confirm it for you.

The rabbinic scholar Malbim, writing in his 1860 commentary, adds:

The Lord will not reveal His secrets through His prophets about the chosen place unless they make endeavors to locate it, and only after such preparation, will He inspire them to disclose it.

Mystic Judaism also advances this cooperation of the human and the divine. Chaim Richman of the Temple Institute explains:

You have the concept of the masculine waters and the feminine waters. Feminine waters that rise, masculine waters that descend, in order to elicit a divine response. In an allegorical sense, we [Jews] are the feminine aspect, and God is the masculine aspect. The feminine aspect has to arouse, and the masculine aspect has to respond. ... The whole prophetic experience in Jewish mysticism ... always entails a great deal of preparation and purification. A person can't expect any gifts gratis; a person has to expect to put in the effort.[5]

On this basis, Gershon Salomon defends his activist attempts to immediately rebuild the Temple by arguing that his detractors suffer from a Diaspora mentality:

Physically they are in Israel, but spiritually they are in the Diaspora. The Jewish people have always brought about divine intervention through their own actions. The Red Sea did not split until the children of Israel walked into it.[6]

Return to the Land

One of the requirements of Maimonides for the rebuilding of the Temple was that the Temple could not be built until a majority of the Jewish people lived in the biblical land of Israel. Until recently this was thought to be a major obstacle, since only about 30 percent of world Jewry live in Israel. But the miraculous return of Ethiopian Jews through Operation Moses and Operation Solomon and the enormous exodus of Soviet Jews to Israel have greatly brightened the prospects for fulfilling this requirement. As a result, Sergio Della Pergola, a Hebrew University demographer, has said that in another ten years it is very likely that the majority of the world's Jews will be living in Israel.[7] This statistic assumes that the rate of immigration will continue as at present. If for some reason events promote a massive influx of Jews to Israel, then the time for the fulfillment of Maimonides' requirement would be shortened.

Given the obstacles, we might conclude that every preparation to rebuild the Temple at present is an exercise in futility. The same was once said of the attempts of the early Zionist movement to reestablish a Jewish presence in the Holy Land. Who at that time would have dreamed that an independent Jewish State, almost five million strong, would have arisen and stood against the sea of hostile Arab nations for more than four decades? The very fact that Scripture affirms that the Temple will be rebuilt indicates that a way will be found to rebuild! Let us now consider some of the ways that this rebuilding might take place.

Chapter 14

Temple Mount Alternatives

To all persons of the Jewish faith all over the world—A project to rebuild the Temple of God in Israel is now being started. With Divine Guidance and Help the 'Temple' will be completed. Jews will be inspired to conduct themselves in such a moral way that our Maker will see fit to pay us a visit here on earth. . . . God will place in the minds of many persons in all walks of Jewish life the desire to participate in this work.[1]

—*Advertisement*, Washington Post

*T*he statement above appeared as an advertisement in large bold letters in the Washington Post *shortly before* the reunification of Jerusalem in 1967. It called for Jews worldwide to unite together and rebuild the Temple. It has been a quarter of a century since that call was issued, yet to this day no effort of the magnitude needed to rebuild the Temple has been organized. In that time, other strategies to remove some of the obstacles presented by the Islamic presence on Temple Mount have been thrust into the cauldron of thought concerning the third Temple.

A New Home

One idea has been to build the third Temple at a site other than the present Temple Mount. A suggestion such as this, to locate the new Jewish nation in Africa, was made to Theodor Herzl, the father of the modern effort to reestablish Israel as a nation. But all of Jewish history and tradition weighs against this. If moving the Temple, even within Jerusalem, had ever been seriously considered, the third Temple would be standing today. Jerusalem's Great Synagogue was raised without difficulty in the heart of the New City, and if the Orthodox believed that the Temple could have been erected anywhere else, it would have been built immediately after statehood was declared on May 14, 1948!

As we saw in our survey of the history of the Temple, the Lord chose the spot for the establishment of the Temple as Mount Moriah (Genesis 22:2 with Deuteronomy 12:14), David executed God's choice by purchasing the site, and Solomon continued the work by building the first Temple upon it. Since the destruction of the second Temple, no Orthodox Jew has considered any place for the third Temple but the Temple Mount.

Purchase the Temple Mount

After the Israeli liberation of the Old City in 1967, an American group called the Masonic Temple Order offered the Muslim Council in Jerusalem the reported sum of $100 million for the Al Aqsa Mosque and the Dome of the Rock. This offer was refused, since as we have said, any territory that has formerly been in Muslim hands must forever remain in the possession of Islam. However, Arabs did sell vast tracts of land to Jews when the Zionist movement began its immigration to Israel, and today Arab inhabitants of the Moslem Quarter have sold property to the Atara L'yoshna group, so this restriction is not completely inviolable. Still, it is hard to believe that Islam's third and fourth holiest sites would ever be put on the auction block!

Move the Muslim Buildings

An alternative to purchasing the Muslim sites is a proposed plan to dismantle them and reassemble them in a place designated by the Islamic Council. The technology now exists to dismantle the Muslim sites stone by stone and reassemble them in Mecca (Islam's most holy place). Though a costly undertaking, it would be a small price to pay to appease the Arabs and clear the Temple Mount for the third Temple. The difficulty lies in the Arab conviction that their holy sites cannot be moved since the very ground under these sites has been hallowed by their prophet and leader's prayers, and can never fall into the hands of infidels (including Jews). The fact remains, however, that Israel has technically had sovereignty over the Temple Mount since 1967, and under the right circumstances, could force the Arabs to leave (although the present Israeli government is completely opposed to this idea).

Destroy the Muslim Buildings

It is the contention of some that the Temple can only be built after the Muslim buildings are removed. Many people in Jerusalem hoped that during the Iraqi attack on Israel a misdirected Scud missile might accidentally fall on the Dome of the Rock and destroy it! There have also been attempts in recent years by extremist groups to blow up the Muslim sites (in 1982 by Meir Kahane's Kach Party), and one deranged individual was successful in setting fire to the Al Aqsa Mosque in 1969. A natural destruction is also possible, since in past times the Dome of the Rock has suffered repeated damage due to earthquakes and, in the time of Justinian, explosive gases.

Rabbi Getz believes that just such a future event will destroy the Dome of the Rock and make possible the rebuilding of the Temple without interference. He says:

In the time of the Redemption, there will be a huge earthquake. Everything will blow up! The mosques—everything! It is written in the Zechariah chapter 14. It is the same as the Christian [interpretation]. But all of the churches around will [also] be destroyed by the earthquake. And the Temple Mount will be raised up, and there will be no mosques then—so of course we'll have enough opportunity to build the Temple.[2]

But should these Muslim sites be destroyed by a natural disaster or by human agency, either accidentally or on purpose, there is every reason to suspect that the Muslims would simply rebuild them as they have done repeatedly in the past. The solution to the rebuilding of the Temple must rest on a greater event, one that dramatically affects the religious and political situation in Israel.

The Possibilities

Despite the obstacles that remain at present to thwart rebuilding, proponents of the cause are adamant that the Temple will soon be rebuilt. Rabbi Kahane says: "An idea whose time is come nothing in the world can stop!" Gershon Salomon adds: "I do not have the slightest doubt that the Temple will soon begin to be built!"

But how will such a rebuilding take place in the troubled Middle East of today? The answer is that the Middle East of today will be radically changed. We have witnessed such world changes in Eastern Europe and the Soviet Union almost overnight. Given the volatile nature of the dispute over the Temple Mount, is it so hard to believe that a similar transformation will soon occur in the religious and political situation between Israel and the Arab world? In talking with the major spokesmen among the groups committed to the rebuilding of the Temple, only two possible scenarios of change were voiced: war and peace.

The Evolution of Peace

There is a Jewish parable that teaches that because the second Temple was destroyed by rivalry and discord, the third Temple will have to be built by peace and unity. A popular belief is that the Temple cannot be rebuilt until all is right with Israel and the world:

> Not until mankind and the people of Israel achieve a higher state of peace, freedom, and dignity, with respect for humans and closeness to God, will the final fulfillment [rebuilding of the Temple] be at hand.[3]

The Lubavitcher Hasidic group recently published a full-page advertisement in the *Jerusalem Post* that promoted this viewpoint (see Figure 10). The advertisement, which capitalizes upon the new messianic consciousness among Hasidim, pictures the word *Moshiach* ("Messiah" in Ashkenazi-accented Hebrew) as a connect-the-dot-pattern, with each dot being a recent current event. "Draw Your Own Conclusion," proclaims the headline. The text of the advertisement reads in part:

> Yes, we are living in the most extraordinary times—as our world evolves toward a state of peace, and mankind thrives toward a state of perfection. The times are changing—not just for the better, but truly for the best. A cornerstone of Jewish faith is the belief that, ultimately, good and peace must triumph. This is the essence of "Moshiach"—who will usher in the final redemption ordained in the Torah. The Lubavitcher

The Fall of Communism   Mass Exodus of Soviet Jewry   Triumph of Democracy and Freedom   Military Mobilization For Humanitarian Relief

Lightning Victory in Gulf War   Israel Unscathed by Scud Attacks   End of the Cold War

Draw Your Own Conclusion

These are amazing times.

The Iron Curtain tumbled...Iraq is humbled...The people of Israel emerge whole from under a rainstorm of murderous missiles...An entire beleaguered population is airlifted to safety overnight...A' tidal wave of Russian Jews reaches Israel...Truth and justice take center stage, with America emerging as the leading global power...Nations around the world turn to democracy...Plus countless other amazing developments that are taking place in front of our eyes.

Any one of these phenomena by itself is enough to boggle the mind. Connect them all together, and a pattern emerges that cannot be ignored.

Yes, we are living in the most extraordinary times – as our world evolves toward a state of peace, and mankind thrives toward a state of perfection. The times are changing – not just for the better, but truly for the best.

A cornerstone of Jewish faith is the belief that, ultimately, good and peace must triumph. This is the essence of "Moshiach" – who will usher in the final redemption ordained in the Torah.

The Lubavitcher Rebbe, Rabbi Menachem Mendel Schneerson, emphasizes that these remarkable events are merely a prelude to the final Redemption, culminating in unity among people, domestic harmony, and cessation of hostilities between races, neighbors and nations.

And these developments can be accelerated through the small but important acts of goodness and charity that are within the reach of every man, woman and child. It is our job to lift ourselves, our communities and our societies toward the great dawn we are all witnessing. And it doesn't take much to move forward – a kind word, a gift to the needy, treating others with respect, strengthening our commitment to the Torah and its directives.

The Era of Moshiach is upon us. Learn about it. Be a part of it. All you have to do is open your eyes. Inevitably, you'll draw your own conclusion.

FRIENDS OF CHABAD LUBAVITCH
For more information contact your local Chabad Lubavitch Center
Sponsored by Joseph Gutnick, Melbourne, Australia.

August 31, 1991   THE JERUSALEM POST INTERNATIONAL EDITION

Figure 10: Messianic Advertising Campaign: Advertisement placed in the Jerusalem Post by Jewish Hassidic Organization, August 1991. Believing that current events are the fulfillment of biblical prophecies, the word "Moshiach" (Messiah) is spelled out by symbolically connecting these events. The ad is part of an international campaign to prepare Jews worldwide for the coming of the Messiah.

Rebbe, Rabbi Menachem Mendel Schneerson, emphasizes that these remarkable events are merely the prelude to the final Redemption, culminating in unity among people, domestic harmony, and cessation of hostilities between races, neighbors and nations . . . The era of Moshiach is upon us.[4]

Many Israelis have given up much for a "higher state of peace," and believe that peace in the Middle East is worth the price. Other Jews, while desiring peace, feel that Israel cannot sell its security for a peace that could not be guaranteed. All controversy aside, the Israeli ideal has been the path of peace, because this path is considered to be the only practical alternative. Nahman Kahane explains:

If it [the Arab-Israeli conflict] ends in war everyone is going to lose. So it has to end in peace, for if it ends in war, the whole world will end up in war. In my opinion, the most important thing we learned from the Persian Gulf War was that the world's store of technology, of smart bombs and the like, revealed the next level of warfare . . . ultimately, the atomic weapon. Once you start throwing around this type of weaponry, nothing will be left, so the only alternative is to solve things in a peaceful way.[5]

The biblical prophets predicted a time of universal peace emanating from Jerusalem.[6] Isaiah 11:6-9 presents the classic passage of the wolf lying down with the lamb, a picture of idyllic peace. This is followed by words that promise an ingathering of the Jewish people from all the nations of the world at the coming of the Messiah. "Then it will come about in that day that the nations will resort to the root of Jesse, who will stand as a signal for the peoples; and His resting place will be glorious. Then it will happen on that day that the Lord will again recover the second time [the first was the return from exile under Zerubbabel] with His hand the remnant of His people who will remain, from Assyria, Egypt, Pathros, Cush, Elam, Shinar, Hamath, and from the islands of the sea. And He will lift up a standard for the nations, and will assemble the banished ones of Israel, and will gather the dispersed of Judah from the four corners of the earth" (verses 10-12).

Many people in Israel believe that they are seeing the partial fulfillment of these verses today. Gershon Salomon says:

> God is acting! The prophets say that there will come a time when I [God] will bring [the Jewish people] from all the corners of the world. From the north, I will say open your gates, and give My people back to this country. And it happens. Word by word it is fulfilled. It says I will bring your people back from Cush, which means Ethiopia . . . and you can see it! See what has happened in Russia, in Romania? . . . A process is now starting, and soon you will see that the revolution will not only happen in Romania, but in all the Western world.[7]

This type of fulfillment is often seen as part of a greater fulfillment of spiritual revival that is presently sweeping the world. Chaim Richman says:

> I think that what is going on here in our [Temple] Institute and Jerusalem in general, is being felt every year in Israel and all over the world. I think that there is a huge spiritual awakening, and that it is a major drama in the process of building the Temple.[8]

Nahman Kahane describes this reawakening as a force that has brought, and will continue to bring, profound spiritual change on a worldwide scale:

> God gives a spirit of peace into the world. No one knows why these things start or how . . . it's unpredictable. It is a movement in the world which began with the Jewish return to the Holy Land. This movement of spirituality in the world is coming on strong, and everybody feels it. Jews and Gentiles, everybody feels it, and as this spirituality grows stronger it draws people to spiritual ideas like a magnet. The height of this spiritual idea is the Temple. . . . People are coming back to religion. Judaism's return to the Torah is getting stronger among the Jewish people of Eastern Europe. I think the United States is awakening. . . . I think it is a sign that the Christian world is interested . . . an indication of the spirituality that is in the world. It would seem that we are on the threshold of great times.[9]

Some believe that this spiritual reawakening will bring those outside of Judaism into the fold. Kahane suggests:

> As ridiculous as it may seem, and as imaginary as it may seem, one day something might happen to Islam, and maybe Christianity too, and they will recognize the superiority of Judaism.[10]

I (Randall) have heard this same proposition put forth by many religious Jews: One day the Arabs and the Christians will all convert to Judaism and help build the Temple! While those who advance this prospect admit that this would be the greatest of miracles, there is a feeling that the miracles witnessed in the return of Soviet and Ethiopian Jewry and the deliverance from the Scud attacks will continue in the years to come and eventually assure such a worldwide conversion.

Kahane, recognizing that nothing less than a radical change would allow for the resumption of Temple worship, believes that religion is the only solution:

> The only alternative to war is peace, and religion might be the peaceful way. Someone said . . . the next century will be the century of religion. If it is not, there simply will not be another century. Religion has got to come back, and then religion will find a way [for men] to come together.[11]

The basis for this viewpoint is derived from such Scripture texts as Isaiah 2:1-4, which speak of all the nations coming to Jerusalem to learn the Jewish Torah from an exalted Israel whose God will have ended war and insured universal peace. Interestingly, Kahane proposes a religious "United Nations" be established in Jerusalem for the intermediate resolution of peace:

> I suggested once . . . that Israel should make a religious United Nations in Jerusalem like the political one in New York. We should have a unity among the nations built on the sanctity of religions. It would not exist to convert one another, but to try to solve human problems through our common belief in God. Of course there will be an argument about who will become chairman, but that will be a secondary argument.[12]

While there will be a literal future fulfillment of the Isaiah's prophecy, other events which precede this era of peace in which Messiah reigns have yet to be fulfilled. Current events do not portend the true and lasting peace such as that spoken of by the prophet, but they do include the realization of the proposal of some type of religious "United Nations" put forth by Kahane.

Israel has agreed that the European Economic Community (EEC) be represented alongside the United States and the former Soviet Union in any peace negotiations, such as those begun in Madrid in 1991. The EEC has stated that since it will have to live with this Middle East peace treaty, it ought to have a part in its creation. The Luxembourg foreign minister stressed that the more international the treaty, the better its chances of success. Interestingly, according to many prophetic authorities it will be a figure who arises representatively out of Europe who will make the "covenant of peace" with Israel, an act which will set in motion the rebuilding of the Temple and the days of tribulation.

In summarizing the possibility of peace, the view is that the Temple movements in Israel and abroad are simply part of an ongoing spiritual process which began with the Zionist movement and will climax with the rebuilding of the third Temple. This spiritual revival, in our interpretation of Scripture, will find its ultimate fulfillment when Jesus the Messiah will have set up His millennial reign from the restored Temple in Jerusalem.

War on the Horizon

A more ominous possibility exists, however, and that is the possibility of war. Those who dream of spiritual revival have nothing but a mystic idealism to offer as a hope for resolving the ages-old animosity that has divided the sons of Isaac and the sons of Ishmael. Those who caution that another war is on the horizon rely upon the rationalism of political analysis and the understanding of Islamic religious ideology.

The August 26, 1991 edition of *U.S. News & World Report* headlined its report on the Middle East: "A Holy City's Holy Wars." This article stated:

A medieval map shows Jerusalem as the heart of a clover consisting of Asia, Africa and Europe. Yet Jerusalem's universality has never fostered an ecumenical desire to share its sovereignty. And because it sits in a part of the world that does not separate the spiritual from the temporal, Jerusalem has rarely known peace.[13]

Observers of the Islamic world understand that religious and political thought cannot be separated as they are in the West. The concept of *Jihad* or holy war, is fundamental to Muslim religious and political thought. In Islamic tradition, the complete military domination of all non-Muslim lands is commanded by Allah:

> Hear, O Muslims, the meaning of life. Shall I not tell you of the peak of the matter, its pillar, and its topmost part? The peak of the matter is Islam itself. The pillar is ritual Rakatin prayer. And the topmost part is Ji'had—holy war.[14]

This holy war is especially directed against the Jews, as Haj Amin el Husseini, the Mufti of Jerusalem, declared after the United Nations recognized Israel's independence in 1948:

> The entire Jewish population in Palestine must be destroyed or driven into the sea. Allah has bestowed upon us the rare privilege of finishing what Hitler only began. Let the Ji'had begin. Murder the Jews. Murder them all.[15]

In like manner, Dr. Abdul Halim Mahmoud, head of the Academy of Islamic Research and rector of the Islamic University, Al Azhar, in Cairo, wrote in 1974:

> Allah commands the Muslims to fight the friends of Satan wherever they are found. Among

189 of Mount Alternatives

the friends of Satan—indeed, among the foremost friends of Satan in our present age—are the
Jews.[16]

The power struggle between Islamic Arab and Jew is not
viewed as a reconcilable matter. Rather it is a matter of
existence or annihilation, for in Muslim theology Jihad will
never end until the Day of Resurrection. Hashemi Rafsan-
jani of Iran reveals this basic tenet of Islamic thought when
he says:

> Every problem in our region can be traced to
> this single dilemma: the occupation of Dar al
> Islam [House of Islam] by Jewish infidels or West-
> ern imperialists. Every political controversy,
> every boundary dispute, and every internal con-
> flict is spawned by the inability of the Umma [true
> believers of Islam] to faithfully and successfully
> wage Ji'had. The everlasting struggle between
> Ishmael and Isaac cannot cease until one or the
> other is utterly vanquished.[17]

This call to Jihad is incumbent upon every Muslim, wherever he lives, and for all time. With such an imperialistic
ambition and irreconcilable religious hatred for the Jews, it
is inconceivable that any peace process could be successful
or adequately sustained. The Palestinian Liberation Organization (PLO), which claims to represent the "Palestinian"
people in Israel, is dedicated to this concept of Islamic
Jihad. Salah Khalaf (Abu Iyad), the PLO's second-in-com-
mand, said in a 1991 speech:

> Now we accept the formation of the Palestin-
> ian state in part of Palestine, in the Gaza Strip
> and West Bank. We start from that part and we
> will liberate Palestine, inch by inch.[18]

The imperative of Jihad can be temporarily forestalled by a truce, but any concept of a peaceful negotiation is not acceptable. This has been reaffirmed with the advent of the Middle East peace talks. Islamic fundamentalists have turned their rhetoric against any Arab body attempting reconciliation with Israel. In November 1991, a group of Muslim clerics gathered in Jerusalem and issued a leaflet condemning an Arab-Israeli peace agreement. The religious opinion or *fatwa* contained in the leaflet cites numerous passages from the Qur'an against Muslims making peace with Jews including the following:

> The Moslem ruler chosen by the nation can conclude a truce for the benefit of the nation [but] he is not authorized to make a permanent peace, and any such pact is forbidden, null and void. ... Such a peace is a grave sin and a betrayal of God and his messenger to the believers.[19]

Whatever the political outcome of the Arab-Israeli talks, the religious position of Muslims will remain in opposition to any permanent peace.

It has been stated more than once that the Muslims on the Temple Mount have sworn that they would defend their holy places to the last drop of blood. If this is so, then a means other than peace must loom on the horizon to pave the way for the rebuilding of the Temple.

After the recent events with Saddam Hussein in the Gulf, it should not surprise anyone that a war will soon sweep over the Middle East. What is surprising is that an Armageddon did not occur with this conflict, as predicted by even some of the most secular analysts. Hussein still has the ability to launch a deadly missile attack on Israel, and may soon have nuclear capability. Although Iraqi power has been severely weakened in the Middle East, it has not been rendered inoperative.

Most people in Israel fully expect another war in the near future. In fact, a 1991 *Jerusalem Post* article announced, "Scuds could strike again." The article reported that the United States may not be able to prevent Israeli retaliation against Iraq if Baghdad resumes missile attacks.

This prospect is also fully anticipated by some of the leaders in the Temple movement. Gershon Salomon believes that we are on the verge of seeing the prophecy of the battle of Gog and Magog predicted in Ezekiel 38-39 fulfilled. Concerning this imminent possibility he says:

> This will be, maybe, the last and biggest war, not only of the Middle East and the land of Israel, but in all the world. And as Ezekiel says, God will show to all the nations . . . what is the right way to worship God. . . . I feel it is very close.[20]

Among the ultra-Orthodox, especially those of the Hasidic group Chabad Lubavitch, this prophecy and others in Isaiah and Daniel have received special attention since the Gulf War. Leaders of the Lubavitcher group have announced that the Messiah will soon appear.

In the 1980's the Brooklyn headquarters issued bumper stickers and posters that read: "We Want Moshiach [Messiah] Now!" Today, in John the Baptist language, the legend "Prepare for the Coming of Moshiach" is emblazoned in giant black letters on a hundred-foot yellow sign perched high above the Rakevet turnoff of the Ayalon highway in Tel-Aviv. The purpose of this massive billboard, according to Menachem Brod, who spearheads public relations and publications for the Chabad Youth Organization, is to put Messiah into the national consciousness. With thousands of Israeli motorists passing this sign daily the indoctrination is well underway. Brod, serious about the outcome of this "messianic campaign," stresses that getting people excited about the coming of Messiah and spurring them to action will actually hasten the arrival of the long-awaited era. In a *Jerusalem Post* interview, he announced to readers: "Dear Jews, Moshiah is about to arrive! The dream of millions of Jews for centuries is upon us, and we all need to be ready for it!"[21]

During the Gulf War, this group's magazine, *Chai Today*, highlighted the new messianic consciousness when it published an article titled: "The Gulf Crisis: A 2,000 Year-Old Prophecy?" The article included a passage from an A.D. 1521 rabbinic commentary on Isaiah 60:1, which read:

> In the year in which our King, the Messiah will reveal himself, all of the kings of the world will be at odds with each other. The king of Persia [Iraq] will be at odds with an Arab king, and the Arab king will go to Aram [Syria] to seek counsel with them. The king of Persia will return and destroy the whole world. This is the year in which the Messiah will come."[22]

This same commentary makes a prophetic statement concerning the intervention of the Messiah to bring deliverance in this great end-time battle. Notice that the text indicates that the third Temple is already standing at this time:

> Seized by consternation, the Jewish people will ask, "Where shall we go?" The Almighty will answer them: "My children have no fear. . . . Why are you afraid?" . . . Mashiach [Messiah] will stand on the roof of the Holy Temple and proclaim, "Humble ones: The time for your redemption has arrived!"[23]

This time of trouble and tribulation has been traditionally referred to by Jewish messianists as the "birth pangs of the

Messiah" (*chevlei Mashi'ach*). This period of time, which is to precede Messiah's coming, has been applied to times of massacre in the past and has given rise to periods of fervent messianic expectations and movements. These "pangs of the Messiah" will be fulfilled in the coming time of tribulation which will host the battle of Gog and Magog spoken of in Ezekiel 38–39.

When war comes to the Temple Mount, what will happen? Since Muslims have sworn to defend the site to the last drop of blood, will Temple Mount see the biggest blood bath in its history? We put this question to Gershon Salomon, who witnessed the 1967 war with the Muslims on the Temple Mount and who is an authority in the area of Islamic studies. Surprisingly, he suggests a very different outcome:

> I believe that the Arabs will defend the Temple Mount "until the last drop of blood" like they did in '67. . . . The real feelings of Moslems, all their religious traditions, go back to Mecca, not to Jerusalem. [In 1967] no Arab soldier died defending the Temple Mount; they all ran away and left everything on the Temple Mount. When I first came to the Mount, a Jordanian Muslim came up to me and acted very friendly. He spent hours showing me all the Jewish places on the Mount.

> After a time I asked him why he didn't show us the Moslem places, only the Jewish, and he said that it was an old Arab tradition from generation to generation that it was written in the holy Moslem books that one day by the will of God the Israelis would come back to this country, and the Arab history here would be finished. So, in the Six-Day War I believe they did not speak about "the last drop of blood." They knew that something happened here and that they must leave Israel. They were ready to accept every change

Israel would have made to the Temple Mount as well as other places.[24]

According to Salomon's view, in the event of war the Muslims would abandon the Temple Mount, and Israel would be able to clear the site of Muslim buildings and rebuild the Temple. Perhaps we will awaken some morning and find that just such a war has begun.

Permission for Rebuilding

Gershon Salomon has also said he soon expects permission to be received to rebuild the Temple.[25] But how would permission to rebuild be obtained today? And more importantly, *permission from whom*? The Israeli government cannot give permission because control of the Temple Mount has been given over to the Muslim Wakf. The Wakf cannot give permission because it does not recognize the right of Israel to exist, much less construct a Temple. According to other Temple activists, permission from human authorities is not possible and therefore unnecessary. Permission has already been granted from *heaven*, and heaven will make clear the proper time for rebuilding.

A prelude to this has been suggested by an interesting situation that accompanied the 1968–1979 excavations in the shadow of the Temple Mount. These were the first excavations by Israelis in this area since the destruction of the Temple nearly 2,000 years ago. When director Meir Ben-Dov faced the first winter of the dig, he faced the certainty of cold, heavy deluges that disrupt work daily during these months of Israel's rainy season. Yet he was amazed to find that the rain stopped in time for the daily work, and resumed only when the work day had ended. He writes:

> Incredible as it may sound, the days went on like that for ten successive winters, and we lost

only an average of six or seven work days a year, since it had a way of raining mostly at night. Even more uncanny was what Josephus Flavius, the first-century Jewish historian, had to say about this phenomenon: "When they built the Temple, our fathers tell us, it only rained in Jerusalem at night." Josephus believed that this was the hand of Providence helping the operation along. Perhaps that was so. . . . It was as true now as it had been two millennia ago.[26]

Does this extraordinary account suggest, as many believe, that heaven has already sanctioned the rebuilding of the Temple, and that those who act in accordance with that design, even archaeologists, will be given supernatural assistance? We know only that when the next Temple is begun, the permission that will be received—in the form of a pact with the coming world ruler, the Antichrist—will appear to have been heaven sent.

Chapter 15

The Tribulation
and Beyond

Let no one in any way deceive you, for it will not come
unless the apostasy comes first, and the man of lawlessness is revealed, the son of destruction, who opposes and
exalts himself above every so-called god or object of
worship, so that he takes his seat in the temple of God,
displaying himself as being God.

—2 Thessalonians 2:3,4

*W*hile it is interesting to survey some of the current
events relating to modern-day Israel's efforts to rebuild the third Temple, it is the fact that the Bible predicts
just such a Temple which causes us to take these matters
seriously. The Bible mentions four Jewish Temples in Jerusalem. We have already noted the first two, Solomon's
Temple and Herod's Temple. The final two have yet to
appear. The tribulation Temple (the third Temple) will be
next, while the millennial Temple (the fourth Temple) will
appear after Jesus the Messiah returns to planet Earth and
builds it to use during His messianic kingdom.

Biblical Passages Supporting
a Tribulation Temple

There are no Bible verses that say, "There is going to be a

198 ◆ *Tribulation and Beyond*

third Temple." Rather the fact that there will be a Jewish Temple in Jerusalem at least by the midpoint of the seven-year tribulation period is supported by at least four scriptural references:

Daniel 9:27 says, "And he [Antichrist] will make a firm covenant with the many [the nation of Israel] for one week [seven years], but in the middle of the week [three-and-a-half years] he [Antichrist] will put a stop to sacrifice and grain offering; and on the wing of abominations [the Altar in the Temple] will come one [Antichrist] who makes desolate, even until a complete destruction, one that is decreed, is poured out on the one [Antichrist] who makes desolate." This passage predicts a future time period of seven years, during which the "Beast," or Antichrist, defiles Israel's Temple by an evil act at the three-and-a-half-year point. In order for this to happen, there must be a Temple in Jerusalem. Therefore, we can conclude from this future event that the third Temple must be built and functioning by this time.

Prophecy scholar John Walvoord notes that the "temple of that future day will be desecrated much as Antiochus desecrated the temple in his day in the second century B.C., stopping the sacrifices and putting the temple to pagan use."[1] Daniel 12:11 is a related passage: "And from the time that the regular sacrifice is abolished, and the abomination of desolation is set up, there will be 1,290 days." In the same way Daniel 9:27 speaks of a future event, so also "the regular sacrifice" being abolished and "the abomination of desolation" being set up will occur in the third Temple.

Christ tells us in *Matthew 24:15,16*, "Therefore when you see the abomination of desolation which was spoken of through Daniel the prophet, standing in the holy place (let the reader understand), then let those who are in Judea flee to the mountains." Jesus is speaking of the same event to which Daniel refers in Daniel 9:27 when He speaks of "the abomination of desolation . . . standing in the holy place." "The holy place" is a reference to the most sacred room within Israel's Temple. What Temple? The third Temple, since it is a future event. Prophecy teacher Tim LaHaye tells us that "Matthew 24:15 portrays the 'abomination of desolation,' when the Antichrist desecrates the rebuilt temple in Jerusalem," adding, "Obviously it has to be rebuilt in order to be desecrated."[2]

The apostle Paul gives us perhaps the clearest passage relating to the third Temple in *2 Thessalonians 2:3,4*. "Let no one in any way deceive you, for it [the day of the Lord] will not come unless the apostasy comes first, and the man of lawlessness is revealed, the son of destruction [Antichrist], who opposes and exalts himself above every so-called god or object of worship, so that he takes his seat in the temple of God, displaying himself as being God." In this passage we see for the third time a description of "the abomination of desolation." This time it is referred to as the event in which Antichrist "takes his seat in the temple of God." Once again, which Temple? The clear answer is the future third Temple. Theologian Charles Ryrie tells us that at "the midpoint of the tribulation period the Antichrist will desecrate the rebuilt Jewish temple in Jerusalem by placing himself there to be worshiped."[3] This act of self-deification is "the abomination of desolation."

The final passage referring to the third Temple is *Revelation 11:1,2*. "And there was given me a measuring rod like a staff; and someone said, 'Rise and measure the temple of God, and the altar, and those who worship in it. And leave out the court which is outside the temple, and do not measure it, for it has been given to the nations; and they will tread under foot the holy city for forty-two months.' " Since the section of Revelation in which this passage appears takes place during the tribulation period, this is a reference to Israel's third Temple in Jerusalem.

Why does God command John to measure the third Temple during the tribulation period? Old Testament passages such as Ezekiel 40 and Zechariah 2 link measurement with a spiritual evaluation of the people. As bestselling prophecy author Hal Lindsey has noted, God's "appraisal of this future Temple therefore determines whether it's truly fulfilling its intended purpose. Unfortunately, it turns out to be an apostate place of worship. Its reconstruction is not based on a recognition of Jesus as the Messiah, but on a nationalistic desire to once again possess a national religious symbol and draw the people back to a belief in their God."[4]

Some Bible interpreters say that the reference to the Temple in Revelation 11:1,2 is not to a future third Temple, that it refers instead to the second Temple or is a figure of speech for an apostate spiritual entity such as Israel or the church. But if these verses refer to the second Temple of Christ's time, then the whole book of Revelation and virtually all New Testament prophecy would have already been fulfilled, as some people do teach. Most Bible scholars believe that Revelation was not written until well after A.D. 70, which would make this interpretation impossible. It is even more unlikely that virtually the whole book of Revelation has already taken place.[5] If Revelation has already been fulfilled, then the early church, not to mention nearly all of the church since, has lived through this time unaware that these things had come to pass.

The "spiritual Temple" view, whether referring to Israel or the church, is incorrect because the Temple in these contexts is not intended to be taken figuratively. For example, in Matthew 24 Jesus is speaking about a literal Temple, since in the context of the passage he is standing and looking directly at the second Temple. The abomination of desolation was something that took place the first time through

Antiochus Epiphanes in the second century B.C. when he stopped the sacrifices and desecrated the second Temple by sacrificing an unclean pig on the altar and setting up in its place a statue of Jupiter. This literally fulfilled Daniel 11:31. Therefore, these future events will be similar in kind to the prototypes—they will be real, historical events in a last days' Temple.

Sharing the Blessings

As we noted earlier, since the church is the spiritual Temple of God, indwelt by the Holy Spirit, some Christians teach that Scripture passages speaking of a future Temple in Jerusalem are not to be taken literally. Is this so?

While it is true the Bible teaches that the church is a spiritual Temple, indwelt by the Holy Spirit, it does not necessarily follow that other passages speaking of a future literal Temple are not also true.

Ephesians 2:19-22 clearly teaches that the New Testament church *is* a spiritual Temple in which the Holy Spirit dwells. "So then you are no longer strangers and aliens, but you are fellow citizens with the saints, and are of God's household, having been built upon the foundation of the apostles and prophets, Christ Jesus Himself being the corner stone, in whom the whole building, being fitted together is growing into a holy temple in the Lord; in whom you also are being built together into a dwelling of God in the Spirit." And it is also true that the New Testament metaphor pictures the corporate collection of believers down through the history of the church as Christ's body (1 Corinthians 12), and His Temple or building which He indwells. This and similar passages in the New Testament teach that the church in the church age is a partaker of the blessings and promises made to Abraham, but not a usurper of these blessings and promises.

Paul answers an emphatic no to the question about whether God has rejected His people Israel (Romans 11:1).

He teaches that Israel's rejection of Jesus as the Messiah is only temporary and that when the right time comes, God will resume His plan for Israel and bring them to Messiah (Romans 11). God has not rejected Israel forever. Nowhere in the New Testament does the Bible teach that the church and Christians are the "New Israel." Nowhere is the word "Israel" ever used to refer to the body of Christ—the church.

The Bible does teach that Christians in the church age are the spiritual seed of Abraham (Galatians 3:29). "Spiritual seed of Abraham" is not the same as "spiritual Israel." Abraham came before Israel. He was the founder, along with Isaac and Jacob, of Israel. But he is at the same time the spiritual father of all redeemed people through Christ, whether Jew or Gentile. God's inclusion of the Gentiles does not mean that God will never restore Israel to favor. He will, because He has promised to do so! He is now in the process of accomplishing this, even though He is offering redemption during the current age to both Jew and Gentile, using the church as His instrument. As Paul says, "I say then, they [the Jews] did not stumble so as to fall, did they? May it never be!" (Romans 11:11). Therefore, just because God currently indwells a spiritual Temple in the church does not mean that His future plans for an earthly Jewish Temple have been set aside.

Would a Rebuilt Temple be Blasphemous?

Some Christian theologians contend that it would be blasphemous for a new Jewish Temple to be rebuilt. Based on statements in the book of Hebrews which speak of Christ's work on the cross, they contend that His act satisfied once and for all time that which the Temple sacrifice only foreshadowed. According to this reasoning, the rebuilding of a third Temple would deny that Jesus' atoning work on the cross made the Temple sacrifice void.

No true Christian would deny that Jesus' work on the cross abolished the need for Temple sacrifice. Christians who look with interest to the Jews rebuilding their Temple are not in any way denying Christ's saving work through His death. Rather, they view the rebuilding as a prophetic sign of the times. The Jews will rebuild the Temple, in part, because of their rejection of Jesus as the Messiah, but what they do in unbelief will fulfill God's sovereign plan of having a Temple in Jerusalem for the Antichrist to defile.

Christians who are excited about recent Jewish developments to rebuild the Temple in no way compromise orthodox Christian belief, since they do not see it as relating to the forgiveness of sins, once and for all accomplished in Christ. Instead they see it as related to God's prophetic plan.

When Will the Third Temple Be Built?

The last few years have seen a growing interest within Israel to rebuild the Temple. But does this have significance in relation to the timing of biblical prophecy? If we are able to establish from the Bible when the third Temple must be rebuilt in order to fulfill its role during end-time events, we will have a reference point from which to answer the question concerning the timing of the rebuilding.

We have already seen that all references to the third Temple occur during the future seven-year period known as the tribulation. We also know that these references are related to the time when Antichrist will defile the Temple. Daniel 9:27 tells us that this defilement will take place three-and-one-half years into the final "week" or seven-year period which has been decreed for Israel. This seven-year period begins when the Antichrist signs a "firm covenant" with Israel (Daniel 9:27). Since the other passages relating to the third Temple either support a midtribulation timing for the Antichrist's defilement of the Temple or do not indicate a time frame, this passage is our only direct reference. From it we learn that the Temple must be functioning three-and-one-half years after the beginning of the seven-year tribulation period. It *could* be erected at any time, but it *does not have to be* in place until midway into the tribulation.

Is the impending rebuilding of the Temple a sign that the rapture is near? No, because there are no biblical signs that must take place before the rapture can occur. But the fact that Israel is returning to the Land, that most of Jerusalem is under the control of Israel, and that there is a growing Jewish movement desiring to see the Temple rebuilt, would certainly lead one to believe that the beginning of the *tribulation* may be near. These signs relate to Christ's return to the earth at the *end* of the seven-year tribulation. Since the rapture will occur before the *start* of the tribulation, these events, while not denoting any precise time, certainly heighten expectation that God is on the verge of completing His long-awaited program for Israel. Just as the return to the land of Israel by the Jews was an indicator of the times, so the revival of Jewish attempts to rebuild the Temple fosters an anticipation of end-time events.

What About the "Times of the Gentiles"?

Jesus, in speaking of the destruction of Jerusalem in A.D. 70 predicted that the Jews would "fall by the edge of the sword, and . . . be led captive into all the nations; and Jerusalem . . . be trampled under foot by the Gentiles until the times of the Gentiles be fulfilled" (Luke 21:24). The "times of the Gentiles" began in the sixth century B.C. when Israel was taken into captivity by Babylon. In its context Luke 21:24 indicates that the "times of the Gentiles" would continue through the destruction of the second Temple, and would end when Messiah came at the end of the tribulation period to rescue Israel and judge the nations as recorded in Revelation 19. So far the "times of the Gentiles" has lasted almost 2,600 years.

Some prophetic writers have proposed that the "times of the Gentiles" ended with Israel's recapturing of Jerusalem in the Six-Day War of 1967. However, the verses that follow Luke 21:24 speak of the second coming of Messiah at the end of the tribulation. In addition, while Israel recaptured the whole city, Israeli General Moshe Dayan gave the Temple Mount back to the Arabs, hoping to appease their hostile attitude toward the Jewish nation. Of course, this did not succeed, and today Jews do not control their most holy site, so it could be said that the Temple Mount is still being trampled down by the Arab Gentiles.

The Arab occupation today prevents Israel from completely fulfilling the biblical prophecy of a return to the Land, since such a return ultimately involves a return to spiritual worship at the Temple Mount in a restored Temple (Ezekiel 37:21-28). This return will be fulfilled during the tribulation, with the spiritual revival occurring at Messiah's coming (Isaiah 66:7,8; Zechariah 12:8–13:2). What we do see today is the partial fulfillment of the promise, and an indication that the events which will complete its fulfillment will soon follow.

What About the Temple in Ezekiel 40–48?

There is another major section in the Old Testament which speaks about a future Temple. Ezekiel 40-48 refers to yet another Temple, one we might call the fourth Temple. The Bible indicates that this will be the final Temple in Jewish history.

This fourth Temple, often referred to as the millennial Temple, will be approximately one mile square, many times larger than the first three Temple complexes (Ezekiel 42:15-20). It will be built by Jesus the Messiah and will likely be the most beautiful structure in the history of the world. Zechariah 14:4-8 speaks of a major topological reconstruction of the Mount of Olives and the Temple Mount in Jerusalem, presumably to provide the real estate needed for the fourth Temple.

The Shekinah glory, which departed from the first Temple in the eighth century B.C. (Ezekiel 9-11), was absent from the second Temple, and will be absent from the coming third Temple, will return to the fourth Temple. The third Temple will be defiled by the Antichrist in the tribulation, but the fourth Temple will be consecrated by the Messiah Himself for His millennial reign on earth. Jesus the Messiah will return to the Mount of Olives and enter the Temple Mount through the Eastern Gate (Ezekiel 43). He will shine forth His Shekinah glory and cleanse the site for worship. A unique priesthood and sacrifices (Ezekiel 40-48) will be set in place, and the Temple will be the focal point of international worship.[6] The Messiah, the God-Man, Jesus of Nazareth, will be present so that anyone will be able to visit Him, talk with Him, and know Him directly.

Why Two More Temples?

One reason why God will allow Antichrist to have his brief moment in history is to demonstrate that the way of evil is futile, fruitless, and fleeting. The dark reign of Antichrist over the land of Israel and the world from the third Temple for a meager three-and-a-half-year period will furnish a contrast with the light of Messiah's thousand-year reign. His kingdom will shine forth with true peace and lasting solutions to the problems of this world—problems which were initiated by mankind and which came to their ultimate fruition under the dominion of Antichrist. This lesson of history will be reinforced by the further contrasts of the third and fourth Temples.

The third Temple will be employed by Antichrist when he makes his false claims to be Messiah and sets up his false image in the Holy of Holies, defiling the sanctity of the Temple. This event will give rise to the final three-and-one-half years of the tribulation which will be the greatest time of persecution Jews and Gentile believers have ever known. While the third Temple will be *a* last days' Temple, it will not be *the* last, but will lead to the final Temple that planet Earth will see—the Messiah's millennial Temple, "the house of prayer for all the peoples" (Isaiah 56:7).

This millennial Temple will not be built by men, but by the Messiah. This agrees with the various Jewish traditions that the Temple envisioned by the biblical prophets would "descend from heaven," be "made of fire," and "personally constructed by Messiah." This Temple will never be defiled and will last for the final thousand years of human history.

Chapter 16

Jewish Predictions for the End-Time Temple

In Israel we have rabbis called Mikubalim [Kabbalists] who have a special way to count the days and years and know exactly when the Messiah will come and when the Temple will be rebuilt. According to their count, which they made according to Daniel, Yehezkiel [Ezekiel] and other prophets, this year, 1992, will be the year of the Messiah and the rebuilding of the third Temple. I have a book in my library which was written 56 years ago, and in this book the man says that this year, 1992, will be the year. Other scholars in Israel are also saying the same thing. We expect it![1]

—*Gershon Salomon*

*S*peculation and prediction about end-times events are usually avoided in Judaism, but many people in Israel today are making very precise predictions about both the coming of the Messiah and the rebuilding of the third Temple. What has brought about this startling change in Jewish viewpoint about predictions of prophetic fulfillment? More importantly, what are their predictions and do they have any significance for Christians?

A Change in Perspective

The traditional skepticism in Judaism toward predicting

the timing of events in the last days is similar to that of many Christians. In the past such attempts have usually ended in embarrassment. For example, Rabbi Akiva mistakenly proclaimed that the Jewish revolutionary Bar Kokhba was the Messiah in A.D. 132. There was also a prediction that the "pangs of Messiah," including the battle of Gog and Magog would begin on the fourteenth day of Nisan in the Jewish year 4291 (A.D. 531). As a result of such failed calculations, the Messiah was included in Jewish teaching among "three things that will come unawares" (Sanhedrin 97a). In addition, a prohibition against prophetic speculation was advanced in the Talmud which put Israelites under an oath "not to make known the end, and not forcibly to hasten the advent of the end" (Kethubim 111a). One such warning reads: "May the bones of those who calculate the end rot" (Sanhedrin 97b).

Nevertheless, prophetic predictions continued in Jewish mystic circles until the seventeenth century when Shabbetai Zevi, who was proclaimed publicly as the Messiah, not only failed to fulfill the messianic hope, but converted to Islam. This was an immense embarrassment to the European Jewish community and consequently, even mystic Jewish groups began to oppose speculation on when the Messiah would come. In the eighteenth-century writings of the Rabbanite Ashkenaz, readers are warned:

> If you see that a man has prophesied the advent of the Messiah, know that he is engaged either in sorcery or in dealings with devils. . . . One has to say to such a man: "Do not talk in this manner." . . . Eventually he will be the laughingstock of the whole world.[2]

Yet biblical prophets had spoken about the last days and had given details of events that could be foreseen. And the expectation that world events might be an indicator of heaven's timing for the return to the Promised Land and the fulfillment of the prophets' predictions continued to provoke popular speculations. To resolve the problem, the rabbis offered a *midrash* (interpretive story) to explain the correct Jewish perspective.

This midrash tells the story of a father and son who set off on a journey with a coach and driver. They had scarcely left the city when the boy childishly asked, "How long till we get there?" The only reply he received from the father was a sharp smack to the mouth. Many miles later, the driver of the coach asked the father, "How long till we get there?" and received a kind and courteous explanation. Puzzled, the boy protested to the father, "When I asked you the same question I got a smack, but when he asked, you kindly told him all!" "Yes," replied the father, "but when you asked we were hardly just begun, but now we are almost there."

The point of the story for predictive prophecy is that when one is far from the fulfillment of the prophecy the events are unclear, and it is better not to ask about them. However, when one is coming around the bend, and the events themselves are within sight, then it is proper to consider the time of their fulfillment. Many Orthodox Jews feel that it is now proper to set dates for the coming of the Messiah.

Many Jewish and Christian interpreters believe the final vision given to Daniel was speaking of greater understanding of prophecy as end-time events approach. "Go your way, Daniel, for these words are concealed and sealed up until the end time" (Daniel 12:9). Daily the pieces required for the fulfillment of end-time prophecy seem to be falling into place with the unfolding of contemporary events.

The Prediction of *Tisha B'Av*

Among those Jews who believe that the Temple will someday be rebuilt, it is universally acknowledged that the

Temple will in some way be the product of Providence (the intervention of heaven). Dr. Asher Kaufman has said that he believes the very reason the Temple Mount has been preserved in its present state through the millennia is because God has reserved it for the eventual rebuilding of the Temple. Christians, Muslims, or Turks during their respective rules could have destroyed the large esplanade of Herod, expanding their cities over the area and making future discovery of the original site, much less the rebuilding of the Temple, an impossibility. Yet today this platform, built to support the Temple, continues to mark that sacred spot until its destiny is fulfilled.

Providence has been especially observed in the instance of one particular date in history, the Ninth of Av (*Tisha B'Av*),[3] a day of mourning for all Jewish people throughout the world since the destruction of the Temple.

Five events of national tragedy have been associated with this date. The first of these national tragedies, and the supposed cause of all that followed, was the failure of the Israelites to enter the Promised Land under Moses (Numbers 14). Because the report of faith by the two spies, Joshua and Caleb, was not believed, and the report of fear from the other ten spies *was* received, God denied entrance to that generation and condemned them to wander and die in the desert. When Moses delivered this word to the people they "mourned greatly" (Numbers 14:39). Since oral tradition preserved in the Mishnah recounts that this lamentation took place on the Ninth of Av, a midrash sought to explain the providential succession of events that later occurred on this same date from this text. The midrash says that God, angered by the needless weeping, said: "You have cried before Me without cause; I shall determine this to be a time of weeping for you for your generations." So began a phenomenal sequence of disasters that has resulted in nearly 20 centuries of annual mourning.

The next four events occurring on the Ninth of Av all relate to the Temple. The second and third disasters involve Solomon's first Temple and Herod's second Temple, which were both destroyed on the same day 656 years apart.[4] The last two disasters occurred 65 years later on the same day (A.D. 135). The first of these was the defeat of the army of Bar Kokhba at Betar. The second followed as a consequence of the first. It was the plowing of the site of the Temple Mount by the Roman governor of Judea, Tineius Rufus, as a means of signifying the utter destruction of the Jewish city. As a result, the Ninth of Av was solemnized as a national day of mourning for the destruction of the Temple. Yet the Providence that brought such a sure end to the Temple is the same Providence that will just as surely bring its new beginning.

In the second century, it is said that a group of Jews were standing on the Mount of Olives overlooking the ruined Temple Mount and weeping (possibly on the Ninth of Av). The venerated Rabbi Akiva comforted his companions by citing Zechariah's prophecy of future redemption: "Thus says the Lord of hosts: There shall yet old men and women sit in the broad places of Jerusalem" (Zechariah 8:4). Rabbi Akiva's statement exemplified the hope for a restored Temple that 2,000 years of mourning has only strengthened.

While Judaism has attached great importance to the observance of the Ninth of Av, its existence as a national symbol of mourning serves to prepare the way for national rejoicing in the future. Indeed, Jewish tradition states that "the Messiah will appear on Tisha B'Av, and the day of mourning will become a national day of rejoicing with the rebuilt Temple."[5] If one date in Jewish history can bind together past and future in such an aspect of providential certainty, then surely the possibility of making similar predictions along other lines exists. Let us now consider one of the more startling contemporary Jewish predictions.

Jewish Date-Setting

In the opening chapter of this book we quoted the statement of Rabbi Leon Ashkenazi made with respect to the Gulf War's fulfillment of many Bible texts, and that in his view the preparation for the Messiah had begun with the Balfour Declaration in 1917, followed by the unification of Jerusalem in 1967, and would be completed in 1992 with the rebuilding of the Temple. We opened this chapter with a quote from Gershon Salomon that the Kabbalistic rabbis in Israel have also predicted the same date. While we are not advancing this date for *Christian* speculation, it may be considered here as an example of the current trend toward *Jewish* date-setting.

This prediction of the coming of the Messiah and the rebuilding of the Temple in 1992 is based on a series of complex computations involving the interpretation of significant events in Jewish history and the reckoning of certain biblical festival days. These reckonings come from several Jewish chronological works, such as the *Seder Olam* ("Order of the World"). The *Seder Olam (Rabba)* is the oldest Jewish chronicle, being edited by Jose ben Halafta who died in A.D. 160. It lists the biblical and post-biblical events until the Bar Kokhba revolt.

Computations are also based on biblical texts, such as Daniel 9-11, Ezekiel 34-48, and Jeremiah 30-33,50,51. These passages are interpreted according to both literal and Kabbalistic (numerological) methods, and according to the interpretations of especially revered rabbis of the past and present. Kabbalistic methods, as we will see, involve mystical interpretations of specific dates. A recent example of this is that of the Lubavitcher Rebbe, Rabbi Menachem Schneerson, who has made much of the recent date 5751 (equivalent to our A.D. 1991) on the Hebrew calendar.

The Hebrew calendar calculates years from the beginning of the world. Since Hebrew letters are used interchangeably with numbers in Hebrew dates, Schneerson interprets the letters comprising 5751 (*tav, shin, nun, aleph*), to indicate the phrase, *"This year will surely be a year in which [God] will show you wonders."* Members of Schneerson's Lubavitcher group, who believe that the Temple will soon miraculously descend from heaven, have said that one need only consider the "miracles" that have already taken place recently: the collapse of the Iron Curtain, the ingathering of thousands of Jewish exiles to Israel, and the divine protection of Israel during the Persian Gulf conflict. According to their view, this is the "era of miracles" that immediately precedes the "era of the Messiah."[6]

Gershon Salomon agrees with this reckoning and has said:

> We are in the year 1991, *tav-shin-nun-aleph*, "the year in which I will show miracles," and so I think the Temple will be built this year, or next year—we are very close.[7]

This specific date can also be derived from a traditional interpretation from the intertestamental period that fixes 1992 as a Jubilee year. Every fiftieth year on the biblical calendar was a Jubilee year, a time of redemption and liberation in which no sowing or reaping was done, all slaves were freed, land reverted to its original owners, and all debts were canceled (Leviticus 25:8-55). It is easy to see how this time of release could be viewed prophetically as that time in which all the land will be returned to the Jewish people, the Jews of the Diaspora would be returned to Israel, and Israel would enjoy its spiritual and physical redemption. Therefore, this early system of reckoning divided the history of the world into a great number of jubilees in order to establish when the "messianic end" would come.

This Jubilee date of 1992 was obtained from the computation of the date of the first Jubilee, held 14 years after the entrance of the Israelites into Canaan under Joshua in 1463 B.C. A Jubilee year has historically ended in either a 2 (Hebrew letter *beth*) or 52 (Hebrew letter *nun beth*), thus the current calendar date 5752 (1992, which actually began with the Jewish New Year, *Rosh Ha-shanah*, on September 9, 1991) is thought to be a Jubilee year. The expectation of the Jewish interpreters who have publicized this view is that this Jubilee year is a "year of release" that will include the release of the Temple Mount for the rebuilding of the Temple.

Another means of reckoning used to interpret the nearness of the messianic age is mentioned in the Talmud: "This world will exist for 6,000 years, 2,000 of which will be a period of desolation, 2,000 of Torah, and the last 2,000 the messianic era."[8] This "biblical" chronology is defended by Orthodox advocates using the same scientific arguments for a recently created or "early earth" as those posited by Christian creationists.[9]

After the first 6,000 years are complete, there will be a thousand years of renewal.[10] This "great sabbath week" of 7,000 years is patterned after the six days of creation (6 days = 6,000 years) and the rest on the seventh day (the last day = 1,000 years). God is said to hide behind the *'olam ha-zeh* ("this present world" of 6,000 years), for the three Hebrew root letters that make up the word "world"— *ayin*, *lamed*, *mem*—indicate a "vanishing," not of God, but of God from the world.

In the last 1,000 years, the *'olam ha-ba* ("world to come"), God will not be in the background, but will appear and transform the natural order into one that is spiritual. It is in this context that the prophecy in Isaiah 11 about the wolf lying down together with the lamb will be fulfilled. In Jewish terms this time is referred to as the "messianic millennium," a period of peace on earth that precedes the final Day of the Lord. In Christian parlance it is called the millennial kingdom, or simply, the millennium.

Regardless of whether or not these calculations turn out to be correct, they do illustrate an increased expectancy among many Jews within the last few years. It is significant to note that an increasing number of Jews are crying out and looking for the coming of their Messiah.

Christian Date-Setting

Some Christian interpreters have also adopted this last Jewish method of reckoning. One of the earliest Christian pseudepigraphal writings, *The Epistle of Barnabas*, outlines just such a scheme. This concept is employed today by some evangelical scholars, and one popular version advances the same date as that posed by its Jewish counterpart. We may arrange this scheme in chart form as shown in Figure 11.

In the chart we can see that the 6,000 years for the existence of the present world has the year A.D. 2,000 as its endpoint. Assuming there are no gaps in the chronology of biblical genealogy, the world was created in 4,000 B.C. If it is 2,000 years from Adam to Abraham, and 2,000 years from Abraham to Christ, there yet remains another 2,000 years to complete the 6,000-year period. Of this 2,000 years, 1,992 have already elapsed, leaving 8 years until the termination. If we subtract seven years for the tribulation period, we arrive at 1992 as the year that precedes the beginning of the tribulation. The final thousand years are reserved for the age of the millennial kingdom.

Another Christian scheme is based on the statement in Matthew 1:17 that the generations from Abraham to David, and David to the Babylonian captivity, and the Babylonian captivity to Christ are each 14 generations. These three periods times 14 equals 42 generations. Employing Thiele's Chronological Tables, which calculates this same period from Abraham to Christ to be 2,160 years, it is a simple step to divide the years by the number of generations (2,160 by 42) and arrive at 51 years, 4 months as the length of a

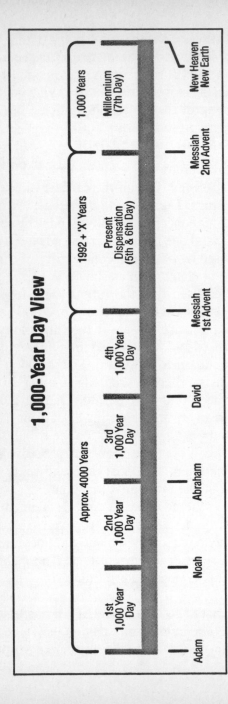

1,000-Year Day View

Adam	Noah	Abraham	David	Messiah 1st Advent	Messiah 2nd Advent

| 1st 1,000 Year Day | 2nd 1,000 Year Day | 3rd 1,000 Year Day | 4th 1,000 Year Day | Present Dispensation (5th & 6th Day) | Millennium (7th Day) | New Heaven New Earth |

Approx. 4000 Years — 1992 + 'X' Years — 1,000 Years

Figure 11: Thousand-Year "Days." This chart illustrates the popular teaching based on 2 Peter 3:8 and Talmudic references, that prophetic history is divided into "thousand-year" periods of time. According to this view, four consecutive thousand-year "days" from Adam are divided by covenants made with great men of the Bible, concluding with Christ and the New Covenant. Since no further covenants were made, the fifth and sixth "days" occupy a space of two thousand years. According to the Gregorian calendar, this "cosmic" or "creation" order is about to see the commencement of the seventh thousand-year "day," the day of God's rest, or the messianic era of peace called the Millennium. The Tribulation Temple, built shortly before this period begins, will be rebuilt by the Messiah according to the specifications of Ezekiel 40—48 and stand during the millennial reign of Christ.

generation. Now if we accept May 1948 as the date for the beginning of the modern State of Israel, and add one generation we arrive at 1999 plus nine months. Subtracting seven years for the Tribulation we arrive at September 1992. According to the Jewish calendar this date ends the year 5752 (1992), and accords with the prediction for the beginning of the rebuilding of the Temple by Rabbi Ashkenazi.

Finally, 1992 is the date set for the formal political unification of United Europe. Many prophecy students believe this European unity will give rise to the one-world government, now loosely heralded as the new world order. From this international union will come the Antichrist, who will sign a peace treaty with Israel and ultimately defile the rebuilt Temple.

Politics and Predictions

Many people believe the timing for any predictions of the rebuilding of the Temple must take into account the political climate in Israel. The founders of the State were not religious people, but secular socialists. In fact, they were at odds with religious Jews who opposed the Zionist cause. Former director of the Israeli government press office, Mordcchai Dolinsky, acknowledges this when he says:

> The fact is that most political leaders of Israel were secular humanists, and the one thing most of them lacked was some sense of a historical perspective. That's true of the press in Israel and of many of the politicians in Israel, and without a historical perspective you tend to lose any reasonable political perspective.[11]

Today, however, not only are many of Israel's politicians more historically informed, but many are religiously observant Jews. This change began with former Prime Minister

Menachem Begin and may be setting the stage for the
realization of Jewish predictions. When recently asked
about how this new climate favored the rebuilding of the
Temple, Mordechai Dolinsky stated:

> Many political realists in this country have a
> great deal of faith in the Lord, and when the time
> comes, the actual political work [for the rebuild-
> ing of the Temple] will start. One needs a sense
> of historical perspective and faith. . . . It will be
> done.[12]

Dolinsky feels that to this point Israeli politicians have
been particularly sensitive about world opinion. This attitude may change as Israel's relationship with the United
States is adversely affected by West Bank settlement and
turbulent relations with its Palestinian Arabs. Alienated by
its only democratic ally, Israel's politicians may disregard
international censures and find a new boldness to act upon
their religious inclinations. With the political perspective of
some officials presently aligned toward the rebuilding of the
Temple, it would take only such international isolation to
move these leaders to press for the realization of their
desire.

A Great Awakening

No one can predict with certainty what date will usher in
the beginning of the messianic era; however, the recent
prediction of a definite date by Jewish rabbis exemplifies the
dramatic precedent that has now been set by Jewish prog-
nostication. Soon after the liberation of Jerusalem in 1967,
the Jewish historian Israel Eldad was quoted by *Time* magazine as saying:

> We are at tne stage where David was when he
> liberated Jerusalem. From that time until the

construction of the Temple by Solomon, only one generation passed. So it will be with us.[13]

Now that we are approaching the end of the generation of those who liberated Jerusalem, we can expect to see increased activity among date-setters as we move into days portending significant changes in the Middle East.

The point we should not miss is that these activities signal an unprecedented awakening within the hearts of Jews to seriously look and long for their expected Messiah. The fact that they are thinking about and relating these activities to rebuilding of their Temple as never before is a good indication that Messiah is preparing the Jewish people and the land of Israel for His soon visitation. It appears that it won't be long until Israel "looks upon Him whom they have pierced." All of humanity stands at the crossroads of history, Jews, and non-Jews alike. The question is, Are we ready?

Chapter 17

The Temple and the New World Order

Further global progress is now possible only through a quest for universal consensus in the movement towards a new world order.

—*Mikhail Gorbachev*
Address to United Nations,
December 7, 1988

Out of these troubled times, our fifth objective—a new world order—can emerge.... We are now in sight of a United Nations that performs as envisioned by its founders.

—*George Bush*, President of the
United States

*T*he recent war in the Persian Gulf not only displayed the amazing superiority of American military technology, but also brought to prominence an emerging idea called by President Bush "a new world order." What is this new world order and how does it affect Israel and the Temple? According to President Bush, who has been using the term in speeches since early 1990, there will be "a new world order, where the rule of law, not the law of the jungle, governs the conduct of nations."

"We will have invigorated a United Nations that contributes as its founders dreamed," declares Bush. "We will have established principles for acceptable international conduct and the means to enforce them. In short, we will have taken a major step toward a community of nations bound by a common commitment to peace and restraint."[1]

This new world order involves globalism, a one-world order of cooperation in which the international community of nations marches to the same drumbeat. In such an order there is no place for independent campaigns of conquest, such as the type of imperialistic aggression practiced by Iraq in its invasion of Kuwait. As President Bush explains, "Our success in the Gulf will shape the new world order we seek."[2]

Former Soviet president Mikhail Gorbachev appeared to be in agreement with Bush when he announced, "Further global progress is now possible only through a quest for universal consensus in the movement towards a new world order." Most of the key players on the world scene appear to be in harmony with the desire for global cooperation, which will be the fruit of a new world order. It is no wonder then, that a primary concern in the formation of this new world order is the situation in the Middle East. The importance of global cooperation was particularly highlighted at the Middle East Peace Conference in Madrid when the representative of the European Economic Community was seated at the first position on the right side of the podium, the closest position to the Soviet Union and the United States. Also present at this peace conference were U.N. observers. Before the Gulf War the United Nations was viewed as divided and inept; however, that conflict has given the organization new life. The United Nations exercised unusual control over Iraq as it stripped the country of its sovereignty. Is this a foretaste of the new world order?

Israel—the Obstacle

Despite all the efforts toward global peace, one major player is often out of step with the aims of a new world order.

The rapid breakup of the Eastern bloc and of the Soviet Union has brought a relief to the West from the Cold War. President Bush and other international leaders have tried to remove the remaining obstacles, such as the Iraqi aggression against Kuwait, so that this new world order will be able to function. The major remaining problem is the Arab-Israeli conflict. Israel is the one party that will not negotiate in order to resolve the roadblock. The Jews' desire to build their own ancient homeland and to live independently cannot be tolerated in an international community in which no flag flies but that of the new world order.

With the collapse of Communist control in the former Soviet Union and the formation of the Commonwealth of Independent States, full diplomatic relations with Israel have begun and new pressure has been exerted on Israel to join the path to peace in the Middle East. Recently Amnon Rubinstein, a member of the Knesset, voiced the new challenge to his countrymen in a "world without Communism":

> The greatest challenge which now stands before every society, including the State of Israel, is simple and acute: to what part of humanity does it want to belong? To that which combines human values with economic growth, or to the world of poor tribes fighting, each under its own flag, over hallowed borders?[3]

Is Israel to give up its land, its "hallowed borders," for peace, and join the new humanity of the new world order? At present this appears to be the call upon Israel from every nation of the world, including its foremost ally, the United States. If Israel refuses to capitulate, where will its denial take the Jewish people?

Today charges of racism are being leveled against Israel by the world community. Though the United Nations reversed its resolution equating Zionism with racism, will such charges, as others brought against the Jewish people in the past, become grounds for renewed attacks of anti-Semitic violence? It appears that we are heading in the direction indicated in Scripture: Israel (and in particular, Jerusalem) against the world.

Jerusalem Against the World

During the coming seven-year tribulation period, world history will continue to revolve around the tiny nation of Israel. The Lord said through the prophet Zechariah, "Behold, I am going to make Jerusalem a cup that causes reeling to all the peoples around; and when the siege is against Jerusalem, it will also be against Judah. And it will come about in that day that I will make Jerusalem a heavy stone for all the peoples; all who lift it will be severely injured. And all the nations of the earth will be gathered against it" (Zechariah 12:2,3). While these events will specifically be fulfilled in the tribulation, the world currently seems to be setting the stage for this grand finale.

In 1988, Israel celebrated its fortieth birthday as an Independent State. This fortieth year has been regarded by many people as particularly significant for Israel's future. In Scripture the number 40 was often indicative of oppression for Israel. So we read in the Bible that it rained 40 days during the flood, that the Israelites wandered for 40 years, and that during the cycles of the Judges, Israel "rested 40 years" (during the time of administrations of Othniel, Deborah, and Gideon) but afterward suffered 40 years of oppression. During modern Israel's first 40 years, it has been at a formal state of war with nearly all of its Arab neighbors, and has actually engaged with them in five wars. Almost immediately after the wars ended the Palestinian uprising began, and Israel's political conflict with the Arabs has since escalated to embrace the nations of the world. In the fall of 1991, Secretary of State James Baker used some of the harshest rhetoric ever with Israel as he strong-armed the nation into the Madrid Peace Conference with the Arabs. With the dismantling of the Soviet Union, it is no longer imperative to have Israel as an ally against a Soviet threat. The censure of Israel's West Bank settlements and the withholding of loan guarantees to supply the needs of new immigrants are signs that the United States is distancing itself from Israel.

Israel, with only four million people in a land about the size of America's smallest state, Rhode Island, occupies a place of extreme significance in modern history and biblical prophecy. Events in the last days will center upon Israel, Jerusalem, and the third Temple. Before we suggest a scenario for the rebuilding of the third Temple, let's consider an overview of God's plan for the last days.

The Rapture of the Church

The opening event in the last days' drama will be the moment in time when those who are believers in Jesus as their Messiah will be caught up in the air to be with Him. The rapture is necessary for several reasons. First, since God's plan for Israel was put on the back burner after the church began on the day of Pentecost, the way He will resume His unfinished work with Israel is to dramatically remove the church from the scene. Just as the beginning of the church was said in the Bible to be a surprising mystery, so the end will be as at the first, an any-moment surprise. Second, God's wrath during the tribulation is said to be for the world that has rejected Christ as their Messiah during the church age. Therefore, the church must be removed or this could not be the case since God's wrath would fall upon those members of the church who were promised relief from it. Third, the church is said to be in heaven with the Lord while the events of the tribulation transpire. Fourth, a return to a pre-Christian society would enable Israel to fulfill the calling which God had for the nation in the beginning. Jews will become the main instruments of evangelism during the tribulation and so fulfill their destiny as a nation of priests.

The Tribulation

Sometime after the rapture, the seven-year tribulation will begin as the satanically inspired Antichrist, a world political leader from Europe, signs a peace treaty with Israel. The Jewish people will accept this man as their Messiah. Already they are being readied for this event.

For several years there has been a worldwide campaign spearheaded by Chabad Hasidism to prepare Jews everywhere for the coming of Messiah. Menachem Brod, who heads this public relations campaign for the Chabad Youth Organization, explains the type of Messiah for which his organization is preparing the Jewish people:

> People who believe Moshiah will raise the dead are stupid. . . . The true Moshiah will be a great leader of the Jewish people. He will be such a great charismatic leader that the whole world will unite behind him. . . . [However] the people may only realize that Moshiah has arrived after the fact; after we see his actions.[4]

The actions that will convince the Jews that this "charismatic leader" is the Messiah will be his ability to do what has been before humanly impossible—negotiate a treaty that will temporarily resolve the Middle East crisis under a guise of world peace. As a result of this treaty, Israel will appear to have finally been reinstated in their Promised

Land with their religious institutions in operation. They will believe that their Day of Redemption, prophesied of old, has arrived, and that with the appearance of their Messiah (really the Anti-Messiah or Antichrist), the era of messianic peace has come. However, this peace will only last for a period of three-and-a-half years.

The Abomination of Desolation

At this midpoint in the seven-year tribulation, the Antichrist, who will have befriended the Jewish people and been accepted as their Messiah, will turn against them and persecute them ruthlessly. Then he will place his own image in the Holy of Holies in the rebuilt Temple. This is none other than what the prophet Daniel foretold would be "the abomination that makes desolate" (which means the desecration that defiles the Temple). Daniel's prophetic outline is diagrammed in Figure 12. His religious representative, known as the false prophet, will then demand that the Jewish people, along with the rest of the world, worship the Antichrist. The revived Judaism that will dominate Israel in that day will refuse, joined by all Jewish and Gentile tribulation believers. But the rest of the world will accept, and in recognition of their "faith," will take the infamous "mark of the Beast," 666, on their right hand or forehead.

The Persecution of Israel

The rebellion of Israel and Gentile tribulation believers against the world order of Antichrist will result in the greatest persecution of the Jewish people and believers that the world has ever seen. Perhaps one justification for the persecution of the Jews will be their rejection of their Messiah (the Antichrist) who "redeemed" them (politically) and rebuilt their third Temple. If so, it will be in character with past satanically inspired persecutions of the Jewish people for rejection of their Messiah.

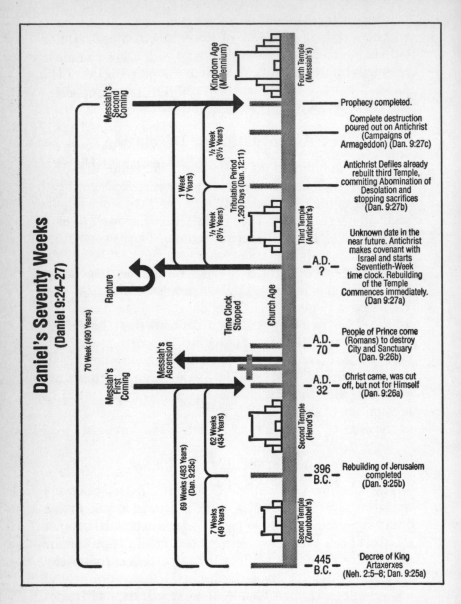

Daniel's Seventy Weeks
(Daniel 9:24–27)

Messiah's Second Coming

Rapture

Messiah's First Coming

Messiah's Ascension

70 Week (490 Years)

69 Weeks (483 Years) (Dan. 9:25c)

7 Weeks (49 Years)

62 Weeks (434 Years)

1 Week (7 Years)

½ Week (3½ Years)

½ Week (3½ Years)

Tribulation Period 1,290 Days (Dan. 12:11)

Time Clock Stopped

Church Age

Kingdom Age (Millennium)

Fourth Temple (Messiah's)

Third Temple (Antichrist's)

Second Temple (Herod's)

Second Temple (Zerubbabel's)

Prophecy completed.

Complete destruction poured out on Antichrist (Campaigns of Armageddon) (Dan. 9:27c)

Antichrist Defiles already rebuilt third Temple, commiting Abomination of Desolation and stopping sacrifices (Dan. 9:27b)

A.D. ? — Unknown date in the near future. Antichrist makes covenant with Israel and starts Seventieth-Week time clock. Rebuilding of the Temple Commences immediately. (Dan 9:27a)

A.D. 70 — People of Prince come (Romans) to destroy City and Sanctuary (Dan. 9:26b)

A.D. 32 — Christ came, was cut off, but not for Himself (Dan. 9:26a)

396 B.C. — Rebuilding of Jerusalem completed (Dan. 9:25b)

445 B.C. — Decree of King Artaxerxes (Neh. 2:5–8; Dan. 9:25a)

Figure 12: Daniel's Seventy Weeks

The coming of Israel's true Messiah, Jesus, to the earth will be a time of judgment on a world which has rejected Him as the Messiah (Revelation 19). It will also be a time in which He will punish the world for the persecution of His people, Israel. This intervention will fulfill the prophesied end-time rescue of the Jews.

Just as Joseph's leadership over Israel was rejected by his brothers when it was revealed that he would rule over the family, so Israel rejected Jesus the Messiah at His first coming. However, many years later, after Joseph had been received by the Gentiles and became the savior of his family, he revealed his identity in secret, and they wept upon each other. In the same way the Jewish people will receive Jesus as their Messiah when He causes them to "look upon Him whom they have pierced; and they will mourn for Him, as one mourns for an only son" (Zechariah 12:10).

The Rescue by Messiah

The Antichrist's persecution of Israel will be so intense and widespread that only the return of the true Messiah will save a remnant of the Jewish people and tribulation believers from this final holocaust. Matthew 24:22 says, "Unless those days had been cut short, no life would have been saved; but for the sake of the elect [the Jews] those days shall be cut short."

Jesus taught that His return to the earth would include delivering Israel from the fury of the Gentile nations of the world in what is known as the battle of Armageddon. At this time, Jesus declared that He would "send forth His angels with a great trumpet and they [would] gather together His elect [the Jews] from the four winds, from one end of the sky to the other" (Matthew 24:31).

Shortly before the Messiah's coming, the Jews will experience a true spiritual revival, a "rebirth" (Ezekiel 37:14). Realizing that Jesus is their promised Messiah, they will turn to Him (Zechariah 12:10). Their return to Him prompts His return to them, and He comes to defend and establish His people (Zechariah 12:4-14). Perhaps it will be Israel's realization that they have followed a false Messiah (the Antichrist) that will help open their eyes to the fact that Jesus of Nazareth really is the one spoken of by their own prophet, Zechariah.

The Millennial Kingdom

Upon His return to earth, Christ will set up His kingdom in Jerusalem (Isaiah 2:3,4; Zechariah 14:9) with Israel as the head of the nations of the world (Isaiah 2:2; Zechariah 8:21-23). He will rule the entire earth for a thousand years. In Jewish theology this is called the Days of Messiah, a golden age of spiritual life predicted by the prophets in which Israel fulfills its divine purpose as the "servant of the Lord" by being a light to the nations. In Christian theology this thousand-year period of the reign of Christ is called the millennium (see Revelation 20:1-6).

A Suggested Prophetic Outline
for Contemporary Events

Today, religious and secular Jews are looking for the appearance of a man who will be able to negotiate a peace in the Middle East and make possible the rebuilding of the Temple. Some Israelis have said that whoever gets the Temple rebuilt will be the Messiah. Many are also predicting another war, which they interpret as the battle of Gog and Magog, out of which will result the peaceful and secure future promised to Israel. What will soon occur in the Middle East that will enable these events to happen? We would now like to offer a possible real-life scenario, interpreting the current world situation in the light of the prophetic model we have presented.

The Next Event

The next event on God's prophetic calendar is the rapture of His church. The rapture will result in great chaos, and God's current restraint of evil will cease. Then the Antichrist will be revealed (2 Thessalonians 2:4,5). The Antichrist will be in charge of a revived Roman Empire (the present European Common Market) which will seek to impose the new world order. This attempt at one-world government will revive the same spirit which once united mankind in rebellion against God at the tower of Babel (Genesis 10-11).

The War on Israel:
The Russian-Arab Alliance

Ezekiel 38-39 tell of an end-time invasion led by a people "from the remote parts of the north with all its troops" (38:6). The Bible says that this invasion of Israel will be led by a ruler named "Gog of the land of Magog" (38:2). Many scholars have shown that the descendants of Gog include the modern people known as Russians (especially from those provinces within the former southern Soviet Union). Gog will lead the invasion, but will have an alliance with him consisting primarily of an Arab coalition. Such a coalition is conceivable at the present time as Russia has become the heir of the 8,040 known nuclear warheads in the wake of the dismantling of the former Soviet Union, and Israel's Arab neighbors are hastening to acquire their own nuclear arsenals. Shlomo Avineri, former director-general of the Israeli Foreign Ministry, and now professor of political science at the Hebrew University, has observed that this rise of the Russian republic to a position of dominance calls for new thinking and an alignment of Israel since "Russia itself is vulnerable from its own eastern Moslem regions."[5] Such a Muslim threat is becoming a serious concern not only to

Russia but to all in the Middle East. Israel Defense Forces spokesman Ehud Barak recently warned of Syria's chemical threat to Israel and of Saddam Hussein's ability to make Iraq a nuclear power again.[6] One newspaper quoted a college professor as saying, "Don't doubt that if [Saddam Hussein] had a nuclear weapon he'd drop it on Israel. Don't doubt that Israel has nuclear weapons and would retaliate. It would be Armageddon in the Middle East."[7]

Barak's warning was reinforced in January 1992 by Maj. Gen. Amnon Shahak. While stating that there was no immediate nuclear threat in the Middle East today, he acknowledged that the disintegration of the Soviet Union has advanced the day of Arab nuclear capability. He also noted that there was a significant rise in the use of firearms and explosives by Palestinian terrorists in Israel, with 1991 recording the highest number of Israeli soldiers and civilians killed since the inception of the Intafada.[8] With the new rule in Algeria by Islamic fundamentalists, increased conflict with Israel seems certain.[9] The possible scale of this conflict is suggested by the building of a weapon-producing nuclear reactor by China and Korea in the Algerian Sahara. The danger of war in the Middle East is rapidly escalating, despite the current attempts at negotiation, and will eventually erupt in an invasion of Israel by a Russian-Arab league.

Ezekiel tells us that this invasion will take place "in the latter years" of Israel's history after the Jews have been regathered from the nations to which they have been scattered. However, the expected victory by the invaders will meet with resounding defeat from the hand of God as He protects the people of Israel. Thus, in keeping with the divine goal of manifesting the knowledge of God's sovereign lordship to the world, it is written, "I shall magnify Myself, sanctify Myself, and make Myself known in the sight of many nations; and they will know that I am the Lord" (Ezekiel 38:23).

Israel's Victory

There are differing views among scholars concerning when this battle will take place in relation to God's plan for the last days. It is most likely that this battle will occur during a relatively short time span just after the rapture, but before the start of the tribulation, which will gain European sympathy for Israel. Israel's great losses, particularly under a Russian-Arab league, will be compensated with complete sovereignty over the Temple Mount and permission to rebuild the third Temple. Likely, control of the Temple Mount for Israel will be part of a settlement gained in negotiations between Israel and the European leader (the Antichrist), which when signed will start the seven-year tribulation period (Daniel 9:24-27).

This scenario solves the problem of how to remove the Arabs and their Dome of the Rock from the Mount, since Israel will receive it as a result of war. Israel will also have permission from the West to rebuild. Since the Temple has only to be built by the midpoint of the seven-year period, Israel will have had plenty of time, especially in light of preparations now being made. This time the Jewish people will not delay or return the Temple Mount to the Arabs as Moshe Dayan did in 1967.

We are not saying this is the only way events could transpire; we are offering what we think is the best possible scenario in light of biblical prophecy. The Temple could be built before the rapture of the church, but we are inclined to think that it will be started after that event.

The traumatic events of the battle will cause a religious revival in Israel and be interpreted by all Jewish sects as the imminently expected Day of Redemption and the beginning of the messianic era of peace. The Antichrist, who will have led the negotiation of the peace treaty with the Arabs, and provided for the rebuilding of the Temple, will be heralded as the Messiah.

This kind of situation would fit the war/peace climate required to break the present stalemate over the Temple Mount, and remove the Arab presence (including the Muslim religious buildings) for the rebuilding of the Temple. It would also provide three-and-a-half years, sufficient time given modern technology, to build the Temple. This third Temple would then be on the scene for its role in God's last days' drama. The more prepared Israel becomes to rebuild the Temple, the closer the day dawns when believers in Jesus the Messiah will be taken home in the rapture of Christ's church.

Chapter 18

Wisdom for Our Times

> There are growing numbers of Christians, many organized into small churches and larger groups, who see the construction of a third Temple as the cornerstone of their beliefs. Though there is a clear divergence in religious belief between these Christians and Jews who work toward the rebuilding of the Temple, they willingly and enthusiastically cooperate.
>
> —*Jerusalem Post*, September 30, 1983

This book has been primarily written for Christians to inform them of what is currently being said and done by Israelis concerning the building of a third Jewish Temple. Many Christians have heard sensationalized reports concerning Temple rebuilding, and some have been involved in the efforts to rebuild the Temple, but our purpose has not been to stir up Christian activism on behalf of Temple rebuilding organizations. Some of the groups associated with Temple research that once discouraged Christian involvement, publicity, and contributions are now both welcoming and encouraging it. But *should* Christians be involved in the Jewish efforts to rebuild?

Qualified Support

Whenever the media reports on the preparations being

made to rebuild the Temple, it invariably links Christians with Jews. For example, one of the first articles to appear on the subject in an international magazine said, "Temple restoration is also a fixation for literal-minded Protestants, who deem a new Temple the precondition for Christ's Second Coming."[1]

In like manner, when the Religious News Service sent out a story to local papers about the rebuilding of the Temple in 1989, it stated: "The project . . . has united ultra-Orthodox Jews with fundamentalist Protestant Christians, both of whom share the dream of a third Jewish temple."[2]

In 1988, Wesley Pippert, former senior UPI Middle East correspondent, reported: "Some Christian fundamentalists in the United States have raised money to support a project to rebuild the temple. This is the central purpose of a group called 'The Jerusalem Temple Foundation,' which is incorporated in the United States. Its theme is 'Build Thy Temple Speedily.'"[3]

Many Christians who refer to themselves as "Christian Zionists" support without reservation any act taken by Temple activists. For example, an American branch of the Jerusalem Temple Mount Foundation, under the name of Committee of Concerned Evangelicals for Freedom of Worship on the Temple Mount, purchased a full-page advertisement in the *Jerusalem Post* condemning the Israeli government for the March 10, 1983 arrest of a group of Temple activists who had sought to penetrate the Temple Mount through the Huldah Gate passageway in the area known as Solomon's Stables.

Members of this group are rumored to have paid the legal fees of those arrested and the next year funded a group known as the Lifta Band, who tried to blow up the Al Aqsa Mosque and the Dome of the Rock. While such actions represent only a radical Christian fringe group, their uncritical attitude toward sponsoring civil disobedience and violating Israeli law (such as that protecting the freedom of worship and places of worship in Israel), is alarming.

General support for Israel among Christians is sometimes intertwined with specific support for Temple movement organizations. A recent case of Christian involvement was reported by the *Jerusalem Post* in September 1991.[4] During a trip to Israel by 100 Christian leaders to prepare for the March 1992 Jerusalem Prayer Breakfast, a group of evangelical Christians came apart independently from the group to dedicate a house in the Moslem Quarter. Bought with Christian funds, this house was given to the Ateret Cohanim Yeshiva, the very organization that is involved in settlements to establish a Jewish presence near the Temple Mount and in training priests for the future Temple. In recent years other Christian groups have also openly demonstrated their unqualified support for Temple rebuilding during annual "Feast of Tabernacle Pilgrimages" to Jerusalem, offering spiritual and financial support to leaders of the Temple movement.

We remind our Christian brethren that while we believe the third Temple will be rebuilt in accordance with the Christian Scriptures, the very groups that are preparing for this event are in opposition to the Christian gospel and to the believing Messianic (Jewish-Christian) community in Israel. The nature of Christian support for Israel as part of God's prophetic program must be qualified by the same Word that has announced that program to Christians (Romans 11:28).

Beware the Christian Cults

Evangelical and fundamentalist Christians have been joined in their support for Temple rebuilding by the Christian cults. I (Randall) was given a video tape by Gershon Salomon, the head of the Temple Mount Faithful, which was made by a group to which he had recently been invited to speak. The tape was produced by the Jehovah Witnesses, and was a propaganda film seeking to prove how Jehovah Witness founder Charles Taze Russell was influential in the Zionist cause and the eventual establishment of the State of Israel. Salomon also addressed a branch of the House of Yahweh, a cult whose members met him at the airport dressed in full religious garb.

One of the most actively supportive cult groups in the United States is the Benai Noach ("Children of Noah"). Coming from mostly evangelical roots, these "Christian" congregations have defined themselves as Gentiles who have turned to the God of Israel and observe the seven Noahic commandments. In the past several years they have sought to gain acceptance from the Chief Rabbis in Israel, once bringing some of these rabbis to America, and in the summer of 1991 sending a contingent to Israel.

One of the Israeli men who accompanied several of these rabbis to America has said that the group has made significant advances toward Judaism, but are not yet acceptable because many still cannot give up Jesus. One of the Benai Noach representatives, Dr. James Tabor of the Religious Studies Department of the University of North Carolina, has become a liaison for the Temple Institute with the Christian community. Openly critical of the motive for evangelical Christian support for Temple rebuilding, he states:

> It is interesting at this time in history that both Christians and Jews have an interest in the building of the Temple. What is ironic about this is that these are rather strange bedfellows in that many Christians only want to see the Temple built to fulfill a prophetic scenario that Hal Lindsey has popularized in the Western world. They do not share with the Jews the spiritual aspects of the Temple. The way I see it is that if you want the Temple built only to fulfill a prophetic scenario,

you haven't read your scriptures very carefully . . .
the Temple makes up a very important part of the
biblical faith.[5]

But is Temple worship (and possible sacrificial service) a
"very important part of the biblical faith?" It is certain that
Christians will not offer sacrifice in the tribulation Temple,
and it is not even clear that Christians will share with Jewish
believers in the *spiritual* aspects of the millennial Temple.
Tabor raises his objection largely because evangelical Christians do not subscribe to Jewish legal observance. The Benai
Noach share more in common with Judaism than Christianity, and therefore adopt a critical stance toward evangelicals who seek to separate support for God's prophetic
program from accommodation to Jewish practice. If evangelical groups are accused of supporting Temple rebuilding
for their own prophetic agenda, may we not suspect that
Benai Noach and other Christian cults also have self-serving
motives, aligning themselves with such organizations to
gain recognition of their religious status?

The accusation leveled against prophetic teachers such as
Hal Lindsey might better be charged to the Jehovah Witnesses, who intend to *replace* the Jews on a restored earth in
the millennium. Certainly their interest in a Jewish rebuilding of the Temple is only to realize their own supposed
prophetic destiny—with themselves as the sole rulers of the
earth!

There is real danger in the association of undiscerning
Christians with Christian cults in the mutual advancement
of the Temple movement. Israeli and Jewish leaders do not
differentiate between Christians and Christian cults, and
may well give preference to the latter who appear more
sympathetic with Jewish faith (for example, anti-Trinitarianism and rejection of the deity of Jesus) and practice (for
example, following Kosher and Sabbath observances). In
light of this, Christians who want to show support for

Jewish Temple-related organizations should exercise caution when receiving so-called "Christian" spokesmen representing these groups.

Pray and Provoke

Because Christians have historically used the destruction of the Temple to prove that Christianity is superior to Judaism, many Christians have held that a rebuilt Temple would contradict the purpose of God in replacing Israel with the church. This theological position led to the Temple Mount being turned into a dung heap during the Byzantine period, and has led many Christians since to deny a unique prophetic destiny for Israel.

Christians who seek to distance themselves from this unscriptural position must support what they perceive is the fulfillment, whether in part or in whole, of prophetic events contained within the Old and New Testaments. This includes support for a rebuilding of the Temple in Jerusalem. At the same time Christians must remain distinctively Christian, and not become entangled in political or religious ideology that would cause a compromise of the Christian position.

In an emotional moment, Gershon Salomon, one of the most active leaders in the Temple movement, remarked that he has felt such acceptance from Christians toward Israel and the Temple's rebuilding that he sees very little difference between the two. Alas, a great difference *does* exist. Most religious Jewish leaders recognize this and have traditionally kept their relations with Christian supporters quite reserved. In fact, all of the Israeli rabbis interviewed for this book made it clear that Jews and Christians can only go down the path so far together; after that the Christian mandate to see Jews come to faith in Jesus as the Jewish Messiah separates Jews and Christians completely.

Christians look for the fulfillment of God's prophetic purposes, which includes the Jews embracing Christ, while

Jews look for the coming messianic era in which they see Christians embracing Judaism. That an observant Jew of the stature of Gershon Salomon is seemingly able to dismiss this distinction[6] may indicate that Temple support is beginning to outweigh, for both Jews and Christians, the theological agreement once thought necessary for mutual work in religious endeavors. Christian support for Israel and the rebuilding of the Temple must not eclipse the Christian responsibility to "provoke [Israel] to jealousy" (Romans 11:14) and to "pray . . . for their salvation" (Romans 10:1).

Proclaiming the Messiahship of Jesus

While making a statement of friendship to Jews and Israelis, a statement of faith must not be avoided. The first-century message delivered by the Jewish disciple Peter to the people at Pentecost remains the same today: "And now, brethren, I know that you acted in ignorance, just as your rulers did also. But the things which God announced beforehand by the mouth of all the prophets, that His Christ [Messiah] should suffer, He has thus fulfilled. Repent therefore and return, that your sins may be wiped away, in order that times of refreshing may come from the presence of the Lord; and that He may send Jesus, the Christ [Messiah] appointed for you [Israel], whom heaven must receive until the period of restoration of all things about which God spoke by the mouth of His holy prophets from ancient time" (Acts 3:17-21).

The terms "times of refreshing" and "period of the restoration of all things" relate specifically to the Jewish hope for *Yemot ha-Mashiach* ("times of the Messiah"), the messianic millennium that follows the coming of Messiah. Since the prerequisite to the Messiah's coming is Israel's repentance,[7] and this "change of mind" is toward Jesus as the Messiah, Christians must not compromise their message, but "let all the house of Israel know for certain that God has made Him both Lord and Christ [Messiah]—this Jesus whom you crucified" (Acts 2:36).[8]

Further, while Christians must show support for Israel in its irrevocable calling as "beloved of God" (Romans 11:28), and pray for the "peace of Jerusalem" (Psalm 122:6; Romans 10:1) which will come in accordance with the prophetic word (Zechariah 14:11; Isaiah 2:4; Romans 11:26,27), they must continue to pray for the salvation of Arabs and Muslims and Palestinians as well, and support humanitarian causes for their aid that does not conflict with Scripture. After all, many of the Arab nations also are included in future blessing in biblical prophecy (Isaiah 19:18-25).

The Suitability
of Contributions

Christians in the past have contributed significantly to Zionist efforts to establish and develop the State of Israel, and in recent times to Jewish causes (such as Hadassah Hospital) and toward relief work among new immigrants (such as the Soviet and Ethiopian Jews). Such financial support is commendable, and should be encouraged not only as a worthy humanitarian gesture, but especially as a testimony of Christian solidarity with God's program for Israel.

The rebuilding of the third Temple, however, is strictly a Jewish endeavor and, while Christians may support its preparation and eventual establishment as part of the certain fulfillment of Scripture, it is their primary responsibility to support the "household of the faith" (Galatians 6:10). Since we believe that the third Temple will *not* be the millennial Temple—the "house of prayer for all people" (Isaiah 56:7)—but the tribulation Temple, Christians should take no part in the spiritual aspects of the Temple promoted by the Temple movement. It is likewise questionable whether Christian individuals or groups should financially contribute to Temple rebuilding efforts in view of the nature and destiny of the third Temple.

This being said, we do believe that we should pray for and encourage the rebuilding of the Temple as part of the future purpose and plan of God. This is in harmony with Christian prayers for the coming kingdom (Matthew 6:10; Luke 11:2; 2 Peter 3:12), which of necessity includes the tribulation period and the tribulation Temple. Indeed, the present preparations for the rebuilding of the Temple encourage us as Christians that the Day of Redemption for Israel is about to dawn, and that our own salvation, and the coming of the Lord, is nearer than when we first believed (Romans 13:11).

Standards for Christians

If as Christians we understand the current Temple fervor as a "sign" that these are indeed the last days before the end of the age and the return of the Messiah, this belief should be translated into practical behavior. We need a standard by which to measure Christian conduct in view of Christ's coming.

In Titus 2:12-14 we find three such standards for living in light of the Lord's return.

1. *Our actions in Christian responsibility are in direct proportion to our attitude toward Christ's return.* Titus 2:12,13 instructs us "to deny ungodliness and worldly desires and to live sensibly, righteously and godly in the present age, looking for the blessed hope and the appearing of the glory of our great God and Savior Christ Jesus." Notice the words "live" in verse 12 and "looking" in verse 13. These words reveal the relationship between prophetic anticipation and practical action in the Christian life: We are to "live . . . *looking!*" Our fervent expectation of Messiah's coming should produce a faithful execution of all Messiah's commands.

2. *As the world grows more ungodly, we as Christians must grow more godly.* The end of this age is clearly that of increasing apostasy. However, as this age is readied for judgment, the resulting fear of losing personal affluence and security will tempt Christians to sink their roots deeper into this world's system to maintain their positions. Jesus reminds us that during the tribulation period, "because lawlessness is increased, most people's love will grow cold" (Matthew 24:12). As the system unravels, the tendency will be for people to focus on themselves in an attempt to secure their own place and possessions. They will exclude other people as competitors and threats.

Such thinking is unbiblical in light of Titus 2:12,13. As believers we are to *deny* all temptations to hold on to this world and to *live* with a desire for the world that is coming with the Lord's return. This self-denial wedded to genuine Christian deeds demonstrates to a watching world the phenomenon of true faith, a faith that cannot be explained without reference to Messiah and His supernatural work. As we move closer to the Lord's coming, this witness will likewise grow, for as the "outlook" for this world decreases, the Christian's "uplook" will increase.

3. *As we wait patiently for Messiah at the conclusion of this age, we must work productively for Messiah during the course of this age.* Titus 2:14 says: "Who gave Himself for us, that He might redeem us from every lawless deed and purify for Himself a people for His own possession, zealous for good deeds." The conduct that is motivated by Messiah's coming is not an idle waiting for a rescue from this world, but an industrious working for the redemption of this world.

At the ascension of Jesus, angels who appeared to announce His eventual return asked the watching crowd, "Why do you stand looking into the sky?" (Acts 1:11). Here was a gentle admonishment for Christians to get their heads out of the clouds and to be about the Lord's business until He comes.

Prophecy is not meant to be a pastime, but to purify and provoke Christians to active witness. If the rebuilding of the Temple is near, the end of the age is near, and with it an end of the opportunities to work for the Savior. Let us who long for the Day of Redemption labor in the time that remains to bring Messiah's redemption to a dying world.

Conclusion

*M*any churches hold a tract of land upon which they expect to build a new facility at a later date. Usually a sign announces this fact with the words "Future site of . . ." Though the actual building may be delayed because these churches lack the necessary finances to build, or face zoning problems, or similar obstacles, these congregations confidently assert that they are ready to rebuild! In like manner Israel now holds a tract of land called the Temple Mount. The present preparations for the third Temple described in this book are equivalent to the sign announcing their future plans to rebuild on that site. Great difficulties may prevent the actual rebuilding today; however, this does not restrain Jews from confidently reporting that they are now *ready* to rebuild.

As you watch the news in the days ahead, expect to see conditions arise that will remove the difficulties to rebuilding one by one. It seems that only yesterday we witnessed the impossible collapse of the Berlin Wall and the demise of Communist control of the Soviet Union. Perhaps tomorrow we will wake to see impossible changes in the Middle East that will make possible the erection of the Temple. And as we Christians see the Jews ready to rebuild, we ourselves should look up, for our redemption draweth nigh!

> *Come Almighty to deliver,*
> *Let us all Thy life receive;*
> *Suddenly return and never,*
> *Never more Thy Temples leave.*

Charles Wesley, 1747

A
Temple
Chronology

Major Events Connected
with the Temple Mount

Before the Temple

c. 2000 B.C.   Abraham and Isaac offer a ram on
               Mount Moriah (Genesis 22:1-19).

c. 1400 B.C.   Moses describes service to be per-
               formed at the future central sanctuary
               (Temple); Deuteronomy 12:5-21;
               15:19,20.

996 B.C.   David makes Jerusalem his capital and
               moves the Ark to a site adjacent to
               Temple Mount (2 Samuel 5:6-12; 6:1-17;
               1 Chronicles 11:4-9; 15:1–16:38).

c. 993 B.C.   David desires to build the Temple;
               Solomon designated as builder
               (2 Samuel 7:1-13; 1 Chronicles 17:1-14).

c. 990 B.C.   David purchases threshing floor of
               Araunah the Jebusite as site for the
               first Temple (2 Samuel 24:18-25;
               1 Chronicles 21:18-26).

c. 960 B.C.   David makes material preparations for
               the first Temple and charges Solomon
               to build it (1 Chronicles 22).

The First Temple

950 B.C.   Solomon builds the first Temple
            (1 Kings 5-8).

910 B.C.   Temple treasures taken by Egyptian
            pharoah Shishak (1 Kings 14:25-28;
            2 Chronicles 12:1-11).

835 B.C.   Jehoash (Joash), king of Judah, and
            Jehoiada effect repairs to damaged
            parts of Temple (2 Kings 12:5-14;
            2 Chronicles 24:12-14).

826 B.C.   Jehoash (Joash), king of Israel attacks
            Judah, breaks down the walls of Jerusa-
            lem, and plunders the Temple,
            removing the Temple treasury to Sa-
            maria (2 Kings 14:13,14).

720 B.C.   Ahaz closes Temple, empties Temple
            treasury, breaks up Temple furnishings
            and vessels to pay tribute to the As-
            syrian king Tiglath-Pileser, and defiles
            Temple with a pagan Syrian altar
            (2 Kings 16:8-18; 2 Chron-
            icles 28:21,24).

715 B.C.   Hezekiah opens Temple doors, cleanses
            Temple, returns Temple vessels, re-
            stores ritual and Passover, and builds
            storehouses for Temple contributions
            (2 Chronicles 29:3-19; 30:1-27;
            31:11,12).

711 B.C.   Hezekiah is forced to give Temple trea-
            suries and strip gold off Temple doors
            to pay tribute to the Assyrian king Sen-
            nacherib (2 Kings 18:15,16).

622 B.C.   Josiah repairs Temple; Hilkiah the
             priest discovers book of the law hidden
             in Temple that brings spiritual revival
             (2 Kings 22:3–23:3; 2 Chronicles 34:8–
             35:19).

605 B.C.   Babylonian king Nebuchadnezzar pil-
             lages the Temple, taking articles and
             depositing them in the Babylonian
             temple (2 Chronicles 36:7).

597 B.C.   King Nebuchadnezzar returns and fur-
             ther plunders the treasures of the
             Temple (2 Kings 24:13; 2 Chron-
             icles 36:7).

586 B.C.   King Nebuchadnezzar invades Jerusa-
             lem a third time and destroys the
             Temple.

The Second Temple

573 B.C.   Ezekiel in Babylonian exile has vision
             of millennial Temple (Ezekiel 40–48).

539 B.C.   Babylonian king Belshazzar desecrates
             Temple vessels at a pagan feast (Daniel
             5:1-4).

538 B.C.   Daniel in exile in Babylon receives vi-
             sion of the defiling of the future third
             (tribulation) Temple by Antichrist's
             placement of an image of himself in the
             Holy Place (Daniel 9:24-27); Daniel
             also receives vision of the defiling of
             the future second Temple (Zerub-
             babel's) by Antiochus Ephiphanes'
             placement of a statue of Zeus in the
             Holy Place (Daniel 11:31).

515 B.C.   Zerubbabel, descendant of David, rebuilds first Temple (hence, a "second" Temple) and Persian king Darius returns Temple vessels taken by Nebuchadnezzar (Ezra 6:3-15).

332 B.C.   Alexander the Great conquers Jerusalem, but spares Temple.

169-167 B.C.   Selucid ruler Antiochus IV (Epiphanes) pillages Temple; soldiers of Antiochus defile Temple; sacrifices stopped and pagan rituals instituted in Temple.

164 B.C.   Temple cleansed and rededicated by Judas Maccabee (Hanukkah) after successful revolt against Selucids (1 Maccabees 4).

67 B.C.   Arisobulus besieges Jerusalem and substitutes pig for sheep in attempt to end Temple sacrifices (which were stopped on the seventeenth of Tammuz). The result of this fraticidal war between Aristobulus and his brother Hyracanus led to the intervention of Rome and the end of Jewish independence.

63 B.C.   Roman emperor Pompey conquers Jerusalem and enters Holy of Holies.

20 B.C.   Herod the Great begins work to rebuild and extend Temple (second Temple); work continues on Temple until c. A.D. 64 (Matthew 24:1; Mark 13:1; Luke 21:5; John 2:20).

c. 4 B.C.   Jesus dedicated in Herod's Temple; recognized there as Messiah by Anna the prophetess and Simeon (Luke 2:22-38).

c. 8 A.D.   Jesus makes pilgrimage to Temple at Passover and remains there three days to talk with Jewish teachers (Luke 2:41-51).

c. 26 A.D.   Jesus at the commencement of His ministry is tempted by Satan by being taken to the pinnacle of the Temple (Matthew 4:5; Luke 4:9) and drives moneychangers from outer courts of Temple (John 2:13-17).

c. 29 A.D.   Jesus comes to Temple courts at Hanukkah (John 10:22,23); enters Temple Mount through Eastern Gate (Matthew 21:1-11; Luke 19:37-44); casts out moneychangers a second time (Matthew 21:12,13; Luke 19:45,46); teaches and heals daily in Temple (Matthew 21:14,37; Luke 19:47); predicts destruction of second Temple (Matthew 23:37,38; 24:2; Mark 13:2; Luke 21:6, 20-24) and defiling of third (tribulation) Temple (Matthew 24:15; Mark 13:14); crucified on mountains of Moriah, adjacent to Temple Mount (Matthew 27:33); Holy of Holies is torn (Matthew 27:51); Peter preaches in court of the Gentiles in Temple at Pentecost (Acts 2); Peter heals lame man at the Nicanor Gate leading from Court of Gentiles to Court of Women in Temple (Acts 3:1-11).

40 A.D.   Roman emperor Caligula fails in his attempt to defile Temple by erecting a statue of himself.

56 A.D.   Paul goes to Temple with men completing Nazerite vow and is wrongly accused of defiling the Temple by taking a Gentile there (Acts 21:26-28)

70 A.D.   Roman general Titus destroys second (Herodian) Temple.

After the Temple

132-135 A.D.   Roman emperor Hadrian reneges on promise to rebuild Temple for Jews and sparks Bar Kokhba rebellion; possible rebuilding of second Temple by Bar Kokhba; Hadrian retakes Jerusalem, destroys Bar Kokhba Temple, and desecrates Temple Mount by erecting pagan temples.

135 A.D.   Tinneius (Turnus) Rufus, Roman governor of Judea plows up the site of the Temple Mount on the Ninth of Av (Tisha B'Av) to signify the utter destruction of the Jewish city and signal the birth of Jerusalem as the Roman colony Aelia Capitolina.

326 A.D.   Byzantine emperor Constantine builds Church of Holy Sepulchre to overlook Temple ruins as example of Christianity as new spiritual center.

363 A.D.   Pagan emperor Julian (the Apostate) allows Jews to attempt rebuilding of Temple to counter Byzantine Christianity; effort fails.

443 A.D.   Hopes that Emperess Eudocia would permit a rebuilding of Temple prompts letter calling for Jewish return and messianic revival.

614 A.D.   Jewish support of Persian conquest of Jerusalem leads to favored status of Jews and hopes for rebuilding Temple.

637 A.D.   Muslims conquer Jerusalem and Caliph
            Omar discovers Temple Mount and site
            of Temple (Rock) covered in centuries
            of dung and debris.

691 A.D.   Muslim caliph Abd al-Malik completes
            Dome of the Rock on Temple Mount.

715 A.D.   Al Aqsa Mosque is completed over
            Jewish/Christian remains at southern
            end of Temple Mount.

1099–1118 A.D. Crusaders take Jerusalem and transform
            Muslim Dome of the Rock into Chris-
            tian church and Al Aqsa Mosque into
            headquarters of Knights Templar.

1187 A.D.   Saladin recaptures Jerusalem for Mus-
            lims.

1537 A.D.   Sultan Suleiman the Magnificent embel-
            lishes Dome of the Rock and builds
            perimeter walls around Old City.

1854 A.D.   Crimean War (Turkey, France, En-
            gland, Russia) fought to resolve
            jurisdiction of Jerusalem's holy places.

1855 A.D.   Duke of Brabant becomes first non-
            Muslim to tour Dome of the Rock since
            1187 expulsion of the Crusaders.

1867-70 A.D. Palestine Exploration Fund conducts
            first underground exploration of the
            Temple Mount.

1873-74 A.D. Discovery of Temple inscription forbid-
            ding Gentile entrance.

1891 A.D.   Report on clearance of Eastern Gate by
            Ottoman authorities.

1917-1948 A.D.   Jerusalem is conquered by British; continual struggles between Arabs and Jews over access and control of Western Wall of Temple Mount; Israeli independence granted May 14, 1948, but no access to Western Wall or Temple Mount; both Dome of the Rock and Al Aqsa Mosque damaged by bombs in War of Independence.

1951 A.D.   King Abdullah of Transjordan is assassinated in the Temple area; succeeded by Hussein.

1958-1964 A.D.   Egypt, Jordan, and Saudi Arabia underwrite extensive repairs of the Dome of the Rock.

1961-1967 A.D.   British archaeologist Dame Kathleen Kenyon conducts excavation at southwest corner of Temple Mount.

Modern Events

June 7, 1967   Israel during Six-Day War liberates Temple Mount on third day of fighting; hopes of rebuilding Temple revive, but are dampened when Defense Minister Moshe Dayan orders Israeli flag removed from atop the Dome of the Rock.

June 8, 1967   Sometime shortly after capture of Temple Mount, Rabbi Shlomo Goren and team carefully measure the dimensions of the Temple compound based on available archaeological remains compared with measurements recorded in Josephus, Mishnah tractates Middot and Shekalim, Maimonides, and Sa'adia Gaon.

June 17, 1967	Moshe Dayan meets with leaders of Supreme Moslem Council in Al Aqsa Mosque and returns Temple Mount, especially site of the Temple, to sovereign control of the Wakf as a gesture of peace; agrees that Jews can have access to Mount, but cannot conduct prayers or religious activities.
June 28, 1967	Israeli government officals meet with Muslim and Christian authorities and place administration of Jerusalem's holy sites under control of respective religious leaders.
August 1-8, 1967	Israeli police are asked to regularly enforce public order at Temple Mount and other religious sites in Jerusalem after reports of improper visitor conduct; Ministry of Religious Affairs committee given oversight of holy places.
August 15, 1967	Rabbi Shlomo Goren leads group, including army chaplains, to pray on Temple Mount. Based on his measurements taken on the Mount in June, he contends that he knows where the Holy of Holies is located and that rabbinic ban against entering the Temple Mount is no longer applicable.
August 22, 1967	Chief Rabbinate seeks to enforce religious ban on entrance to Temple Mount by posting signs at ramp leading to Temple compound.
February 29, 1968	Israeli archaeologists Benjamin Mazar and Meir Ben-Dov begin extensive excavations south and southwest of the Temple Mount 100 years after first British excavation. Significant finds relating to the Temple include the

original entrance to the Temple Mount through the Huldah Gates and Temple priests' tunnels.

July 15, 1968   Moslem Court of Appeals rejects $100 million offer by American Masonic Temple Order to build their "Temple of Solomon" on the Mount.

December 19, 1968   Prayers are offered on Temple Mount at Hanukkah by nationalistic Jewish group.

April 15, 1969   Temple Mount Faithful file legal action against Police Minister Shlomo Hillel to allow Jewish prayer services on Temple Mount; Israeli State Attorney upholds police enforcement of government prohibition of prayer on basis of national security and political concerns.

August 23, 1969   Australian Christian cultist, Denis Michael Rohan, sets fire to the Al Aqsa Mosque; Arab demonstrators, and later Muslim legal representatives, accuse Israel of deliberately setting the blaze in order to rebuild the Temple.

August 27, 1969   Wakf closes Temple Mount to non-Muslims for two months.

September 9, 1970   Israeli High Court decides not to adjudicate in Jewish prayer on Temple Mount case, allows government restriction to remain.

March 11, 1971   Gershon Salomon of Temple Mount Faithful leads group of students to pray on Temple Mount; results in minor disruption.

August 8, 1973   Knesset member Binyamin Halevi and Rabbi Louis Rabinowitz pray on Temple Mount in protest of government ban.

January 30, 1976   Lower Court (Magistrate) acquittal of Betar youths arrested for holding prayer service on Mount affects ruling on whether or not Jews are permitted to pray on Temple Mount; Police Minister Shlomo Hillel rejects court ruling.

February 9-23, 1976   Arab East Jerusalem schools protest the Lower Court ruling resulting in over 100 arrests; Arab shops close in strike, riots in West Bank; court ruling is appealed on February 11.

March 4, 1976   UN Secretary Kurt Waldheim pledges to introduce Islamic contentions against Israel's interference with Muslim holy places.

March 8, 1976   Gershon Salomon and Rabbi Rabinowitz attempt to lead group to Temple Mount but are turned back by police.

March 11, 1976   Muslim councils in Ramallah, El Bireh, and Nablus protest police action against Arabs who demonstrated against the Lower Court ruling permitting Jewish prayers on the Mount.

March 17, 1976   Lower Court ruling is overturned by District Court but upholds the historical and legal right of Jews to pray on the Temple Mount if the Ministry of Religious Affairs can regulate such activity to maintain public order.

August 14, 1977   Gershon Salomon leads 30 members of *El Har Hashem* ("To the Temple Mount of God") in an attempt to conduct a Tisha B'Av service on the Temple Mount, but is turned away by police.

March 25, 1979	Rumors that Meir Kahane and Yeshiva students would hold prayer service on Temple Mount provokes a general strike among West Bank Arabs; 2,000 Arab youths brandishing stones and staves riot at Temple Mount and are dispersed by Israeli police.
August 3, 1979	Several Jewish nationalist groups are prevented from holding prayer service on Temple Mount.
August 6, 1980	Israeli High Court considers appeal to revoke ban on prayer on Temple Mount based on recent law guaranteeing freedom of access to religious sites.
August 10, 1980	Ultraright activist group *Gush Emunim* ("Bloc of the Faithful"), with 300 supporters attempt to force entrance to the Temple Mount and are dispersed by police.
August 28-30, 1981	Chief Rabbi Shlomo Goren and workers of the Ministry of Religious Affairs trace a leaking cistern to discover one of the original entrances to the Temple (Warren's Gate); Goren closes dig; Yigael Yadin condemns the dig as quasi-archaeological; Arabs seal the cistern, thus preventing entrance to the tunnel.
September 2-4, 1981	Yeshivah students, under orders from Rabbi Getz, break down Arab wall-seal; Getz claims that the treasures of the Temple, including the Ark of the Covenant are hidden within a lower chamber accessed by the tunnel; Arabs clash with Jewish students and police intervene; gate entrance is sealed due to

rioting Wakf protests (September 3); Supreme Moslem Council orders general strike of all Arab schools and shops in East Jerusalem (September 4) to protest excavation under Temple Mount.

September 10, 1981   Wakf seals tunnel from Muslim side to prevent future Israeli entrance.

September 15, 1981   Gershom Salomon and the Temple Mount Faithful attempt another prayer service on the Mount, but are again stopped by police.

April 11, 1982   Alan Goodman, an American immigrant in the Israeli army, opens fire on the Temple Mount "to liberate the spot holy to the Jews." Though ruled mentally unstable by the Israeli courts and later sentenced to life imprisonment, the incident set off week-long Arab riots in Jerusalem, the West Bank, and Gaza, and drew international criticism against Israel.

April 25, 1982   Kach Party member, Yoel Learner, attempts to sabotage a mosque on the Temple Mount. He is arrested and later sentenced to two-and-one-half years in prison.

December 9, 1982   Geula Cohen, a member of Israel's Knesset, raises the charge that Muslim Arabs have caches of ammunition sequestered on the Temple Mount.

March 10, 1983   Rabbi Israel Ariel and a group of more than 40 followers, planning to pray on the Temple Mount (via the Solomon's Stables, adjacent to the Al Aqsa

Mosque), after four youths connected with Yamit Yeshiva are found breaking into the area. Weapons and diagrams of the Temple Mount are recovered in a police search, and numerous arrests are made.

April 1983 The *Jerusalem Post* prints an "Open Letter to the Prime Minister and the People of Israel," drafted by an "evangelical Christian" group, condemning the arrests of the Temple Mount activists of March 10.

May 11, 1983 Israel's High Court reverses a police refusal to grant a license for prayer at the entrance to the Temple Mount to members of the Temple Mount Faithful.

May 22, 1983 Physicist Lambert Dolphin of SRI International in California and his team attempt to use scientific equipment within the Western Wall tunnel area to clarify the Temple's location. Israeli police stop the project as a result of pressure from Muslim officials.

September 17, 1983 Rabbi Shlomo Goren and Moshe Levy conduct a prayer service within the Western Wall tunnel beneath the Temple Mount.

January 27, 1984 Temple activists are arrested for attempting to "attack" the Temple Mount.

January 3, 1985 It is revealed that a secret airlift of 3,000 Ethiopian Jews to Israel was successfully accomplished the previous month. Temple activist groups contend it is a sign of the nearness of the Messiah and the rebuilding of the Temple.

January 8, 1986 — Several members of the Knesset led by Geula Cohen seek to hold a prayer service in the Temple area. The incident provokes a riot and an altercation with Arabs on the Mount.

February, 1989 — The Temple Institute opens a visitor's center for the exhibition of their Temple artifacts on the second floor of a building in the Jewish Quarter.

October 16, 1989 — Gershom Salomon and Yehoshua Cohen, dressed in the priestly garments, and members of the Temple Mount Faithful attempt to lay a cornerstone for the third Temple at the entrance to the Temple Mount during the Feast of Tabernacles. A protest at an Arab school earlier in the day led police to rescind previous permission to conduct the ceremony.

October 16, 1989 — *Time* magazine runs Richard Ostling's article "Time for a New Temple?" describing the Temple controversy and current preparations for rebuilding.

October, 1989 — Israel's Ministry of Religious Affairs sponsors the First Conference on Temple Research at Shlomo (the Great Synagogue).

October 8, 1990 — Preannounced plans by the Temple Mount Faithful to repeat their previous year's ceremony and attempt to lay a cornerstone for the third Temple provoke a riot on the Temple Mount. At the Western Wall where more than 20,000 Jews are assembled for Feast of Tabernacle services, 3,000 Muslim Palestinian Arabs pelt the crowd with stones from above. The result of the melee with Israeli police left 17 Arabs dead and brought condemnation from the United Nations, including the United States. Later, it is discovered that this was an attempt to draw attention away from Saddam Hussein's invasion of Kuwait and justify later aggression against Israel in an attempt to unite the Arab League with Iraq against a common foe.

July-August, 1991

Gershom Salomon and members of the Temple Mount Faithful come to the United States for an extended lecture tour, including a television appearance on Pat Robertson's "700 Club" and numerous other radio, television, and public meetings.

September 24, 1991

The Temple Mount Faithful conduct their third attempt to lay a cornerstone and to pray on the Temple Mount. Met by opposition from harredim who feared a repetition of the 1990 Arab riot and official restraint, the attempt to lay the cornerstone was aborted.

October 1991

El Ad, an Israeli housing association, announced that it had purchased over 50 percent of the property in the Jerusalem village of Silwan (the ancient City of David) and Jewish settlers, including several right-wing Knesset members, occupied more than five buildings in the area. This area includes the Pool of Siloam, where the Temple water-drawing ceremony was conducted.

October 31, 1991   At the Middle East Peace Conference in
                    Madrid, Spain, Syrian Foreign Minister
                    Farouk Al-Shara accuses Israel of at-
                    tempting to blow up the Al Aqsa
                    Mosque and proclaims that there will
                    be no free access to the religious sites
                    on the Temple Mount unless Israel
                    returns all of East Jerusalem to the
                    Arabs.

February 10, 1992   Members of the Ateret Cohanim set-
                    tling in the Arab Silwan Village, the
                    ancient site of King David's city,
                    announce plans to build more than 200
                    homes for Jews. The purpose is to
                    establish a Jewish presence near the
                    Temple Mount for the day when the
                    Temple can be rebuilt.

May 8, 1992   Rabbi Dr. Marvin Antelman of the
                    Weizmann Institute announces that a
                    substance uncovered in excavations at
                    Qumran by Vendyl Jones is a sample of
                    ancient Temple incense. Chaim Rich-
                    man of the Temple Institute argued that
                    the fact that it was not found in a con-
                    tainer, but on the floor of the cave,
                    proved that it had been discarded as de-
                    fective. Jones believes that with this
                    discovery he will soon find other trea-
                    sures of the Temple, including the Ark
                    of the Covenant.

March 1992   The March-April issue of the *Biblical
                    Archaeology Review* prints chief archi-
                    tect of Temple Mount excavations Leen
                    Ritmeyer's article establishing the exact
                    location of the Temple. This is the first
                    published archaeological research on
                    the location of the Temple verifying the
                    traditional site in the last 60 years.

Glossary

Abomination of Desolation (Hebrew, *hashiqutz meshomem* "the abomination that makes desolate"): The expression used to describe the act of setting up an idolatrous image in the Holy Place, thus defiling or "making desolate" the Temple, and ending the offering of all sacrifices. This was done in the past by Antiochus Epiphanes (Daniel 11:31), whose act reflects the future defilement by the Antichrist (Daniel 9:27). Both Daniel and Jesus indicated that this future act would signal the start of the great tribulation (Daniel 12:11; Matthew 24:15; Mark 13:14).

'Acharit ha-yamim ("end of the days"): The Hebrew term used to designate that period of the end time described by the biblical prophets. It includes *Yom YHWH* ("the day of the Lord") in which God's judgment falls upon Israel's adversaries, as well as *Yemot ha-Mashiach* ("the days of Messiah"), the period preceding the judgment. It is followed by *'olam ha-ba* ("the world to come"), the eschatological future world.

Aelia Capitolina: The Roman name of the city of Jerusalem beginning with the reign of Emperor Publius Aelius Hadrianus, or Hadrian (A.D. 117-138). The city, now with the status of a Roman colony, was rebuilt according to Roman city planning, and contained a statue of Hadrian erected on the site of the Jewish Temple.

Aliyah (Hebrew, "to go up, ascend"): The Jewish expression used for the act of returning or making immigration to the land of Israel.

Amidah: The main prayer recited at all services; also known as the *Shemoneh Esreh* ("The Eighteen" benedictions).

Amillennialism (Latin, "no millennium"): The theological view that Christ and His saints will *not* reign for a thousand years in connection with His final return.

Anastasis (Greek, "rising, resurrection"): The name of the rotunda of the Church of the Holy Sepulchre; it marked the site of the cave in which Jesus was buried and from which He arose.

Anti-Semitism: The term applied to the hostile attitude of non-Jews toward Jews, individually and collectively. The consequences of this viewpoint have ranged from restrictive laws against Jews and the social isolation of Jewish groups to pogroms and attempted genocide in the Nazi holocaust. Christian anti-Semitism has historically resulted from an adoption of *replacement theology*.

Apocalyptic Literature (Greek, *apocalypsis*—"unveiling"): Prophetic writings concerning the end of the world and/or God's final judgment, both in and outside the canon of Scripture. In particular it has reference to that body of Jewish prophetic writing that developed between the sixth century B.C. and the first century A.D.

Aqsa (Arabic, "the farther"): Term used for the farther mosque in the Koran (Surah 17). It probably originally indicated a mosque located in the northern corner of Mecca, but the tradition was later moved to Jerusalem, hence the Al Aqsa Mosque.

Ashkenazi (Yiddish: pl. *Ashkenazim*): Those Jews and their descendants who came from Germany or parts of Europe as contrasted with *Sephardi[m]* (Jews from Spain or Portugal).

Atara L'yoshna (Hebrew, "crown to its original [form]"): The name of an activist organization in the Temple movement which seeks to restore Jewish life to its former state, i.e., biblical Judaism with complete Jewish sovereignty and a rebuilt Temple. It is involved primarily with Jewish settlement in the Moslem Quarter.

Ateret Cohanim (Hebrew, "crown of the priests"): The name of an activist organization in the Temple movement that maintains a yeshiva for the training of priests for future Temple service. It is affiliated with Atara L'yoshna in settlement activities.

Azarah (Hebrew, "enclosure"): The term for the sacred precinct of the Jerusalem Temple or its outer court.

Balfour Declaration: The letter authored by British statesman Lord Arthur James Balfour on November 2, 1917, that proclaimed British recognition of the claim of the Jewish people to their historical homeland (Palestine) and favored its establishment.

Basilica (Latin, "portico, colonnaded building"): A long rectangular building with two rows of pillars or columns dividing it into a central nave and two aisles. Common to Roman administrative architecture, its design influenced both that of the royal portico on the Temple Mount and that of synagogues and churches of the period.

Byzantine: The period of Roman Christian rule in Jerusalem (A.D. 313-638) during which Christianity was made the official religion of the Roman Empire, and the center of imperial power was moved to Byzantium. The Byzantine period is divided into the early period (313-491), the great Christian architectural period, and the late period (491-638), which saw a temporary conquest by the Persians, and ended with the Islamic invasion under Caliph Omar Ibn el-Khattab.

Caliph (Arabic, "succeed"): The title of an official successor to Mohammed. Wherever a caliph prayed a mosque had to be built by his followers.

Chabad: The initials of the three Hebrew words *chokmah* ("wisdom"), *binah* ("understanding"), *da'at* ("knowledge"), which are used as the name of the Hasidic movement founded in White Russia by Shneur Zalman of Lyady. Chabad Lubavitch is a specific organization of Chabad, headquartered in Brookyn, New York, whose spiritual leader is Rabbi Menachem M. Schneerson.

Cohen (Hebrew, "priest," pl. *cohanim*): An Israelite descendant of the family of Aaron, which was designated as a priestly line (Exodus 28:1,41). Because this family belonged to the tribe of Levi, they are referred to as the Levitical priesthood. Their functions were ritualistic in nature and revolved around service in the Temple during Temple times.

Devir (Hebrew, "sanctuary," though derived from word meaning "the back part of a room"): The third division of the Temple, namely, the innermost chamber, the Holy of Holies, where the Ark of the Covenant was housed.

Diaspora (Greek, "dispersion"): The term used to describe the area of Jewish settlement outside the land of Israel. Jews today are said to be either "in the Land" (Israel), or "in the Diaspora" (everywhere else).

Dispensationalism: The view of biblical history that maintains one plan of salvation in which God reveals himself to man and deals with man in different ways in each successive period of their relationship or economy (dispensation) of time.

Eastern Gate: The gate of second Temple times that served as the eastern entrance into the Temple. The original name of this gate during that period was the Shushan Gate, which may exist today beneath the present sealed double gate called the Golden Gate or just south of it. The term "golden" was mistakenly applied to this gate because the reference in Acts 3:2 to another inner Temple gate, used the Greek word *horaia* ("beautiful"), which was misunderstood as *aurea* ("golden"). It is thought that this Eastern Gate might also be the Double Gate mentioned in the Copper Scroll, in which are hidden the red heifer urn and a scroll describing the red heifer ceremony.

Eschatology (Greek, "study of last things"): The study of things relating to the end of the world, the final judgment, and the life and world to come.

Eretz Israel (Hebrew, "Land of Israel"): The Hebrew term used by Jews to designate the biblical Promised Land, the historical homeland of the Jewish people.

Even Shetiyyah (Hebrew, "Foundation Stone"): The stone, which according to ancient Jewish sources existed within the Holy of Holies in the Temple and upon which the Ark of the Covenant rested in first Temple times. According to tradition this stone is identified with the rock inside the Muslim Dome of the Rock.

Falasha: Ethiopian Jews who claim descent from Israel through Menelik I, an offspring of a supposed laision between King Solomon and the Queen of Sheba. While their Jewish identity is still disputed by some, the State of Israel has recognized them as "black Jews" and has aided in their immigration to Israel in two operations, Operation Moses and Operation Solomon.

Gihon (Hebrew, "gush" or "burst forth"): The spring on the eastern slope of the Ophel that served as the chief water source for Jerusalem in the days during the biblical period.

Gush Emunim (Hebrew, "Bloc of the Faithful"): The movement to foster Jewish settlements in the West Bank in order to continue the national stream of Zionism. Activist by definition, members of this movement have been involved with attempting to blow up the Dome of the Rock and anti-Arab attacks and demonstrations.

Halakah (Hebrew, "walk," pl. *halakot*): The official or lawful way according to which a Jew ought to conduct his life. The Jewish *Halakah* contains various moral laws and ritual prescriptions, based on the Bible, that embrace all of the teachings of Judaism. It also refers to those parts of the Talmud which deal with legal matters.

Hanukkah (Hebrew, "inauguration"): A post-Mosaic festival, often called the Festival of Lights. It is an eight-day celebration commemorating the victory of Judas Maccabee over the Syrian king Antiochus Epiphanes that climaxed with the rededication of the Temple. In the New Testament it is called the Feast of Dedication (John 10:22).

Haram (Arabic, "enclosure"): The present platform upon which the Dome of the Rock is built and which is thought to approximate the original Herodian Temple platform. The full title used by the Muslims is *Haram es-Sharif* ("The Noble Enclosure").

Hasidism (Hebrew, "righteous, pious"): A religious movement founded by Israel ben Eliezer Ba'al Shem Tov in the first half of the eighteenth century. Originally it was a religious revivalist movement of popular mysticism that began in West Germany in the Middle Ages.

Hasmoneans: The family name of the Maccabean dynasty that ruled in Judea from 141-37 B.C. and especially associated with Mattathias and his five sons, who successsfully revolted against Syrian rule, culminating with the rededication of the Temple on December 25, 165 B.C.

Hechal (Hebrew, orginally from Sumerian *e-gal* "great house" and Assyrian *ekallu*, "palace, temple"): The second division of the Temple, namely, the main room or sanctuary.

Holocaust: Literally meaning "a burnt offering or sacrifice," this is the term applied to the attempted genocide of European Jewry in the ovens of the Nazi death camps during the Second World War. More than six million men, women, and children were systematically exterminated in this sacrifice of Jewish lives.

Hosanna (Hebrew, "save us, please"): An entreaty or prayer taken from Psalm 118:25.

Hoshana Rabba (Hebrew, "Great Hoshana"): The time during the Feast of Tabernacles in which the *hosanna* was recited, once daily for six days and seven times on the seventh (last) day. It was at this time that the water-drawing ceremony was performed.

Islam: A monotheistic religion whose only deity is *'Allah* ("God"), and whose prophet is Mohammed. It venerates certain Old Testament figures and traditions and accepts some traditions about Jesus, who is considered a lesser prophet. Its primary religious text is the Qu'ran, a set of divine revelations made to Mohammed.

Jihad (Arabic, "holy war"): The term used in Muslim religious law for the holy war waged against all infidels until the end of time.

Josephus, Flavius: The Roman name of a Jewish historian and military leader known in Hebrew as *Yosef ben Mattiyahu* (Mattathias). His many historical writings, apparently intended for a Roman audience, constitute the best extrabiblical source for the study of Jewish life during the period of the second Temple.

Lapis Perturbis (Latin, "Pierced Stone"): The term used by early Christian pilgrims to describe the Rock on the Temple Mount in Jerusalem, which the Jews annointed with oil, believing it the foundation stone of the Temple. It was so called because its surface was intruded by a number of holes (many small and one large) that gave it the appearence of being "pierced."

Likud (Hebrew, "union, alignment"): The right-wing bloc or political party in the Israeli system of representation. The present representative of Likud is Prime Minister Yitzhaq Shamir.

Kabbalah: The Jewish mystical tradition; *Kabbalist:* A Jewish mystic or student of the Kabbalah.

Kach (Hebrew, "thus"): The name of the Israeli party created by the late Rabbi Meir Kahane, advocating the deportation of all Arabs from the land of Israel after due compensation. Members of the Kach party have attempted to take over the Temple Mount in the past.

Knesset (Hebrew from Aramaic, "assembly"): The parliament of the State of Israel.

Kotel (Hebrew, "wall," from *kathal* "to join together, make into blocks"): The Western or Wailing Wall, popularly called *Ha-Kotel*, "The Wall." This section of wall after the destruction of the second Temple was the only remnant of the Temple (a retaining wall) accessible to the Jewish people. It first became accessible to Jews for worship in modern times on June 7, 1967.

Mea Shearim (Hebrew, "Gate of the Hundred"): The name of the settlement area in Jerusalem inhabited by a separatist community of ultra-Orthodox Jews.

Menorah (Hebrew, "lamp"; pl. *menorot*): A term used for the seven-branched oil lamp, or candelabra, used both in the Tabernacle and in the Temple.

Messiah (Hebrew, "annointed [one]"): Equivalent to the Greek term *Christos* from which is derived the English "Christ." In traditional Orthodox Jewish definition this is a human political-military deliverer who is sent by God to usher in the age of redemption for Israel promised by the biblical prophets. In historic orthodox Christian definition the Jewish concept is further developed by God the Son being sent to fulfill this role. Thus, Christians accept a divine Messiah whom they identify with the Jewish man Jesus of Nazareth.

Messianic Jews: Orthodox Jews who believe the messianic times are imminent. Most Messianic Jews in Israel are actively preparing for the Messiah's coming through the adoption of more biblical lifestyles and in research and activism toward rebuilding the Temple.

Middot (Hebrew, "measurements"): A tractate of the Jewish Mishnah that deals specifically with the measurements of the Temple.

Midrash (Hebrew, "interpretation"): A written collection of rabbinical interpretation of the Bible compiled by the *Soferim* ("scribes") in the fourth century A.D. The *midrashic* method of interpreting Scripture was employed to clarify legal points or to bring out lessons by the use of stories.

Mishnah (Hebrew, "learning, repetition"): The earliest written collection of Jewish oral law (i.e., Jewish religious and legal teachings handed down orally). It was compiled about A.D. 200 by Rabbi Judah ha-Nasi. It comprises the first part of the Talmud.

Mitzvah (Hebrew, "commandment"): The term for a religious and moral obligation, whether one of the 613 biblical commandments or any other traditional ordinance, observance, teaching, or statute.

Mohammed (from Arabic *hmd*, "to praise," also *Muhammed*): The founder and prophet of Islam who was born in A.D. 570 and died at Medina in A.D. 632.

Moshiach: The Ashkenazi accented Hebrew spelling of Messiah, literally "anointed one."

Moslem (see Muslim).

Muslim (from Arabic *'aslama*, "to submit, convert to Islam"): A believer or follower of Islam.

'Ophel (Hebrew, "hill, mound"): The southeastern spur north of the City of David that is the oldest known part of Jerusalem. It is the section of Jebusite territory captured by King David and was the site of the Tabernacle during his days.

Orthodox (Greek, "straight"): Those holding to religious views that have been traditionally accepted and taught. Orthodox Jews are those accepting the *Tanakh* (Old Testament) as divine revelation, and the *Talmud* as divine direction for the interpretation of the *Tanakh*, and are observant (practioners) of Jewish law. There are many different divisions within Orthodox Judaism today.

Palestine: A pejorative term for the country west of the Jordan River, first coined by the Greeks and Romans after the word *Philistine*, the enemies of Israel who inhabited the Mediterranean coastal plain. The Bible refers to the same territory as *Canaan*, after its pre-Israelite inhabitants, though Jews have always called it *Eretz Yisrael* ("Land of Israel").

Parah ("cow"): Term used for the red heifer that was sacrificed on the Mount of Olives and whose ashes were used in the Temple purification ceremony. It is also the name of a tractate in the Mishnah and of a related book in the Qu'ran dealing with the red heifer.

Pogrom (Russian, "riot, devastation"): A word used since 1881 to describe all violent and anti-Semitic attacks on Jewish communities.

Postmillennialism (Latin, "after millennium"): The theological view that Christ and/or His saints will reign on the earth *before* His final return.

Premillennialism (Latin, "before millennium"): The theological view that Christ and His saints will reign on the earth for a thousand years *after* His final return.

Pseudepigrapha (Greek, "false writings"): A collection of non-canonical works of mystical Jewish-Hellenistic origin, generally composed after the sixth century B.C. These writings were influenced by Persian cosmology (view of the universe) and are highly apocalyptic in nature.

Quds (Arabic, "holy"): Arabic term used for both Jerusalem and the Temple Mount area (the sanctuary), as in *Al Quds*, "the Holy City."

Qur'an (also *Koran*, Arabic, "recitation"): The most holy book in Islam, believed by Muslims to be 114 chapters dictated or recited by the archangel Gabriel to the prophet Mohammed at Mecca and Medina.

Rabbi (Hebrew, "master"): Derived from the Hebrew verb *rabab* "to be great," the term is an honorable title for an ordained Jewish teacher of the law or a leader of a Jewish community. Roughly equivalent to Christian "pastor" or "bishop."

Radvaz: Hebrew abbreviation for the name of Rabbi. The vowels are only supplied for assistance in pronouncing the abbreviation.

Replacement Theology: A theological view among both Catholics and Protestants that the Jews have been rejected and replaced by "the true Israel," the church. Those who espouse this view disavow any distinct ethnic future for the Jewish people in connection with the biblical covenants, believing that their only spiritual destiny is either to perish or become a part of the Christian church.

Rosh Hashanah (Hebrew, "head of the year"): The Jewish festival of the civil New Year celebrated on the first and second days of the month *Tishri* (equivalent to September/October on the Julian calendar).

Sakhra (Arabic, "rock"): Arabic term for the sacred rock within the Moslem dome on the Temple Mount, hence: *Qubbet es-Sakhra*, "Dome of the Rock."

Sanhedrin: The assembly of ordained Jewish scholars which func-
tioned both as a supreme court and as a legislature in Israel before
A.D. 70. With the destruction of the Temple and the end of Jewish
independence, the Sanhedrin ceased to function.

Sephardi (Hebrew: "Spanish"; pl. *Sephardim*): Those Jews and their
descendants who came from Spain and Portugal as contrasted
with *Ashkenazi[m]* (Jews from Germany or parts of Europe).

Shekalim (Hebrew, "shekels" [tax]): The fourth tractate in the division of the Mishnah, which deals with the annual half-shekel
(monetary amount) tax collected for the maintenance of the
Temple. It serves as a valuable primary source of information on
the Temple during the second Temple period.

Shekinah (Hebrew, "dwelling, resting"): A term used for the Divine
Presence of God that was manifested by "dwelling" with the
Israelites, first in the Tabernacle and later in the first Temple.

Shiloah (Hebrew, "the one sent"): Hebrew term for the Greek (New
Testament) *Siloam*, the pool located at the end of the water tunnel
of King Hezekiah which collected water from the Gihon Spring.
During the ancient *Hoshana Rabba* water was drawn from this
source for the libation poured on the Altar in the Temple.

Six-Day War: The war that occurred June 5-10, 1967, when Israel
reacted to Arab threats and blockade by defeating the Egyptian,
Jordanian, and Syrian forces. The Sinai Peninsula, the West
Bank, and the Golan Heights fell to Israel in this conflict. The
Sinai was returned to Egypt in 1979 as a condition of the Camp
David Peace Treaty. For Jerusalem the war was a three-day con-
flict, June 5-7, that resulted in the liberation of East Jerusalem and
the Temple Mount from Jordan.

Sukkot (Hebrew, "booths"): The Hebrew term for the one-week
Feast of Tabernacles; the last of the three pilgrim festivals that
begins on the fifteenth of Tishri (approximately September-
October on the Julian calendar). *Sukkot* were the booths or tabernacles that the Israelites dwelt in during their time of wandering in
the wilderness (Leviticus 23:42).

Surah (Arabic, "chapter"): A division of the Muslim holy book, the
Qur'an.

Synagogue (Greek, "gathering together"): An institution that was developed by Jews in the Diaspora, after the destruction of the first Temple, for worship and study of the Bible.

Tallit: The four-cornered garment, with fringes or tassels on each corner, worn by observant male Jews in accordance with the biblical command. The *Tallit Gadol* ("Great Tallit") is the prayer shawl, and the *Tallit Katan* ("Small Tallit") is the garment worn under the outer clothes.

Talmud (Hebrew, "teaching"): The entire corpus of Jewish oral law including the Mishnah together with a written compendium of discussions and commentary on the Mishnah called *Gemara*. Its teachings and rulings span a period between Ezra in the Old Testament (c. 450 B.C.) and the middle of the Roman period (c. 550 A.D.). Because it includes rulings made by generations of scholars and jurists in many academies in both Palestine and Babylon it exists in two versions: the *Jerusalem* (discussions in the Jerusalem academies) and the *Babylonian* (discussions in the Babylonian academies).

Tanakh: Term used for the Jewish Bible made up of the Hebrew initials for the words *Torah* ("Law"), *Neveim* ("Prophets"), *Ketubim* ("Writings"), the three divisions of the Old Testament.

Tel (Hebrew, "mound, hill"; Arabic *tell*): A technical term in archaeology referring to an artificial elevation of earth which consists of ancient occupational layers buried within.

Temenos: A sacred enclosure intended for formal royal cult practices. It comprised three parts: a podium for a temple structure, a square open area where the main sacrificial altar was located, and side chambers used for ritual, minor sacrifice, and administration. In our usage it is essentially a synonym for the Arabic *haram*.

Tisha B'Av (Hebrew, "Ninth of Av"): A fast day commemorating the destruction of the first and second Temples that occurs on the ninth day of Av, the first month of the Jewish religious year, approximating July-August on the Julian (Christian) calendar.

Topography (Greek, "study of place"): The description of a particular place, including its physical structures and elevation.

Torah (Hebrew, "law"): Used either of the first five books of the Old Testament, the Pentateuch, or of the entire body of traditional Jewish teaching and literature.

Tribulation: That period of time, according to the premillennial interpretation of prophecy, which follows the rapture of the church. Lasting for seven years, the first three-and-one-half years are a time of peace which witness the rise of Antichrist and the rebuilding of the Jewish Temple. The last three-and-one-half years are a time of divine judgment known in the Old Testament as "the time of Jacob's trouble." At the end of this period, climaxed by the battle of Armageddon, Christ returns to rescue Israel and set up His millennial kingdom.

Tzitzit (Hebrew, "fringes"): The tassels attached to the four corners of the *Tallit*, the traditional prayer shawl or garment, with a blue thread included in each tassel, to remind Jews to keep God's commandments (Numbers 15:37-39).

Ulam (Hebrew, from Akkadian *ellamu*, "front [porch]"): The first division of the Temple, namely, the forecourt or main entrance porch.

Wakf (also *Waqf*): The Supreme Moslem Council, which maintains religious jurisdiction over Islamic holy places, and in particular the Temple Mount.

Yeshiva (Hebrew, "sitting"): A Jewish traditional academy, or school, devoted primarily to the study of the Talmud and rabbinic literature; roughly equivalent to a Christian seminary.

Yom Kippur (Hebrew, "Day of Atonement"): The most solemn day of the Jewish year, celebrated on the ninth day of Tishri (September-October on the Julian calendar). Considered the day of judgment and reckoning, it is a time when Jews individually and as a nation, are cleansed of sin and granted atonement. It was on this day alone that the high priest was permitted to enter the Holy of Holies in the Temple.

Zion (Hebrew disputed): Originally the hill area north of Jerusalem, the *'Ophel*, where the Tabernacle resided. Through poetic usage it became a synonym for the city of Jerusalem and Israel itself, and spiritually as the eschatological ideal of God's chosen place on earth.

Zionism: The movement to establish an autonomous Jewish national home in the land of Israel, so called because of the historical desire of Jews to return to Zion. Zionism as a political movement of world Jewry (The World Zionist Organization) began with the first Zionist Congress (1897) convened by Theodor Herzl. With the establishment of the State of Israel, political aspirations were attained, and the organization now assists in development of the State and as a bridge between Israel and Jewish communities in the Diaspora.

Notes

Chapter 1—Tomorrow the Temple
1. As reported by Kenneth L. Woodward, "The Final Days Are Here Again," *Newsweek*, March 18, 1991, p. 55.
2. For more information on this incident see the video *The Real Story: The Attack on the Western Wall Plaza* (IRTF Film Associates—Mattus Heritage Institute Productions, 1991).
3. This contention is supported by the investigation of the International Relations Task Force.
4. Stobe Talbott, "How Israel Is Like Iraq," *Time*, October 29, 1990, p. 50.
5. Finding of the Zamir commission reported by David Bar-Illan in "Temple Mount Provocation," *Jerusalem Post (International Edition)*, August 10, 1991, p. 7.
6. Anne Marie Oliver and Paul Steinberg, "In the Forest of Symbols," *Jerusalem Post (Weekend Supplement)*, June 21, 1991, p. 22.
7. *Newsweek*, July 22, 1991, p. 48.
8. Irving Greenberg, "Some Thoughts on the Meaning of the Restoration of Israel and Jerusalem for Days of Commemoration," in *Jerusalem: City of the Ages*, Alice L. Eckardt, ed. (New York: American Academic Association for Peace in the Middle East, 1987), p. 281.
9. As cited by John Phillips, *Exploring the World of the Jew*, revised ed. (Chicago: Moody Press, 1988), p. 189.

Chapter 2—Christian Controversy
1. Irenaeus, *Against Heresies:* Book V, Chapter 30, Paragraph 4.
2. David Chilton, *Paradise Restored: An Eschatology of Dominion* (Tyler: Reconstruction Press, 1985):224.
3. Robert L. Wilken, "Jerusalem, Emperor Julian, and Christian Polemics" in *Jerusalem: City of the Ages*, Alice L. Eckardt, ed. (Lanham, Maryland: University Press of America, 1987), p. 242.
4. Ibid., 242-43.
5. Ibid., 243.
6. Ibid.
7. *Letter to the Community of the Jews*, No. 51, 396-398 in W.C. Wright, *The Works of the Emperor Julian* (3 Vols. 1913-1923).
8. *Letter to a Priest*, 295c.
9. Jerusalem Talmud, Ta'anim 65a; Hor. 47c; Yoma 21b.
10. Jerusalem Talmud, Ma'as. Shabbat 56a.
11. Philip C. Hammond, "New Light on the Nabateans," *Biblical Archaeology Review* (March/April, 1981), p. 23.
12. Wilken, "Jerusalem," p. 248.
13. Reverend Warburton, *Julian. Or a Discourse Concerning the Earthquake and Fiery Eruption, Which Defeated That Emperor's Attempt to Rebuild the Temple in Jerusalem* (London: J. and P. Knapton, 1750), pp. 156-59.
14. Sozomen, *Church History* V, 22, cited by F.E. Peters in *Jerusalem*, p. 147.
15. Cited in John Wilkinson, *Egeria's Travels in the Holy Land*, p. 167.
16. Lawrence D. Sporty, "The Location of the Holy House of Herod's Temple: Evidence from the Post-Destruction Period," *Biblical Archaeologist* 54:1 (March, 1991), p. 32.

17. Cited by G. Le Strange, *Palestine Under the Moslems*. Reprint of the 1890 edition (Beirut: Khayats, 1965), p. 139.
18. "I consider the prophecy relative to the destruction of the Jewish nation, if there were nothing else to support Christianity, as absolutely irresistible." Mr. Erskine's speech at the trial of Williams for publishing Paine's *Age of Reason*, cited in Holford, *The Destruction of Jerusalem*, title page.

Chapter 3—One House for One God

1. Exodus 25:22; 2 Samuel 6:2; 1 Kings 8:6-11.
2. Josephus, *Wars* 7, 8,7.
3. Dio Cassius, *Roman History*, 6, 65.
4. G. Ernest Wright, "The Significance of the Temple in the Ancient Near East," *Biblical Archaeologist* 7:3 (September, 1944), p. 42.
5. This thought in part was drawn from an excellent article by G. Ernest Wright, "The Significance of the Temple in the Ancient Near East (Part III: The Temple in Palestine-Syria)," *Biblical Archaeologist* 7:4 (December, 1944), p. 71.
6. Psalm 132:1-5; 2 Chronicles 12:13; 28:19; 2 Samuel 7:1,2.
7. 1 Kings 11:32,36; 14:21.
8. Jonathan Z. Smith, *To Take Place: Toward Theory in Ritual* (University of Chicago Press, 1987), pp. 83, 84.
9. Cf., Psalms 2:6; 125:1; Isaiah 2:2-4; Joel 3:9-17; Zechariah 14.
10. 2 Samuel 7:4-5; 1 Chronicles 14:4.
11. Genesis 13:14-17; 17:7,8.
12. See also 1 Chronicles 21.
13. Shaye J.D. Cohen, *From the Maccabees to the Mishna*, Library of Early Christianity, Wayne A. Meeks, ed. (Philadelphia: Westminster Press, 1987), p. 106.
14. Berakot 321.
15. Pirke Avot (Ethics of the Fathers) 1:2.
16. *Jerusalem to Jabneh: The Period of the Mishna and its Literature* (Ramat-Aviv: Everyman's University, 1980), Unit 1.3, p. 15.
17. Mishna Avodah Zarah 8b and Sanhedrin 14b (the ruling is based on Deuteronomy 17:8).

Chapter 4—The Temple Destroyed—The Temple Rebuilt

1. Our calculation is based on the long or royal cubit which was about 52.5 cm. or 20.9 in.
2. The Mishnah states that this rock had been at the site since the time of the early prophets (i.e., David and Solomon), and that it was three finger breadths higher than the ground (Yoma 5:2).
3. Radbaz, Responsa, 2 (1882), nos. 639, 691.
4. This is based upon the theory that the rock under the present-day Muslim Dome of the Rock is not the *Even Shetiyyah*. If the rock seen today was the foundation for the Altar, then the Holy of Holies would have stood to the west of it (see chapter 12 for a more indepth study of the relationship between the Rock, the Altar, and the Holy of Holies).
5. Josephus, *Antiquities of the Jews*, 20, 1:2.
6. Josephus, *Contra Apion* 2:23, Sec. 193.
7. Tacitus, *Historiae* 5, 9:1.
8. R.C. Sproul, *The Holiness of God* (video series), Ligonier Ministries, Orlando, Florida: Tape 1.
9. Talmud, Succah 51:b.
10. Michael Avi-Yonah and Menahem Stern, "Jerusalem: History of the Second Temple Period," *Encyclopedia Judaica* 9:1379.

Chapter 5—The Temple in Transition
1. F.E. Peters, *Jerusalem* (New Jersey: Princeton University Press, 1985), p. 122.
2. Jacob Neusner, *A History of the Mishnaic Law of Holy Things: Studies in Late Antiquity*, Vol. 30, Part VI (Leiden: E.J. Brill, 1980), p. 283.
3. *Sibylline Oracles* 5:46-50.
4. Genesis Rabbah 64:10.
5. R.M. Smallwood, *The Jews Under Roman Rule: From Pompey to Diocletian* (Leiden: E.J. Brill, 1976), pp. 434-436.
6. Michael Avi-Yonah, *The Jews of Palestine* (Oxford: Basil Blackwell, 1976), p. 13.
7. The nineteenth-century Lithuanian Rabbi, Samuel Shtrashun (R'shash) made this assertion in his Talmudic commentary on Pesachim 741. It is supposed his source was the Roman historian of the period, Dio Cassius.
8. Leibel Reznick, *The Holy Temple Revisited* (New Jersey: Jason Aronson Inc., 1990), p. 156.
9. *Paschal Chronicle* P.G. 92, 613; cf. also, Benjamin Mazar, *The Mountain of the Lord* (New York: Doubleday & Co., 1975), p. 236.
10. Dio Cassius, *Roman History*, 69:12.
11. Jerome, *Commentary on Isaiah 2:9*.
12. John Wilkinson, "Christian Pilgrims in Jerusalem During the Byzantine Period," *Palestinian Exploration Quarterly* 108 (1976): 77, emphasis added.
13. Meir Ben-Dov, *In the Shadow of the Temple* (Harper & Row, 1982), p. 219.
14. From a chronicle composed by the Syrian monk Bar-Yoma, published in *Revue de l'Orient Chretien* (1913-1914).

Chapter 6—The Temple and Islam
1. *U.S. News & World Report*, August 26–September 2, 1991, p. 33.
2. Gaalyah Cornfield, *The Mystery of the Temple Mount* (Jerusalem: Bazak Israel Guidebook Publishers, Ltd., n.d.), pp. 9-10.
3. Mirain Ayalon, "Islamic Monuments in Jerusalem," in *Jerusalem: City of the Ages*, p. 82.
4. This explanation was offered by the historian Ya'qubi in A.D. 874; cf., G. Le Strange, *Palestine Under the Moslems*. Reprint of the 1890 edition (Beirut: Khayats, 1965), p. 116. While repeated by later Muslim authors and accepted by most Western historians, the account suffers by virtue of the fact that no other contemporary historians are aware of Ya'qubi's story, but instead offer entirely different explanations.
5. Ibid., p. 83.
6. Translation from Yehudah Even Shmu'el, *Midreshey Ge'ula* (Jerusalem, 1954), p. 189.
7. *Al-Muqaddasi: Description of Syria, Including Palestine*. Translated from the Arabic and annotated by G. Le Strange. Palestine Pilgrims Text Society 3. Reprint of 1896 edition (New York: AMS Press, 1971), pp. 22-23, as cited in F.E. Peters, *Jerusalem*, p. 1985.
8. Shelomo Dov Goitein, "The Historical Background of the Erection of the Dome of the Rock," *Journal of the American Oriental Society* 70:2 (April-June, 1950), p. 107.
9. Al-Tabari, *Annals of Kings and Prophets*, Arabic text, edited by De Goeje, Permia Series, Vol. V, p. 2408 (translation by Hava Lazarus-Yafeh in "The Sanctity of Jerusalem in Islam," in *Jerusalem: City of the Ages*, p. 324).

Chapter 7—Why Rebuild?
1. *Time* magazine interview, October 16, 1989, p. 65.

2. Ibid.
3. *Guide to the Treasures of the Temple Exhibition* (Jerusalem: The Temple Institute), p. 3.
4. Josephus, *The Jewish War*, 2, 12, 1 and *Antiquities* 20, v. 3.
5. Pinchas Peli, "What Does Jerusalem Mean to My Faith," *Jerusalem: City of the Ages*, pp. 272-275.
6. Interview with Gershon Salomon, June 24, 1991.
7. API interview reported in *Midland Times*, May 8, 1989.

Chapter 8—Gathering Momentum
1. Interview with Nahman Kahane, June 23, 1991.
2. Interview with Chaim Richman, June 23, 1991.
3. Isaac Herzog, *The Royal Purple and the Biblical Blue, Argaman and Tekhelet: The Study of Chief Rabbi Dr. Isaac Herzog on the Dye Industries in Ancient Israel and Recent Scientific Contributions* (Jerusalem: Keter Publishing House, 1989).
4. *Jerusalem Post (International Edition)*, August 31, 1991.
5. As quoted in *Time* magazine, October 16, 1989, p. 65.
6. As quoted in *The Dallas Morning News* (Texas), Saturday, October 28, 1989, p. 38A.
7. API interview reported in *Midland Times*, May 8, 1989.
8. Interview with Nahman Kahane, June 23, 1991.
9. Interview reported in *Hadassah* magazine, January 1989, pp. 26-27.
10. Ibid.
11. Rueven Prager, *Proposal for the Revival of the Ancient Jewish Marriage Ceremony*, p. 3.
12. Quoted from literature given by the Harraris concerning their harps.
13. Carol Hogan, "The Harp Makes a Comeback," reprint from *Art and Judaica* (1989), p. 7.

Chapter 9—Activity on the Mount
1. *Jerusalem Post*, April 24, 1990.
2. *Jerusalem Post*, May 14, 1990.
3. *Jerusalem Post*, October 13, 1989, p. 1.
4. Interview with Gershon Salomon, June 24, 1991.
5. Communication from E. Breuer for Temple Mount & Eretz Yisrael Faithful Movement, July 30, 1991, promoting stateside lecture tour of Gershon Salomon.
6. Interview with Gershon Salomon, August 22, 1991.
7. *Jerusalem Post (Supplement)*, April 13, 1991, p. 11.
8. H.J.C. (High Court of Justice; The Supreme Court) 193/86, *The Temple Mount Faithful v. the Commissioner of Police, the Mayor of Jerusalem, the Minister of Education, the Director of Antiquities Authority and the Moslem Wakf*.
9. *Biblical Archaeology Review*, Vol. IX, No. 2 (March/April, 1983), pp. 60-61.
10. *Biblical Archaeology Review*, Vol. XVII, No. 5 (September/October, 1991), pp. 60-68.
11. *Jerusalem Post*, June 21, 1991, p. 9.
12. Interview with Gershon Salomon, June 24, 1991.
13. Ibid., and interview of August 22, 1991.
14. Actually, David entered through the *sinnor* at the Gihon Spring, which was a Jebusite water conduit that brought water from the spring up into the city.
15. Interview with Gershon Salomon, June 24, 1991.

Chapter 10—A Purified Priesthood
1. *The Search for the Ashes of the Red Heifer*, Round Table Discussions featuring Vendyl Jones, with Noah Hutchings and Dr. Emil Gaverluk (Oklahoma: Southwest Radio Church, 1981), pp. 15, 20-21.

2. *Encyclopedia Judaica* 14:12.
3. Talmud, tractate Parah, Yad, Parah Adummah 3:4.
4. Interview with Gary Collitt (by Jimmy DeYoung), July 22, 1991.
5. Interview with Chaim Richman, June 23, 1991.
6. Ibid.

Chapter 11—An Ancient Tunnel Uncovered
1. Meir Ben-Dov, Mordechai Naor, Zeev Aner, *The Western Wall* (Jerusalem: Ministry of Defense Publishing House, 1983), p. 5.
2. *The Western Wall Tunnels*, a descriptive brochure published by the Western Wall Heritage Foundation, 1991.
3. This sign has been replaced with one whose wording is slightly less dramatic. The original is at present in storage in the Public Relations office.
4. For example, the large compound of Herodian public buildings built of well-dressed stones.
5. Interview with Rabbi Getz (by Jimmy DeYoung and Menachem Kalisher), July 18, 1991.
6. Interview with Dan Bahat (by Jimmy DeYoung), July 19, 1991.
7. Interview with Shlomo Goren (by Jimmy DeYoung), July 22, 1991.
8. Interview with Yehuda Getz, July 18, 1991.
9. Interview with Chaim Richman, June 23, 1991.
10. Addis Ababa is the transport point for immigration to Israel. At this writing about 1,500 Falasha awaited transport in Addis Ababa, while another 2,500 in Quara were on their way to Gondar for transport, arriving at the rate of about 100 per week, *Jerusalem Post*, November 21, 1991:5.
11. *Armageddon—Appointment with Destiny* (Frontier Research Publications, 1988, Bantam Books, 1989).
12. Interview with Dan Bahat (by Jimmy DeYoung), July 19, 1991.
13. Interview with Rabbi Getz (by Jimmy DeYoung), July 18, 1991.

Chapter 12—Searching for the Sacred Site
1. Kathleen Kenyon, *The Bible and Recent Archaeology* (London: The British Museum, 1978), pp. 85-86.
2. Michael Avi-Yonah, "Jerusalem of the Second Temple Period," in *Jerusalem Revealed*, edited by Yigael Yadin (New Haven: Yale University Press, 1976), p. 13.
3. J.L. Porter, *Jerusalem, Bethany, and Bethlehem* (London: Nelson, 1887), p. 52.
4. It is an idealized, but *actual* Temple, that might be described as a combination of Solomon's first Temple and Ezekiel's visionary fourth or millennial Temple. For further information on this Temple's plan see Lawrence H. Schiffman, *The Eschatological Community of the Dead Sea Scrolls* (Atlanta: Scholars Press, 1989) and his forthcoming commentary on the Temple Scroll.
5. Meir Ben-Dov, *In the Shadow of the Temple* (New York: Harper & Row, 1982), p. 77.
6. Kathleen Kenyon, *Jerusalem: Excavating 3,000 Years of History* (New York: McGraw-Hill, 1967), p. 55.
7. See the chronological appendix for a listing of the most important of these excavations.
8. Based on his two previously published articles: "Il 'Tempio di Jerusalemme' dal II all' VIII Secolo," *Biblica* 43 (1962): 1-21, and "La Posizione del tempio erodiano de Gerusalemme," *Biblica* 46 (1965): 428-444.
9. Citing Jerome (in Matthew 4:24; cf., J. Migne [ed.], *Patrologia Latina* 26, 180f.f.; *Enchiridion* 445, Bagatti, Il 'Tempio di Gerusalemme' dal II all' VIII Secolo," *Biblica* 43 (1962): 13-14.

10. This is the contention of Michael Avi-Yonah, *Madaba Map*, p. 59, n. 79, although it appears as an objection to Bagatti in Richard M. Mackowski, *Jerusalem: City of Jesus* (Grand Rapids: Wm. B. Eerdmans, 1980), p. 121.
11. *Ariel* 43 (1977): 63-99.
12. Based on interview discussion at Kaufman home (with Jimmy DeYoung), July 21, 1991.
13. This story was related to me (Randall) by Gershon Salomon, who as professor of Oriental Studies at the Hebrew University is an expert on Arab legends connected with the Temple Mount.
14. *Niv Hamidrashia* 15 (1980): 115-130 (Hebrew); *Biblical Archaeologist* 44 (1981): 108-115; *Biblical Archaeology Review* IX:2 (1983): 40-59; *Proceedings of the Ninth World Congress of Jewish Studies*: Jerusalem, August 4-12, 1985 (Division B, Vol. 1), pp., 13-20 (Hebrew); *Har HaBayit ve' atriv* (1989), pp. 179-181 (Hebrew). He has recently published (in Hebrew) a critical edition of Mishna tractate Middot (giving the critical measurements of the Temple) which includes notes based on his findings with accompanying charts and diagrams.
15. Interview with Dan Bahat, July 1991.
16. Leibel Reznick, *The Holy Temple Revisited*, p. 142.
17. Cf., 2 Samuel 24:25; 1 Kings 8:22, 64; 9:25; 2 Kings 16:14, 15.
18. Interview with Rabbi Goren (by Jimmy DeYoung) July 21, 1991.
19. "Judgment on the Temple Mount," *Jerusalem Post*, June 21, 1991, p. 9.
20. e.g., Radvaz.
21. Mishna Yoma 5,2.
22. Tosephta Yoma 3,6.
23. Rabbi Shaul Schaffer and Asher Joseph, *Israel's Temple Mount: The Jews' Magnificent Sanctuary* (Jerusalem: Achiva Press, 1975), p. 95.
24. Interview with Dan Bahat (by James DeYoung), July 1991.
25. Interview with Chaim Richman, June 26, 1991.
26. Interview with Dan Bahat, July 1991.
27. David M. Jacobson, "Ideas Concerning the Plan of Herod's Temple," *Palestine Exploration Quarterly* (January-June, 1980), pp. 33-40.
28. Josephus, *Antiquities*, 8, 97.

Chapter 13—Why the Delay?

1. Warning sign posted at the entrance ramp leading to the Temple Mount. The prohibition is not only for Jews, but extends to Gentiles as well. It includes not only entrance for prayers, but also for tourism and archaeological investigation.
2. Interview in the *Jerusalem Post*, October 17, 1989.
3. Interview with Nahman Kahane, June 23, 1991.
4. As cited in Joan Comay, *The Temple of Jerusalem* (New York: Holt, Rinehart and Winston, 1975), p. 263.
5. Interview with Chaim Richman, June 25, 1991.
6. Interview in the *Jerusalem Post*, October 17, 1989.
7. *Jerusalem Post*, April 1991.

Chapter 14—Temple Mount Alternatives

1. Ad in the *Washington Post* (Washington D.C.), May 21, 1967.
2. Interview with Rabbi Getz (by Jimmy DeYoung and Menachem Kalisher), July 18, 1991.
3. Irving Greenberg, "Some Thoughts on the Meaning of the Restoration of Israel and Jerusalem for Days of Commemoration," in *Jerusalem: City of the Ages*, Alice Eckardt, ed. (New York: American Academic Association for Peace in the Middle East, 1987), p. 283.

4. *Jerusalem Post (International Edition)*, August 31, 1991.
5. Interview with Nahman Kahane, June 25, 1991.
6. Isaiah 2:1-4; 4:2-6; 11:6-16; 60:17.
7. Interview with Gershon Salomon, June 25, 1991.
8. Interview with Chaim Richman, June 25, 1991.
9. Interview with Nahman Kahane, June 25, 1991.
10. Ibid.
11. Ibid.
12. Ibid.
13. Richard Z. Chesnoff, "A Holy City's Holy Wars," *U.S. News & World Report*, August 26–September 2, 1991, p. 29.
14. Mohammed, *Hadith* (Muslim tradition), cited in Thomas W. Lippman, *Understanding Islam* (New York: New American Library, 1982), p. 116.
15. Quoted in Lewis R. Essher, *Exile and Exodus: The Jewish-British Regiments in World War Two* (London: Jackson-Poore Ltd., 1961), p. 84.
16. Abdul Halim Mahmoud, *Al-Ji'had was al-Nasr (Holy War and Victory)*, Cairo, 1974, p. 148.
17. *Al-Qabas Kuwait* (December 19, 1989) as cited in George Grant, *The Blood of the Moon: The Roots of the Middle East Crisis* (Wolgemuth & Hyatt, 1991), p. 56.
18. Salah Khalaf, Fatah Day Celebration speech, Amman, Jordan, January 1, 1991.
19. *Jerusalem Post (International Edition)*, December 14, 1991, p. 11.
20. Interview with Gershon Salomon, August 22, 1991.
21. *Jerusalem Post (Weekend Magazine)*, October 5, 1991, p. 13.
22. Translation by R. Manis Friedman of *Midrash Yalkut Shimori*, Isaiah 60:1, Vol. II, section 499, on Isaiah 60:1, in *Chai Today* (December, 1990), p. 6.
23. Translation from ad by Friends of Chabad-Lubavitch, *Jerusalem Post*, June 21, 1991, p. 5.
24. Interview with Gershon Salomon, May 26, 1991.
25. *Jerusalem Post (Weekend Magazine)*, April 13, 1991, p. 11.
26. Meir Ben-Dov, *In the Shadow of the Temple*, p. 28. Abdul Halim Mahmoud, excerpted from *Our Faith—Our Way to Victory* (Cairo: Egyptian Armed Forces Department of Printing and Publications, June 30, 1973).

Chapter 15—The Tribulation and Beyond

1. John F. Walvoord, *The Prophecy Knowledge Handbook* (Wheaton, IL: Victor Books, 1990), p. 257.
2. Tim LaHaye, *How to Study Bible Prophecy for Yourself* (Eugene, OR: Harvest House, 1990), p. 110.
3. Charles C. Ryrie, *The Ryrie Study Bible, New American Standard Translation* (Chicago: Moody Press, 1978), p. 1812.
4. Hal Lindsey, *There's a New World Coming* (Santa Ana, CA: Vision House, 1973), p. 160.
5. For a rebuttal of this viewpoint see H. Wayne House & Thomas Ice, *Dominion Theology: Blessing or Curse?* (Portland, OR: Multnomah Press, 1988), pp. 217-334.
6. Isaiah 2:2-4; 66:18-20; Zechariah 14:16-19.

Chapter 16—Jewish Predictions for the End-Time Temple

1. Interview with Gershon Salomon, August 22, 1991.
2. *Sefer Hasidim*, J. Wistinetzki, ed. (1924), 76-77, No. 212.
3. The Ninth of Av is not the only date which has manifested divine Providence. For instance, the seventeenth of Tammuz is also associated with five disasters that fell upon the Jewish people (cf., Mishna tractate Ta'anit 29a). We have selected the

Ninth of Av because it is primarily centered in events relating to the destruction and future rebuilding of the Temple.

4. There is discrepancy in the date for the destruction of the first Temple between the Mishnah and the biblical accounts. The Mishnah gives the traditional date of the ninth day of Av, but Kings says the seventh day (2 Kings 25:8-9), and Jeremiah, an eyewitness to the event, records in a parallel passage the tenth day (Jeremiah 52:12). The Jewish sages reconciled these apparently contradictory statements by explaining that Nebuchadnezzar and his troops entered Jerusalem on the seventh of Av, ate, drank, and reveled for three days (seventh, eighth, ninth), finally on the evening of the ninth of Av setting fire to the Temple which burned all through the night and the next day, until sunset on the tenth.

5. Naphtali Winter, ed., "Fasting and Feast Days" in *The Popular Judaica Library* Series (Jerusalem: Keter Publishing House, 1975), p. 77.

6. From an ad entitled "The Time for Your Redemption Has Arrived" placed by Friends of Chabad-Lubavitch, *Jerusalem Post*, June 21, 1991, p. 5.

7. Interview with Gershon Salomon, June 26, 1991.

8. Sanhedrin 97a-b; Av. Zar. 9a; cf., Rosh Hashana 31a.

9. For example see Amnon Goldberg's argument on the date of creation in the "Readers' Letters" section of the *Jerusalem Post*, October 5, 1991, p. 22.

10. Sanhedrin 97b.

11. Interview with Mordechai Dolinsky (by Jimmy DeYoung), July 21, 1991.

12. Ibid.

13. *Time*, June 30, 1967.

Chapter 17—The Temple and the New World Order

1. January 16, 1991 speech by George Bush on national television.

2. March 6, 1991 speech by George Bush on national television.

3. Professor Amnon Rubinstein, "Finding Our Place in a World Without Communism," *Jerusalem Post (International Edition)*, October 12, 1991, p. 7.

4. Menachem Brod, cited in "Announcing the Days of Redemption," by Carl Schraz, *Jerusalem Post (International Edition)*, October 5, 1991, p. 22.

5. *Jerusalem Post (International Edition)*, December 7, 1991, p. 8B.

6. *Jerusalem Post (International Edition)*, December 14, 1991, p. 1.

7. Dr. Byron Augustine, Professor of Geography and Planning at Southwest Texas State University, in *San Marcos Daily Record*, Sunday, September 29, 1991, p. 1.

8. *Jerusalem Post (International Edition)*, January 4, 1992, p. 28.

9. With 75 percent of the Algerian population under 30 years of age (the youngest in the Arab world), Islamic fundamentalism is the wave of the future that may well sweep other Arab nations into the coming invasion of Israel.

Chapter 18—Wisdom for Our Times

1. *Time*, October 16, 1989, p. 64.

2. Steve Rodan, *Religious News Service* (as printed in *The Dallas Morning News*, October 28, 1989, p. 38A).

3. Wesley G. Pippert, *Land of Promise, Land of Strife* (Waco, TX: Word Books, 1988), p. 152.

4. *Jerusalem Post*, September 7, 1991, p. 6.

5. Interview with Dr. James Tabor (by Jimmy DeYoung), July 18, 1991.

6. This is not to imply that Dr. Salomon compromises his orthodox Jewish belief. In theological discussions with us concerning Jesus as a divine Messiah he clearly rejected this Christian premise. His acceptance of us was on the basis of our support of Israel and our research in the rebuilding of the third Temple, and especially our interest in his organization's efforts.

7. The Hebrew term for this act is *teshuva*, literally "the turning" or "return." It signifies "the return to that teaching, way, and direction after having deviated from it, and thus to the relative perfection and innocence possessed before the deviation" (as defined by Moshe Kohn, *Jerusalem Post*, September 7, 1991, p. 10).

8. A note to Jewish readers: The Jewish-Christian spokesman in telling his fellow Jews that they "crucified Jesus" is not singling them out for guilt. The New Testament affirms that the Romans (Gentiles) nailed Jesus to the cross and so are guilty of the crime. That the Jewish Sanhedrin handed Jesus over to the Roman court is also recorded, and in this they share the blame. The New Testament testifies that thousands of Jews believed in Jesus as Messiah, both before, and especially after His death, and gives absolutely no basis for what historically has been called "the blood libel."

Ready to Rebuild Video

Filmed on location in Israel, this comprehensive video documentary visually presents the facts concerning the present preparations to rebuild the Temple presented in the book *Ready to Rebuild*. Hosted by James DeYoung and featuring authors Thomas Ice and Randall Price, this dramatic video includes interviews with leaders of the Temple movement and Israeli archaeologists, along with a tour of the Temple vessels at the Temple Institute.